Also by June Bingham

COURAGE TO CHANGE
*An Introduction to the Life and Thought
of Reinhold Niebuhr* (1961)

THE INSIDE STORY
Psychiatry and Everyday Life (1953, 1960)
(with Fritz Redlich, M.D.)

U THANT

The Search for Peace

JUNE BINGHAM

U THANT
The Search for Peace

NEW YORK   ALFRED·A·KNOPF   1966

L. C. catalog card number: 66–12397

THIS IS A BORZOI BOOK,
PUBLISHED BY ALFRED A. KNOPF, INC.

FIRST EDITION

TO A.M.G.

WHO, AMIDST HER SEVEN SONS,

MANY GRANDCHILDREN AND GREAT-GRANDCHILDREN,

MAINTAINS A NEW ENGLAND EQUIVALENT

OF BURMESE SERENITY,

THIS BOOK

IS DEDICATED

WITH AFFECTION AND ADMIRATION

BY DAUGHTER-IN-LAW NUMBER 7

A United Nations soldier . . . is like no other soldier in the world—he has no mission but peace and no enemy but war.

ADLAI E. STEVENSON
Princeton University, March 23, 1964

CHRONOLOGY

5th century B.C.   Lifetime of the Lord Buddha.

261 B.C.   King Asoka established Buddhism as the state religion of India. From there it spread to Burma and elsewhere.

A.D. *c.* 500   Tibeto-Mongolian peoples started migrating to Burma: Mons, Karens, Burmans, Shans, etc.

1044   Birth of Burman king, Anawrahta, who conquered the other tribes and united Burma for the first time. He also spread Buddhism throughout the kingdom.

1277   Successful invasion of Burma by Kublai Khan, although Burmese guerrillas continued their harassment.

14th century   The Mongols withdrew from Burma. Burmese tribal warfare was resumed.

Mid-16th century   Burma was reunited under Burman king, Bayinnaung. She invaded neighboring territories, including Siam.

17 century   The Mons broke away from Burman hegemony and established their own kingdom. The British established their rule over parts of India.

1762   The Burmans under King Alaungpaya reconquered the Mons.

1769   The Burmans began repelling three further invasions by China.

Chronology

1813   The first American missionary, the Reverend Adoniram Judson, arrived in Burma.

1824–26 The first Anglo-Burmese War. The British in India annexed part of Lower Burma.

1852   The second Anglo-Burmese War. The British annexed the rest of Lower Burma and part of Upper Burma.

1853   Accession of the great Burman king, Mindon.

1860–64 U.S. Civil War cut American rice exports, thereby raising the price for Burmese "paddy'" and encouraging development of the Irrawaddy Delta.

1869   The Suez Canal was opened.

1879   Accession of Burman king, Thibaw.

1885   The third Anglo-Burmese War; all of Burma became a "province" of the "colony" of India.

1905   The Japanese defeated the Russians, thus proving to Asians that they were not inferior to Europeans.

1906   The Young Men's Buddhist Associations were founded in Burma.

1907   U Nu was born.

1909   U Thant was born.

1915   Gandhi returned to India; Aung San was born.

1914–17 First World War. Britain promised limited self-government (dyarchy) to India.

1919   Dyarchy was granted to India but not to Burma.

1920–2 The School Strike in Burma.

1921   The Greater Council of Burmese Associations was formed; U Ottama was jailed.

1923   Dyarchy was granted to Burma, with limited power for Burmese Ministers and legislature.

1926–28 U Thant studied at Rangoon University. The Rangoon University Students' Union was founded shortly before he left.

Chronology

1928   The Simon Commission came out from London to inquire into possibility of "separation" for India and Burma.

1929   Gandhi planned his Salt March; U Wisara died; U.S. stock market crashed, starting world depression.

1930   The Dock Strike; the beginning of Saya San's Rebellion; "separation" was decreed by Great Britain.

1931   U Thant won the Anglo-Vernacular Teachership Examination; the Thakin Movement was founded; the Japanese invaded Manchuria.

1934   U Nu returned to University of Rangoon.

1935   The Government of Burma Act was passed by British Parliament, with greater self-government for "separated" Burma.

1936   Elections were held for new Burmese legislature; Dr. Ba Maw became Prime Minister; Rangoon University Students Strike.

1937   Sino-Japanese War began at Marco Polo Bridge; Burma Road was started; Japanese infiltrators started entering Burma.

1939   Hitler marched into Poland; Britain (including Burma) declared war.

1940   Dr. Ba Maw and U Nu were jailed; U Saw became Prime Minister; Aung San went to Japan.

1941   The Atlantic Charter was signed (Burma being excluded from its provisions by Churchill); the Japanese attacked Pearl Harbor and the Philippines, and invaded Burma.

1942   The British-Burmese government fled to Simla; the Indians in Burma fled; the whole of Burma was captured by the Japanese; U Thant was in Rangoon for three months; the Ba Maw Executive Government was established.

Chronology

1943   Burma's "independence" was declared; her Resistance began to form and its emissary went to India; Mountbatten arrived in India.

1944   The Burmese Resistance was formally established; Battle of Imphal.

1945   The Japanese were driven out of Burma; the end of World War II; the UN was founded; Attlee replaced Churchill.

1946   Anti-Fascist People's Freedom League refused to join Governor Dorman-Smith's Council; Dorman-Smith was replaced by Governor Rance; AFPF League leaders did join the Council and negotiated the Aung San–Attlee Agreement; the Red Flag Communists went underground.

1947   U Thant went to Rangoon to found his magazine; the assassination of Burma's leaders; U Nu prepared to form a government for independent Burma; U Thant became Press Director for AFPF League and then for the Directorate of Information.

1948   Independence of Burma; Burma was admitted to the UN; U Thant was appointed Deputy to Information Secretary and then Director of Broadcasting; the White Flag Communists went underground; the Karen insurgency began; U Thant went behind the Karen lines.

1949   Height of insurgency; U Thant's home was burned; Mainland China became Communist; Burma deplored the Chinese invasion of Tibet; Burma tried to build strong alliances but failed; U Thant became Secretary of Information Ministry, also Chairman of the Burma Film Board.

1950   Beginning of the Korean War; Burma supported several UN Korean resolutions; U Thant accompanied U Nu on good-will mission to India; the U.S.-Burma Aid Agreement was signed.

1951   General elections were held and the AFPF League won overwhelmingly; U Thant went to Indonesia, Thailand, England; Bureau of Special Investigation was formed; neutralism was announced as Burma's national policy.

1952   High point of U.S. aid relation with Burma; U Thant went to UN as member of Burmese delegation; Pyidawtha Plan was announced; the Kuomintang problem became acute; Burma entered the Colombo Plan Organization.

1953   Burma brought the Kuomintang problem before the UN; U Thant was made Secretary for Projects; the end of Korean War and drop of rice price; Burma canceled U.S. aid; Stalin died.

1954   The Sixth Great Buddhist Council began; Burmese barter deals were made with USSR and Mainland China; SEATO was formed; the Colombo Powers joined together; border negotiations with China were opened; U Thant was appointed Secretary to the Prime Minister.

1955   U Thant was appointed Secretary of Economic and Social Board; the Bandung Conference was held; U Nu tried to mediate between U.S. and Mainland China; U Nu and U Thant went to U.S.

1956   Elections were held and AFPF League margin of victory was much reduced. U Ba Swe became Prime Minister; U.S. aid was renewed; Burma took a firm stand on Hungary and Suez.

1957   U Nu became Prime Minister again; U Thant went to the UN as Burma's Permanent Representative.

1958   AFPF League split; the Ne Win Caretaker Government was established.

1959   No official Burmese comment was made on Mainland China's suppression of Tibetan uprising; General Ne Win bore down on politicians and businesses that had broken the law.

1960 General Ne Win stepped down; U Nu won the election and came back in as Prime Minister with the support of the National Unity Front.

1961 U Thant accompanied U Nu to Belgrade; U Thant was elected UN Acting Secretary-General; he dropped contact with Burma.

1962 General Ne Win took over as leader of Revolutionary Council Government; U Thant helped to mediate Cuban crisis; the Congo problem became acute.

1963 The West Irian problem was settled by UN; the Borneo problem was acted on by the UN despite threats by Indonesia; UN troops left the Congo; the partial nuclear test ban treaty was signed.

1964 The Cyprus problem arose; U Thant went back to Burma for three days; the UN financing problem reached critical stage with U Thant as one of the mediators; the UN Trade and Development Conference aided the less developed countries.

1965 The UN financial crisis was eased; problems in Cyprus and along the Arab-Israeli border continued; U Thant sent UN representatives into the Dominican Republic; his offer to travel to Peking in the interest of peace in Vietnam was rejected by the Mainland Chinese; he visited India and Pakistan, helping to win acceptance by both countries of the cease-fire called for by the Security Council in the Kashmir dispute. The Pope made his pilgrimage to the UN.

ACKNOWLEDGMENTS

Gratitude can be expressed but not, in this case, fully conveyed: there is too much of it. The kindness and patience
of the academic community toward the nonacademic re-
searcher is close to unbelievable. It is as if bankers, with no
criterion other than the appealer's need, repeatedly and cheerfully handed out cash. Kindness and patience are also qualities that characterize the Burmese, as well as being the
stock in trade of diplomats from many lands. It is, therefore,
with profound thanks that the following persons are listed:

Among the Burmese, first and foremost is U Khant,*
U Thant's second brother; also in Rangoon, U Thaung and
U Tin Maung, the two younger brothers, and Daw Nan
Thaung, mother of all four; Dr. Maung Maung, Chief Judge
of the Chief Court; U Myo Min, Professor of English, Rangoon University; Dr. Ba Maw, first Premier of Burma under
the British; U Nyo Mya, former editor, *Oway;* and U Aung
Chein, Imperial Police Service (retired). Others include the
late U Aung Than, former Secretary of the Information Ministry; U Nyun, Secretary-General of the UN's Economic Commission for Asia and the Far East (ECAFE); in Washington,
U On Sein, former Burmese Ambassador to the United States;
Dr. Htin Aung,* former Rector of Rangoon University; and
in New York, Ambassador James Barrington, Burma's former

* A single asterisk identifies those who have read part of the manuscript
in one of its many drafts; two asterisks, those who have read it all.

Acknowledgments

Permanent Representative at the UN, Aye Aye Than Doliner, U Aung Thein, and U Thant's wife, Daw Thein Tin, their daughter, Aye Aye, and son-in-law, Dr. Tyn Myint U. A special word of gratitude should be included for General Ne Win, leader of Burma's Revolutionary Council Government, who made it possible for my husband and me to visit Burma in August, 1964.

Among the Americans, foremost is Frank N. Trager,** Professor of International Relations, New York University, and his wife Helen; also in New York, John Scott Everton,** former American Ambassador to Burma, now Vice President, Education and World Affairs; Lionel Landry,** Deputy Director, The Asia Society, and his wife Ruth; Professor Elizabeth Nottingham* of Queens College; Andrew Cordier,** former UN *chef de cabinet,* now Dean of the Columbia University School of International Affairs; Porter McKeever,** Chairman of the Burma Council and Executive Director of the UN Associations; in Washington, Economists Robert R. Nathan and Louis Walinsky, and Thomas Manton;** and in Berkeley, Woodbridge Bingham, Professor of Far Eastern History at the University of California.

Among the UN diplomats, first and foremost is Under-Secretary C. V. Narasimhan; also the then United States Permanent Representative, Adlai E. Stevenson; Ireland's former Permanent Representative, Frederick Boland; Norway's Permanent Representative, Sievert Nielsen; Under-Secretaries Ralph Bunche and Constantin Stavropolous; Gustavo Duran; Ramses Nassif;* the United States Mission's Ambassador Charles Yost, its Senior Adviser on Political Affairs Richard F. Pedersen,* and its former Director of Public Affairs, Clayton Fritchey.*

Thanks also go to the Library of Congress's Chief of the Southeast Asia Section, Dr. Cecil Hobbs; to Yale's Chief of the Sterling Library's Southeast Asia Section, Dr. John Musgrave, and to the Mercantile Library in New York; to Alexander Schnee,** former Deputy Chief of Mission for the United States in Burma; to Henry Clay Childs who, on a visit to

Acknowledgments

Burma in 1963, excerpted some of U Thant's writings unavailable elsewhere; to Mabel L. Rossbach,** Elsa Grossman,** and Jessica Dahlmann** who edited the early, far longer draft; to Judge J. Howard Rossbach* and Adelaide Hixon* who made valuable suggestions on a later draft; to James and Sherry Bingham Bland and June Mitchell Bingham who researched; to Timothy* and Claudia Bingham* who advised (on the basis of their recent college studies); and lastly and mostly to Representative Jonathan B. Bingham,** former United States Ambassador to the UN Economic and Social Council, who provided long-term enthusiasm toward the book's subject, editorial rigor toward the manuscript, and amused tolerance toward its author while she commuted mentally from the Bronx to Burma and by evening was not always fully home again.

Finally there were numerous UN delegates who were of positive or negative help but whose names cannot be revealed because what they took to be a casual conversation at a reception or dinner was really a noteless interview. Also there were several Secretariat officials who, although granting an interview, insisted that it be off the record (as international civil servants they must be discreet). The notes of interviews, as well as the letters from U Khant and others, are being deposited with the Library of Congress, Manuscript Division.

For all sins of omission and commission the author nervously assumes responsibility. The names of many an important Burmese were deliberately omitted; so unfamiliar is their nomenclature that the Western reader has difficulty in bearing in mind even the irreducible few names. One deliberate commission was to conform all quotations, except in the Appendix, to the text, in which Bur*man* applies to Burma's major ethnic group and Bur*mese* to all her citizens; another was to refer to Permanent Representatives at the UN as Ambassador, a title that denotes their rank but not their position (the larger delegations have several Ambassadors but only one Permanent Representative who is the chief). Involuntary mistakes may well cluster around the events that are

[*xv*]

Acknowledgments

described so differently by some British and Burmese sources that one wonders whether they are talking about the same thing (an example is the Burmese role in helping the Allies drive the Japanese out of Burma in World War II; some British sources portray it as peripheral, some Burmese sources as central). In such cases, when possible, a source from another country was used (all sources are listed in the Bibliography). Throughout the book the nationality of the source is given when relevant in the hope that the reader can then discount the unconscious bias that, as U Thant, among others, has insisted, is inevitable in the writing of history.

J. R. B.

New York; Geneva;
Mar del Plata, Argentina;
Washington, D.C., 1962–5

CAST OF CHARACTERS
(*Burmese*)

THE FAMILY OF U THANT
(pronounced *Oo Thont*—as in *font*)

* U Po Hnit	father
Daw Nan Thaung	mother
U Khant ⎫	
U Thaung ⎬	brothers
U Tin Maung ⎭	
* U Shwe Khin	great-uncle
Daw Thein Tin	wife
* Daw Kyè	mother-in-law
Ma Aye Aye	daughter
* Maung Tin Maung	son
* Maung Boh	son
Dr. Tyn Myint U	son-in-law
Ko Saw Lwin	foster son

IMPORTANT BUDDHIST MONKS

* Shin Arahan
* U Ottama
* U Wisara
U Thittila

* Deceased.

[*xvii*]

Cast of Characters (Burmese)

* General Aung San	Burma's George Washington
U Nu	also known as Thakin (accent on second syllable) Nu, first Premier of independent Burma
General Ne Win	leader of Burma's Revolutionary Council Government
U Ba Swe	former Premier
U Kyaw Nyein	former Deputy Premier
M. A. Raschid	former Cabinet Minister
* Thakin Mya	organizer of the peasants, later a Socialist leader
Dr. Maung Maung	former journalist, now Chief Justice, Chief Court of Burma
Dr. E Maung	former Foreign Minister
Dr. Htin Aung	former Rector, Rangoon University
James Barrington	former Permanent Representative at the UN
U Myo Min	professor of English, Rangoon University
* U Aung Than	former Secretary, Information Ministry
* U Tin Tut	ICS Officer; elder brother of Dr. Htin Aung
U Myint Thein	former Ambassador to Peking, another brother of Dr. Htin Aung
Bo Let Ya	former member, Thirty Comrades
U Khin Zaw	Director of Broadcasting, Ministry of Information

Cast of Characters (Burmese)

U Mya Sein   Ambassador to Australia

U Paw Htin   Chargé d'Affaires in Bangkok, Thailand

U Hla Maung   former Secretary, Economic and Social Board

Saya U Ba Khin   Auditor-General

PRIME MINISTERS OF BURMA
UNDER THE BRITISH

Dr. Ba Maw
U Pu
* U Saw
* Sir Paw Tun (acting)

JOURNALISTS

U Nyo Mya
U Edward Law Yone
Daw Mi Mi Khaing
U Tun Pe

COMMUNIST LEADERS

Thakin Soe
Thakin Thein Pe (Myint)
Thakin Than Tun

KAREN LEADERS

Saw Hunter Tha Hmwe
Saw Ba U Gyi

[*xix*]

CONTENTS

Contents

[*xxii*]

ILLUSTRATIONS

(Between pages 166 and 167)

U THANT
The Search for Peace

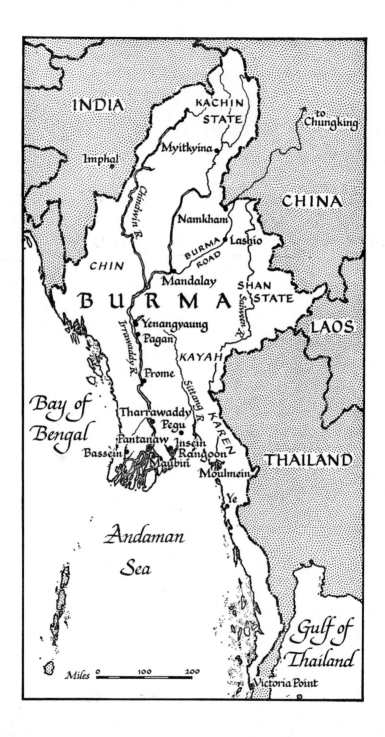

PROLOGUE

From Rangoon
to Turtle Bay

High over the Hudson, in the Riverdale section of the Bronx, stands the large ivy-covered house where the Secretary-General lives. Its curtains are never drawn.

On a raw winter Saturday at six in the evening, my husband, then a UN delegate, and I walked there from our home nearby to deliver the typescript of this book. We were surprised to see through a lighted downstairs window that U Thant was already back from the office. He was on the phone. When he caught sight of us at the door, he waved at us to come in.

Not having expected to see him, I was wearing slacks; his son-in-law, not expecting company, was wearing the Burmese ankle-length skirt (*longyi*). A lady in pants, a gentleman in skirts, the pungent smell of Burmese cooking in the outskirts of New York City—it was all rather cross-cultural and typically UN.

U Thant came toward us with a smile, his gentle brown eyes alight and his perfect teeth gleaming against the apparent sun tan. His face is round, his chin is round, and his mouth, in repose, is round, with a full lower lip. The lenses of his glasses, rimmed only at the top, are also round. I handed him the typescript. Thoughtfully he hefted it and then gave it back. "I think I won't read it after all."

"Why not?"

"Because if I make even a small correction"—he cocked his head—"I mean, if I make a small change, then I would be implicated in the writing of the book."

"But no one would know."

His look, for a moment, was stern. "*I* would," he said.

Of the three qualities listed in the UN Charter as essential for the Secretary-General, the most far-reaching, and humanly the rarest, is integrity (the others are efficiency and competence). U Thant emanates it. Says an American who dealt with him for years in Burma, "U Thant is so honest himself that people find themselves being more honest with him than they might have intended."

Before becoming Secretary-General, U Thant was Burma's Permanent Representative to the UN. Several evenings a week my husband and I would run into him at some diplomatic function. With a cheroot in one hand (U Thant is an enthusiastic smoker) and a daiquiri in the other (he is an unenthusiastic drinker), Ambassador Thant provided an oasis of serenity in an atmosphere humming with national, ideological, and personal tensions. He is both a gay raconteur and, as Under-Secretary C. V. Narasimhan says, "the world's best listener." U

Thant can also charm the ladies without arousing the pique of their husbands, although he will drop the charm —and the ladies—when shop talk is in order.

Unguarded and frankly curious as U Thant is with his friends, he can remain impassive for an indefinite period. He is known as "the Bronze Buddha" among the Secretariat officials, the people who work for the UN, and among the delegates, the peoples who work at the UN. American television viewers too had the opportunity in October, 1962, during the Cuban crisis, to see the effortless immobility of the Secretary-General, except for an occasional steepling of his fingers or attention to his cigar.

So great are U Thant's powers to act as a human shock absorber that some people assume that his detachment means indifference. This is emphatically not so, as his speeches and writings, and his intimates attest. He has potent emotions and his moral underpinnings are unshakable. A UN colleague says, "When you scrape the patina off this Buddha, you find hard metal underneath."

Publicly U Thant is ready to tell the American people that their image abroad is damaged by racial injustice at home, just as he is ready to tell the Russian people that they are not being given all the facts. Sometimes, like an old fire horse that whinnies at the sound of the alarm, U Thant responds to questions at a press conference by reverting to his early role of schoolteacher—some say, of schoolmarm—and lecturing the nations on their sins. Privately he is so scrutable that his wife and daughter describe him as "easy to beat at poker."

His household, when he became Secretary-General on November 3, 1961, after the death of Dag Hammarskjöld, comprised his wife, Daw Thein Tin, a motherly lady with a twinkle in her eye despite high blood pressure and diabetes; a daughter, Aye Aye, a lovely fawnlike creature, recently married to Tyn Myint U, a young aviation engineer; and a son, Tin Maung. One of Tin's friends at the Riverdale School, a Japanese boy, remembers the household as a welcoming one: "Aye Aye's husband, the servants, and even I felt like members of the family."[1]

So much a member of the family was the American chauffeur of the Burmese Mission to the UN that U Thant's American friends nicknamed him "Herman the Burman." Herman, according to one of them, "is a nice boy from Brooklyn who sat with U Thant's family the day the Secretary-General took the oath of office and was as proud, though not as self-contained, as they."[2]

U Thant's wife has never learned English, which her conservative Buddhist parents termed "the language of the heretics." Because she rarely attends UN functions, there is some grumbling among Secretariat wives who have never had a chance to meet her. She and her husband, however, give an occasional luncheon at the Riverdale house and, about once a year, a large dinner in celebration of some Burmese holiday. Then an illuminated shrine to the Lord Buddha, a marquee with multicolored lanterns, Burmese food, and music provide an unusual ambience.

The host's handshake is firm and lasts longer than is customary with Americans. He may take the husband's hand in one of his and the wife's in the other and continue talking happily to both. An American couple, both taller than U Thant's five feet seven inches, once stopped in on their way home from the hospital, where the wife had undergone a minor but potentially alarming operation. So concerned was U Thant about what the doctors had said that he held on to their hands too long, and the

1 Letter from Motoharu Imai, 1963.
2 Interview with Lionel Landry, New York, 1963.

wife started to sway from the effort of standing. Her husband, knowing her proclivity for falling forward in a dead faint, was about to shout "Timber!" "Imagine," he said later, "if the Secretary-General had been felled by a citizen of one of the Cold War nations."

Usually U Thant is empathic, and his knowledge of the human heart is profound. His view of man is based on Buddhist precepts, that there is more evil in man than good, but that with change being a universal law there is always chance of improvement. His view of man is not based on Freud's writings, which have not permeated to Burma, and U Thant, whose tastes in reading run to history, biography, economics, and political science, has no particular interest in studying Freud.[3]

In keeping his judgment free of static from his ego, however, psychiatry would seem to have little to teach him. He receives criticism, for example, with interest and detachment. If the criticism is fair he freely, if ruefully, admits his error, as he did, privately, after publicly referring to Moise Tshombe and his then fellow Katangan secessionists as "a bunch of clowns." If the criticism is unfair but well meant, he rejects it quietly and without rancor. If, however, it is both unfair and intended as intimidation, he rejects it politely at the time but his anger smolders afterward. One such occasion he revealed to a Burmese-speaking friend a whole year later, quoting the day of the month, the day of the week, and the hour of the day when the accusation was made. "What did you say to the Ambassador?" the friend asked.

[3] In addition to *The New York Times*, the New York *Herald Tribune*, the *New York Post*, U Thant reads the weekly editions of his lifelong favorite, the *Observer*, as well as the London *Times*, the *Tribune*, the *New Statesman*, and the *Guardian*. Among American magazines he reads *The New Republic*, *The Nation*, *The Progressive*, *The New Leader*, and sometimes *The Saturday Evening Post*.

"I said if that was the way he felt he should take his complaint to the Security Council."

"Did he?"

U Thant shook his head. *"Kwema tha"* (s.o.b.).

Another time U Thant waited thirty-five years before revealing a painful experience with the arrogance of the British overlord of Burma. "Our attitude," wrote one of these colonials, E. C. V. Foucar, "undoubtedly created an inferiority complex among the Burmese."[4] Aloof and insensitive as the British often were, their attitude did not inevitably have the result Foucar assumed. U Thant, for one, has unusually chipless shoulders. As a result, although he plainly enjoys praise from people he respects, he cannot be cajoled by flattery. In this connection he likes to quote Adlai Stevenson's quip, that "flattery is like smoking—not dangerous so long as you do not inhale."

On the other hand, he has retained a passionate sense of solidarity with his fellow Asians—and with nonwhite people everywhere. On February 4, 1964, for example, he assured an African audience that he could understand "all too well the emotional, even the furious reaction which racial discrimination, supported by physical force, can engender in its victims."

Although he never forgot his own unpleasant experience, he did not let it make him anti-British. Nor did he exploit it politically, as he might have during the Burmese agitation for independence. Racial prejudice, he told the Africans, is "a serious form of mental sickness" and therefore "not a reason for retaliation or violence."

Instead, he believes, it is a reason for long-term moral and intellectual education and for unremitting nonviolent pressure. U Thant had seen at close hand how Burma's

[4] E. C. V. Foucar: *I Lived in Burma* (London: Dennis Dobson; 1953), p. 208.

independence was won, primarily by political rather than violent means. Such means, he believes, should be given a chance to work against racism as well as against colonialism. And when he believes something, neither hell nor high water, unwelcome bed-fellows, nor the example of his cautious-speaking predecessor will keep him from voicing it when he feels the time is right.

He thus combines subtlety in dealing with persons, with forthrightness in dealing with issues. People who approve his speaking out say that he stands in the prophetic tradition, utilizing the prestige of his office to improve the moral climate of the world. People who think that Secretaries-General should be seen and not heard, say that he muddies the international waters with his moralistic comments. In view of the furor he has aroused, he may limit the frequency of his statements. But in view of his having daily risked death, during the Japanese occupation of Burma, to listen to the clandestine radio, it is unlikely that his freedom to speak out will be any less precious to him than his freedom to listen once was.

In some ways, U Thant is like Hammarskjöld, particularly in his dedication to the UN. In other ways, U Thant is very different. Hammarskjöld generated electricity: one vibrated in his presence like a tight wire in a high wind; U Thant tends to defuse people when they are wound up. Hammarskjöld, the Christian, was a mystic; U Thant, the Buddhist, is a pragmatist. (One of the many Hammarskjöld aides who stayed on to work with U Thant compares Hammarskjöld, the aristocrat, to Pope Pius XII, and U Thant, the humanitarian, to Pope John XXIII.)

Hammarskjöld was an intellectual with a highly cultivated aesthetic sense; U Thant, though extremely intelligent, would probably be rated middle-brow by the aesthetic intellectuals. Hammarskjöld, as a French fellow-diplomat said, was "a master of the calculated imprecision" who spoke mostly for the ear of the Foreign Offices; U Thant, the former headmaster, tends to simplify complex issues and to speak for the ear of the people. Hammarskjöld liked authority centered in his own hands; U Thant likes to delegate it. Hammarskjöld, a bachelor, flew all over the world at the drop of a challenge; U Thant, a family man, travels, but only when convinced it is necessary.[5] Hammarskjöld, mercurial, was thrilling to work for but very demanding; U Thant, invariably courteous, is pleasant to work for: "He never even burns off tension by flaunting his ego," says one of his assistants. And Undersecretary Constantin Stavropoulos says, "He trusts us so much that we feel a greater responsibility, and we work twice as hard as we would if he were constantly checking on us."

Only one quality in people arouses U Thant's open anger. This is deceit. A French-speaking delegate phoned one Friday for an interview with the Secretary-General. This could not be fitted in until Monday. The delegate phoned several more times on Friday to ask if it could be hastened. It could not. Before the delegate arrived on Monday he had informed the press that he had tried on four separate occasions to see the Secretary-General, without success. This statement, U Thant told him to his face, was "a lie." (The nervous interpreter informed his Ambassador that the Secretary-General had said it was "inaccurate.")

Most people in the Secretariat, however, do not know

[5] During his first three years in office Secretary-General Thant found it necessary to travel 120,000 miles to thirty-two countries. In 1965, on a Security Council mission to India and Pakistan, U Thant, like any other traveler, discovered at the last minute that he had forgotten his luggage keys; his daughter and son-in-law had to drive hurriedly to the UN to deliver them.

that the "SG" is capable of this much overt anger. So thorough is his self-control that people do not recognize it in operation. Perhaps because he is a person who does not easily feel threatened, he does not make others feel anxious. He can correct a draft without denigrating the drafter; he can receive news of a serious mistake without punitiveness toward the perpetrator. It is as if his daily Buddhist meditation had equipped him to absorb into himself the hurts and disappointments of life and from them to distill pity, not for himself, but for the other people who must suffer from these hurts and disappointments.

U Thant's concern for other people is the chief reason he has no enemies within the UN. A poignant example of this concern was given by his *chef de cabinet,* C. V. Narasimhan:

> It was the 21st of May, 1962, at 11:45 in the morning. Ambassador Schurmann was here talking to the Secretary-General about the West New Guinea problem. When my secretary buzzes twice, it means something really urgent. I left the room. Ramses Nassif, our Press Aide, had gotten word from Rangoon that the son of U Thant had been killed.
> "We must wait," I said, "for confirmation." Before long, there was a cable from U Thant's family. Tin had been killed by falling from a bus. I waited until Schurmann had left. It was the most uncomfortable moment in my life. I told U Thant. His first words were, "my poor wife."[6]

Premature death is more usual in the less developed lands than in the medically proficient West. The Thants had previously lost an infant son from illness. But the anguish of bereavement is the same the world over. Mrs.

[6] Interview with Narasimhan, New York, 1962. Ambassador Carl Schurmann was then Permanent Representative of the Netherlands to the UN. He is now her Ambassador to Washington.

Thant's already indifferent health was undermined, and a year later the few people she consented to see were careful to steer the conversation away from sons. Yet she is a devout believer in Buddhism, which includes the doctrine of rebirth (see Chapter 4).

According to Narasimhan, himself a devout Hindu, "acceptance comes more easily in Hinduism and Buddhism." U Thant's acceptance of heartrending news, whether in his personal life or in his professional life, as when UN casualties were daily mounting in the Congo, is such that he was able to say after two years as Secretary-General, "I have never despaired and I sincerely hope I will have no reason to."[7] So powerful is his resilience under stress that it influences people without their knowing it. A young co-worker received a staggering blow in his own life. When he responded with unprecedented calm a family member asked how he had learned his stoicism. The young man, to his own surprise, found himself saying, "I must have picked it up from U Thant."

U Thant's kind of acceptance includes a disciplined ability to retrieve his balance. On hearing about his son's death, he went home to be with his wife, but the next morning he was back at his desk. Only a few close associates knew how bitterly he regretted that the pressure of work prevented him from going to Rangoon for the funeral. It was more than two years before U Thant, according to a Rangoon newspaper, "accompanied by his mother, Daw Nan Thaung and daughter Aye Aye, laid a wreath on his son's grave. Unable to control her grief, Aye Aye broke down in sobs. U Thant himself was moved to tears."[8] Similarly, when the news came of

[7] David Sureck's interview with the Secretary-General was published in part in *The Saturday Evening Post*, September 21, 1963, and in full in the *United Nations Review*, January, 1964.
[8] *The Guardian Newspaper*, Rangoon, July 27, 1964.

President Kennedy's assassination, a guest at a luncheon U Thant was attending saw tears spring to U Thant's eyes. The Secretary-General left the luncheon and hurried back to work.

Indeed work, as he told Mrs. Heinz Wieschoff, the widow of Hammarskjöld's loyal aide who had died with him in Africa, can sometimes be a solace in time of grief. Gently, he added, "I think these things are always harder on the woman than the man."

U Thant's working day includes his lunch hour. "Every day I have lunch with some Permanent Representatives or Undersecretaries or both."[9] The fact is that he also lunches with presidents and emperors, kings and queens, foreign ministers and leading legislators, but his favorites tend to be intellectuals with liberal sympathies.

Whether his guests are famous or not, U Thant regales them with amusing stories. He also likes puns (the pun in Burma is considered a high form of wit). One of his favorites is about the man who was "Hungary" and asked the waiter for "Turkey" and "Greece"; the waiter replied, "I don't want to 'Russia' but you cannot 'Romania,'" etc.

On the walls of U Thant's living room, in addition to a pointilliste landscape by Aung Khin, there are four humorous, brightly colored pictures reminiscent of the best of Al Capp. One shows the Burmese New Year's festival during which these ceremonious people squirt water over everyone they meet—the more dignified, the greater the dousing.

U Thant's own humor can also throw water on people. An American asked his opinion of a fellow Burmese, a man as loquacious as U Thant is reserved. U Thant, who

9 "A Half Hour with the Secretary-General," *The Secretariat News,* January 16, 1964.

sometimes answers a question with a question, said, "What do *you* think of him?"

The American did not wish to be rude about U Thant's compatriot. "I think" he hesitantly said, "that the man is brilliant but slightly crazy."

"Not 'brilliant,' " U Thant corrected him, "and not 'slightly.' "

Another example may be more revealing of Narasimhan's humor than U Thant's, for it was Narasimhan who spoke, U Thant who laughed. It may also be revealing of the residual resentment against the former overlord that exists in one-time colonies, such as India and Burma. This is not the bitter gallows humor elicited by a cruel dictatorship, but neither is it wholly benign.

U Thant had been puzzling out loud about his then eighteen-year-old son who was not concentrating on his studies. "All that seems to interest him," Thant said, "is photography."

"Wonderful!" Narasimhan said. "He'll probably end up marrying into the British royal family."

After the death of young Tin Maung, U Thant arranged to bring over from Rangoon his foster son, Saw Lwin, together with Saw Lwin's wife and small son and daughter. Saw Lwin too is interested in photography (the reproduction of U Thant's diary page is his), and the sound of his children's laughter helps dispel the loneliness of the Riverdale home.

U Thant is rarely there except on Sunday. His day begins at six-thirty with Buddhist meditation. At breakfast (juice, coffee, eggs, bacon, and toast) he reads the newspapers and then receives phone calls from his office. A little after nine he is driven to the Turtle Bay section of New York where the UN buildings stand, remaining there until about nine in the evening. As Ambassador Thant, he rarely missed a UN reception, but as Secretary-General Thant, he rarely attends one, and then only if it is both in honor of some national day and held in the UN dining room (this chamber, with its separate entrance and exit, is ideally suited to the brief appearance—the current record being under three minutes).

As soon as he gets home he changes into Burmese dress. Dinner is at 9:45, and afterward he reads (he is not a fast reader). "Sometimes," his daughter says, "he watches wrestling or boxing or Danny Kaye on television, but usually he brings a book along." Sometimes on Sunday, despite his enjoyment of nature, he becomes so engrossed in his book that he has to be coaxed outdoors.

U Thant's two forms of exercise are walking and swimming (there is a small outdoor pool on the Riverdale grounds), but like most Burmese he never learned ballroom dancing. "I kept myself very fit as a young man," he boasts. In his mid-fifties he is still trim, with an unlined face, a jaunty walk, and formidable endurance. During his first two years as "SG," the job described by the first man to hold it as "the most impossible in the world," U Thant was ill only once, with the flu, and then only for a few days. But by the end of the third year he developed a peptic ulcer. The one-pint transfusion given to him at a New York hospital caused good-natured ribbing among the UN delegates. "Now U Thant is part American," said a Westerner. An Eastern European shook his head: "We shall have to watch carefully in case his neutralism has been diluted."

U Thant was reluctant to be the subject of a biography, and his decision not to veto this book was a long time in coming—about six months. He is singularly without vanity and totally without hurry. I was able to win his reluctant concurrence only by simulating a Burmese sort of patience, by punning occasionally, and finally by deciding, after preliminary research, that the book should alternate chapters about him and his background, thus covering subjects he would like Westerners to know more about, such as Burma and Buddhism, anti-colonialism and neutralism.[1]

Although U Thant did not veto the project, he had little time to help with it. He did, nonetheless, provide a fat list of books to read and a thin list of people to contact. And on an occasional Saturday morning in Turtle Bay, or during a free moment at a conference in Geneva, he would grant a question-and-answer interview. In these he would answer with frankness and often with humor, but he would never volunteer any information. I complained of being a dowser, tapping blindly along the surface while he bubbled away underneath. He smiled and said, "What's your next question?" I discovered later that keeping one's own counsel is a quality the Burmese have long cultivated, first under their kings, then under British rule and Japanese occupation, and finally today under their own Union of Burma Government, headed by General Ne Win.

On the other hand, U Thant likes old friends to be open with him: regarding a fellow Burmese in the United States, he once complained: "He's not being frank with me." And his own judgments of people are often unequivocal. Kipling, he said, "was artistically gifted but politically naïve."[2] And in contradicting Kipling's prediction that East and West would never meet, U Thant said: "A civilized Asian is no different from a civilized Euro-

[1] That first-class reporter John Gunther devoted less than one page to Burma out of 575 pages of *Inside Asia*.
[2] Interview with U Thant, New York, 1962.

pean or American [though] each of them is very different
from his own uncivilized compatriots."[3]

Among the many bridges between East and West, one
is U Thant's own life. Though he did not leave Burma
until he was in his forties, he was educated in a British-
dominated school system. It was, therefore, often a volume
of Shakespeare that he set down on the bank of the
Pantanaw River before tucking up his longyi and plung-
ing in for a swim. And the human problems faced by
Thomas Hardy's Mayor of Casterbridge, he found, were
no different from those faced by the Myook of Pantanaw,
the town of 4,500 people where he and his family lived.

Burma, moreover, like many neutral countries, if not
a bridge, is at least a buffer between the "West" of the
mixed economies and the "East" of the varying com-
munisms. If Burma had not been unaligned in the Cold
War, her then Ambassador would almost certainly not
have been elected Secretary-General six weeks after the
death of Hammarskjöld on September 17, 1961. U Thant
is quoted as saying, soon after his election, that his quali-
fications were that he stemmed from a nonaligned country
in a strategic part of the world.[4]

When the UN was founded in San Francisco in 1945
with fifty members, few people imagined that its third
Secretary-General might be an Asian. Since 1945 the
UN has more than doubled in size, with the inclusion of
67 new members, mostly African and Asian. Presumably,
for some time, there will not be another European
Secretary-General like the first one, Trygve Lie, whose
country, Norway, is militarily aligned with the West.
Were such a person to be nominated, he would, as would

[3] Speech of June 2, 1963.
[4] Burma is non-aligned also in the struggle between the Soviet Union
and Mainland China.

a Russian, be vetoed in the Security Council. Even if Dag Hammarskjöld from neutral Sweden had lived, UN delegates agree that the Soviet Union, enraged by Hammarskjöld's activities in the Congo, would have blocked his re-election. (Nikita Khrushchev, then Russian Premier, had challenged him after the death of Lumumba to "show courage and resign.")

U Thant is in some ways a typical Burmese, in some ways a unique individual. Similarly, Burma is in some ways a typical Asian country and in some ways a unique one. U Thant, who scrupulously avoids showing the slightest partiality for his native land, cannot avoid viewing some subjects within the context of his country's experience. He says, for example, that Burma's internal struggle against Communist insurgency might have remained the prototype for South Vietnam if the United States had not engaged there in sizable military intervention. "Because," he said on February 24, 1965, "not one American life has been lost in Burma and not one American dollar has been spent for military purposes in Burma in the last seventeen years, there has not been a single instance of outside help to the Burmese Communists." Had Burma received sizable Western military assistance after her neighbor, Mainland China, became Communist in 1949, he continued, "either the country would be divided into two parts or the whole country would have become Communist long ago."[5]

Although U Thant—like many Southeast Asians—disapproves of the type of United States involvement in Vietnam, he still reflects "the reservoir of good will" toward past actions by the United States that the late Wendell Willkie found on his world travels. The prime

[5] This interpretation was challenged by a high State Department official: "U Thant extrapolates the Burmese experience too much to the other countries of Asia."

cause of this good will was the successful waging of the first anti-colonialist war in 1776. Said U Nu, then Burma's Premier, on a visit in 1955 to the United States with his aide, U Thant, who sometimes wrote his speeches:

> The ideas and ideals, the ringing words and slogans of the American Revolution, have a tremendous emotional importance. . . . Those who dream and plot and fight for freedom do so in the name of the eternal principles for which your revolution was fought. In those parts of the world the ideas of the American Revolution are today the most explosive of all forces, more explosive in their capacity to change the world . . . than even atomic bombs.[6]

Vivid too, in Asia and Africa, is the American Civil War and its lesson, bloodily learned, that insurgency by dissident groups must be overcome by the central government before freedom can grow.

More recently, the United States, by freeing her colony, the Philippines, in 1946, made friends in countries recently or still under Western rule (the Philippines chose July 4 as their Independence Day). Twenty years later an American back from Asia reports, "They're not crazy about *us* but they're in love with our *history*."

Americans, in turn, are more concerned with events in Southeast Asia than ever before. Yet, in contrast to the Vietnams, Burma is a country that young Americans know less about than did their parents. "The Road to Mandalay" is not a song they have sung; the Burma Road was not, within their memory, the lifeline to embattled Free China. Today in Burma's military cemeteries lie many Americans who helped drive out the Japanese during World War II. Two countries that had never thought to join their fortunes have already joined their blood.

[6] *An Asian Speaks* (Washington: Embassy of the Union of Burma; 1955), p. 9; U Nu was addressing a Joint Session of Congress.

Three years after the war, Burma achieved independence and soon started receiving American aid in the form of dollars and doctorate holders, technicians and matériel. In exchange some Americans have gained nonmaterial aid from the Burmese. One is the ability, newly sought in the era of automation, to enjoy long periods of leisure. Another is the composure without recourse to drugstore or package store that many Burmese, including U Thant, manifest.

Although U Thant's health is equal to the exigencies of being the UN's chief executive, he describes the job as "a lonely and difficult one." It is not lonely in the sense of solitude. All day long he has appointments with individuals and groups (he never, for example, refuses to see a Permanent Representative). The loneliness stems from the awesomeness of his responsibilities. As Lord Caradon, the British Permanent Representative, often says, "Most problems do not come to the UN until all other methods of solving them have been tried—and have failed." Yet insoluble as some problems appear to be, U Thant keeps patiently working at them. Time, so often considered in the West as an enemy, is often considered in the East as an ally.

After U Thant's last appointment of the day, and before he attacks the pile of cables accumulated on his desk, he sometimes stands thoughtfully at his 38th-floor office window facing east. Halfway around the world is Burma, "the Golden Land." Fosco Maraini says in *Secret Tibet* that in Asia a man's fundamental outlook stems from individual roots that go back to his infancy and social roots that go back for a thousand years.

Once already the fate of East and West together have lain in part in the square sensitive hands of a single Burmese Buddhist. "The Cuban crisis," said the late

Ambassador Adlai E. Stevenson, "was a classic example of performance by the United Nations in the manner contemplated by the Charter. . . . It provided through the Secretary-General . . . the means of conciliation, of mediation, and of negotiation."[7]

One nuclear storm has blown over, but another could arise suddenly and terrifyingly at any time. If so, Secretary-General Thant would again summon from his "individual" and "social" roots the calm, the perseverance, and the courage to use, in the interest of peace, the power that he never thought to seek, but that the members of the UN unanimously voted to assign to him.

[7] WABC-TV, "Adlai Stevenson Reports," December 23, 1962.

CHAPTER ONE

Individual
Roots

At five minutes after midnight, on Friday, January 22, 1909, a man-child was born in Pantanaw in the Irrawaddy Delta, a region so flat that its horizons, like those of the ocean, blend imperceptibly into the sky.

Said one of the few British officials ever to visit Pantanaw:

The public buildings were a courthouse with a police station hard by, a hospital, a schoolhouse, and a bazaar. . . . The rest of the town consisted of native houses. . . . The whole subdivision supported one pony. He lived in ease and affluence, as you could not ride half a mile without coming upon an impassable stream.[1]

[1] Sir Herbert Thirkell White: *A Civil Servant in Burma* (London: Edward Arnold; 1913), p. 36. Because of the impassable streams, travel from Rangoon to Pantanaw today is still solely by boat.

One of the nicest "native houses" in this literally "one-horse town" belonged to the baby's father, U Po Hnit, and mother, Daw Nan Thaung. It was a two-story teakwood house on stilts (against flooding and snakes), and in the garden grew masses of sweet jasmine, shaded against the tropical sun by two mango trees, several guava trees, one coconut palm, and a giant tamarind. The father, aged thirty-six, and the mother, aged twenty-six, also owned four other houses, a hundred acres of "paddy land," and ten acres of "garden land" planted with trees and vegetables. Their livestock comprised fifteen bullocks (travel, when not by boat, was by bullock cart), six cows (for milk), and ten buffaloes (for plowing). As devout Buddhists they would not raise animals or birds to be butchered. On the other hand, they could, with clear conscience, eat fish as well as meat if someone else were sufficiently careless about his next rebirth to make these available (the main course at lunch in the Secretary-General's dining room today is likely to be fish).

The moderate wealth of the family had been amassed by the paternal grandfather and his brother, who established a successful rice mill, and by the maternal grandfather, who exported "cottage industry" products, especially the woven reed and bamboo mats that have served as beds, chairs, and tables in India as well as in Burma. Although both grandfathers died before the baby was born, the great-uncle, U Shwe Khin, was much in evidence: "He was the richest man in town," U Thant remembers, "and the stingiest; he wouldn't even give us a penny to buy sweets." U Thant's father was a business partner of this uncle, who had no children himself.

The Burmese family stands somewhere between the "extended" family of India and the "nuclear" family of the United States. Its head makes certain that its members do not go hungry, but he does not rule their lives. No one, in fact, will rule the lives of Burmese adults if they can help it. Women as well as men are proud of their inde-pendence: as a wife, the woman keeps her own name; as a daughter, she inherits equally with her brothers; as a mother, she is the center of the household. According to Shway Yoe (Sir James Scott), a British civil servant in Burma shortly before U Thant was born, "When anything surprises or pleases a Burmese, he never fails to cry out, *Amé,* mother."[2]

When the baby was a week old his naming ceremony was held. This included having his dark hair washed for the first time. His mother then sat, with him in her arms, in the center of a large circle of family and friends, with her husband nearby. For a time no one spoke. Finally an elder friend of the family suggested the name Thant, a suitable name for a Friday-born child.[3] There was a chorus of approval. "Thant," one person said, is a fine name because it means "clean" (U Thant roughly trans-lates as Mr. Clean, as some American journalists have enjoyed pointing out). Another friend noted that Thant was the name of a popular Royal Pretender who had recently led a courageous but unsuccessful rising against the British. The spontaneity of these suggestions, however, was feigned: the name had previously been chosen by the baby's parents.

Thant, moreover, was the baby's only name. No more than the wife takes the husband's name does the child take the father's. This practice complicates genealogical

---

[2] Shway Yoe: *The Burman: His Life and Notions* (New York: W. W. Norton & Company, Inc.; 1963), Dedication.
[3] Names for Friday-born people begin with *T, Ht,* or *Th,* while those for Sunday-born, for example, begin with *A, O,* or *Au.* At first meeting, therefore, one can judge who, astrologically speaking, would be a suita-ble partner in business or marriage.

research and drives the Post Office to distraction, but it suits the individualism of the Burmese people.

From infancy to young manhood, Thant was prefaced by Maung, which means young, or younger brother (the female equivalent is Ma). Only later was he honored by the U, or Uncle, which is applied after a person has achieved a degree of distinction, or number of years, or both (the female equivalent is Daw). But the Secretary-General still continues the Burmese tradition of signing himself modestly as Maung Thant (a pale Western equivalent is not signing a letter, even to a child or subordinate, as "Mr." or "Mrs."). To his brothers, Thant is either Ako-gyi (big older brother) or Ko (brother). Ko is also used by close friends and classmates.

With only a limited number of names for each day of the week, there is much duplication of names. Nor does a name necessarily reflect the sex of a person: (U Mya Sein is a Burmese diplomat; Daw Mya Sein is a historian). U and Maung, furthermore, besides being forms of address, are also proper names. To add to the confusion, many Burmese, including U Thant, have used pen names (in British days this was sometimes a sensible precaution). Also they may try to ward off bad luck or illness by changing their name; this is easy to do: they simply insert a notice in the newspaper.[4] To distinguish a person from others of the same name, the town of birth may be included. Pantanaw U Thant is the way the future Secretary-General became known in his native land.

The rhyming of names within a family is another frequent practice. When Thant's next brother was born, he was named Khant. Two-year-old Thant's feelings were deeply injured by Khant's arrival. "Why did you have an-

---

[4] In the Old Testament the changing of names was also held to be significant, as with Abram (Abraham) and Sarai (Sarah).

other baby?" he demanded of his mother. "Wasn't I child enough for you?"[5] When two more sons were born, two years apart, their names, Thaung and Tin Maung, rhymed. Each pair resemble each other more than they do the other pair, U Khant being an even handsomer edition of U Thant, while U Thaung and U Tin Maung have narrower heads and more angular features than the elder two. All four today wear glasses, though their mother does not.

The four boys had the typically happy childhood described by Mi Mi Khaing, "playing all day, in the stream and up and down the village streets, stopping only when hungry or tired.[6] When hungry the boys could pull fruit from a tree, orange or banana, guava or pineapple, coconut or mango. Or they could go home where, hot or cold, there was always rice.

So precious is rice to the Burmese that if some grains spill on the floor, no one is allowed to tread on them. The equivalent for "I wasn't born yesterday" is "I grew up eating rice."

Thant grew up eating rice, and his favorite condiment with it was a mixture of fish paste and red peppers. Other of his preferred dishes are sesame seeds, fried peanuts, mashed lobster eggs, and pickled tea leaves. The boys' father, U Khant says, "was an amateur cook":

He took delight in feeding his sons special delicacies. . . . He would cook for us special coconut rice with either mutton or chicken curry . . . ghee-rice mixed with peas, and compatible curries. In Burma we had a very learned Buddhist High Primate, Ledi Sayadaw U Nyana, M.A., D.Litt. He

[5] Interview with Daw Nan Thaung, Rangoon, 1964, U Khant interpreting.
[6] Mi Mi Khaing: *Burmese Family* (Bloomington, Ind.: Indiana University Press; 1962) p. 23. Daw Mi Mi Khaing and her husband later became friends of U Thant and his wife.

toured the country and . . . preached for the abstaining of beef-eating, as cows and oxen were the benefactors of man. When that famous abbot visited Pantanaw, mother was in her teens and we were not born yet. Mother along with some others was so enamoured of the preaching that she pledged before the Sayadaw to abstain from taking beef throughout her life; this pledge she most scrupulously keeps to this day. Our father, on the other hand, liked beef-curries. So mother would cook beef-curries at times, which we all enjoyed.

If there is anything the Burmese enjoy more than putting good things into the mouth, whether as food to eat, betel to chew, or cheroots to smoke, it is laughing. "Get a Burmese to laugh with you," says Professor Frank N. Trager, "and you've made a friend."[7] Burmese humor, direct and lusty, is perhaps more like the American variety than the Burmese have realized. Mi Mi Khaing, for example, maintained that "the funny stories [that] made us roar with delight [were not] of the right type for Western children." But the only Western children she knew were British and reserved, not American and uninhibited. One Burmese story was of "two brothers who wanted to make their grandmother beautiful and bathed her in the hottest water they could produce; the water was boiling and the grandmother emerged clean and fair—and rigid, and the two grandsons dressed her up and propped her in the doorway for all to admire."[8]

Yet halfway around the world, American children had been doubling up over the "Little Willie" verses, one of which was,

> *Little Willie pushed Grandma into the lake*
> *Just to see what a splash she would make.*
> *Mother said, "Now see what you've done";*
> *Father said, "Let the child have his fun."*

[7] Interview with Trager, New York University, 1962.
[8] Mi Mi Khaing: *Burmese Family*, p. 61.

Bathing in the river, whether just splashing or actually swimming, is another favorite Burmese pastime. The youngsters, like those in neighboring Thailand, are virtually amphibious, having been dipped in the river since infancy and having often, like Thant, been taught to swim by older children before the age of six. Since small children in tropical Asia are often semi- or totally nude, they hardly notice when they are wet and when they are dry, and after they start wearing longyis, the sarong-like garments serve also as bathing suits. Mi Mi Khaing recalls an experience Thant and his brothers also enjoyed:

Our use for the longyi was to stand on a diving platform with it open at the bottom, jump feet first and let the air rush in, nicking the longyi in at the ankles as we struck the water. This makes you land with a balloon which floats you for a minute . . . like those swollen celluloid ducks in babies' tubs.[9]

But no matter how clean from swimming, Thant and his brothers had to have their ears and faces washed before bedtime and rubbed with *thanakha,* the unguent made of powdered sandalwood bark that Burmese men, women, and children use to protect their skin from the sun, and that the women also use as a cosmetic. U Khant said in a letter:

Mother used to use thanakha to make our skins soft and our faces beauteous. We were naturally reluctant to have thanakha especially on our ears; but our dear mother would soothe us with the words that by not putting thanakha on our ears, the heavenly angels above would dislike and scold us, so we sons had to undergo the treatment almost every night.

U Thant today deplores the Burmese emphasis on smoothness and beauty for young boys. It was almost as if

9 Mi Mi Khaing: *Burmese Family,* p. 69.

he and his brothers were brought up to be princelings—
or, in Western terms, Little Lord Fauntleroys.

On the other hand, the four boys were not subjected, as
were most Burmese children, to terrifying stories about
the *Nats*. These spirits who live in trees and mountains
vary from the benign to the malign. They are a carry-over
from the animism that prevailed in Burma before the
advent of Buddhism and still exists in some quarters.
"The goblins will get you if you don't watch out" was
alarming enough to Western children, even when they
suspected that the adult concerned did not believe in
goblins; when the adult concerned did believe in Nats,
there was often an orgy of mutually infecting terror. U
Thant and his brothers, as a result of their father's influence, were brought up without the prevailing supersti-
tions.

Their father was the only man in Pantanaw who could
read and write English. He had gone to Calcutta to study
(there was, as yet, no university in Burma) and he had a
sizable library. Other of his interests were education and
world affairs. U Khant in a letter thus remembers him:

Father was Wednesday-born, quiet by nature, kind-hearted
and straight-forward, playful and jovial at times with his
four sons, would not stand any nonsense from any quarter,
was self-less and very compassionate to the poor and needy.

U Po Hnit, in fact, gave so much away that he did not
always reveal the full amount to his wife. U Thant also
remembers his father's sense of humor, his graciousness
to subordinates, and his daily newspaper reading. When
U Thant was asked whether he is like his father, he first
looked thoughtful and then said, "I hope so."

As for the boys' mother, U Khant says in a letter:

Monday-born, she is simple, very religious, very much devoted to her sons, would not hesitate to do household chores

and kitchen work for the comfort of her sons (though she usually had two housemaids). Mother, up till now, unless she is ill, never fails to keep the Sabbath on Buddhist Sabbath days.

The third son, U Thaung, is particularly impressed by his mother's power of recall: As he says in a letter, "Mother has an uncanny memory: she can, for instance, narrate as easily as if it had happened yesterday, what meal she had, when, where, and with whom, though it was an incident that might have happened seventy years ago." She is now in her eighties, a slim, straight-backed Asian equivalent of Queen Victoria, not readily amused, adoring of her husband's memory, and emanating a no-nonsense quality to which the grown sons gently defer. Smoothing his own pepper-and-salt hair, the Secretary-General says proudly, "Mother has less gray than I." When this remark was quoted to Daw Nan Thaung, she showed no pleasure at the implied compliment: "It's true," she said.[1]

The Burmese culture is not a child-centered one, and after infancy, the four boys had to abide by certain rules. One was that before bedtime they should *shikko* (a prostrate obeisance comparable to the Chinese kow-tow) in front of Lord Buddha's shrine and their parents. As U Thant said on American television, "Most people in Burma do not even stand straight in front of their parents. . . . If I have to stand in front of . . . my father or mother seated on a chair . . . I have to bow my back . . . [and similarly] before my teacher."[2]

In Burma respect is also shown to the monks, or *pongyis*. Each morning before dawn U Thant's mother or one of the maids would prepare rice for the orange-robed,

1 Interview with Daw Nan Thaung, Rangoon, 1964.
2 WABC-TV, "Adlai Stevenson Reports," October 29, 1961.

shaven-headed monks who came by with their black
begging bowls.

Small boys too, it seems, were up early and hungry. As
U Khant recalls in a letter:

Every morning mother would give us either tea or coffee
with Huntley and Palmer, or Peak, Frean biscuits. But
strangely we kids usually preferred Burmese hand-made
rough rice-cakes or other delicacies hawked around the town
by seller-women, placed in a wide-open bamboo basket dex-
trously perched on their heads.

Early every morning, we would see sparrows and black
ravens twittering on the trees in front of our house seeking
for food. When as kids we were in some indifferent mood, the
over-observant black raven would come down from its perch
and snatch away the sweets from our hands, and it was more
a rule than an exception that a maid-servant would have to
scare away the raven with a stick.

As kids we were fascinated by the procession of Buddhist
monks . . . making the rounds for alms-food. There were altogether sixteen monasteries in Pantanaw town proper. Sometimes when the elders of the house were busy, U Thant or I
. . . would offer one big Burmese copper spoonful of rice to
each monk.

The big copper spoon was a handsome one. In Burma
traditionally there has been less emphasis on painting and
sculpture as such than on making as artistic as possible
the daily and feast-day utensils, whether of copper or
silver, lacquer or teak.

At the age of six, Thant started walking down the
narrow road, which was paved with burned brick mixed
with coal tar, to the little wooden Primary Vernacular
School. As long as he could remember, he had heard
through its open windows the students' voices reciting in
unison. At last he was of an age to join them. Since
there were no sidewalks he had to move over onto the dirt

shoulder of the road to make way for bullock carts, bicycles, and pedestrians older than himself. But he did not mind. He was on his way to learn to read and write.[3]

Two and a half years later he progressed to the Middle School, which was Anglo-vernacular, meaning that English was taught but was not the medium in which the other subjects were taught. There was no free tuition in Burma in those days except for the monks' schools, but their curriculum was inadequate to prepare the students for the University. The boys' father hoped that all his sons would enter the University—and, indeed, in Asia the B.A. degree is so prized that some people put after their name "B.A.–failed," in order to set themselves off from those not qualified even to have sat for the examination. Today, in Burma, the list of scholars who have achieved their degree appears in the newspaper for days, together with their respective ranks. And on the visiting card of a Burmese, his degree is likely to be included. U Thant, when asked about someone, almost invariably starts out with the person's extent of education.

Young Thant, because of his father's interests, had a head start on his classmates. The first book Thant read in English was an anthology containing the story of the little Dutch boy with his finger in the dike. (This story, curiously enough, is not well known in the Netherlands.) Years later, when Secretary-General Thant's finger, arm, and shoulder were jammed into the Congo dike, he mentioned to Ambassador Frederick Boland of Ireland the deep impression this story had made.

Starting at the age of twelve, Thant became engrossed in authors as varied as Shakespeare and Conan Doyle. Because of the British influence on Burmese education,

[3] In those days, primary school was for ages six to ten; middle school for ages eleven to fourteen; and high school for ages fifteen to eighteen. U Thant finished a year ahead of the average student.

[*32*]

Thant ended up knowing more about London during Shakespeare's day than about the Shan States of Burma during his own. He did not, however, enjoy the books by the British author Charles Garvice, then the rage among his peers. Had he been born a generation later in the United States, he might well have refused to watch the popular television programs. His has long been a relaxed imperviousness to what "everyone else" happened to be doing or thinking. In this attitude he was encouraged by his father, who agreed with Lord Buddha's statement, "Do not believe in anything because it is rumored and spoken by many." To his literary father, in turn, Thant must have been as satisfying as a Little League pitcher is today to a sports-minded American parent. The boy not only loved to read, but also, according to U Khant, "from early childhood wrote a beautiful hand and drew figures like an artist."

Since Thant's teachers were Burmese or Indian, not British, he speaks English in a recognizably Asian manner, pronouncing "certainly" as "suttonly," "work" as "walk," "first" as "fusst," and "committee" almost as "comedy." He did not speak to a Briton until he was eleven years old. An officer of the Irrawaddy Flotilla Company once visited the Pantanaw school. Because Thant was the best in the class, he was delegated to converse with the visitor. They had a fine time, apparently, with the boy showing off and the visitor impressed that British culture was so thoroughly permeating the hinterlands.

Thant was not, however, solely a bookish child. He enjoyed various forms of sport. "I used to hike several miles on Saturdays and Sundays," he recalls. A friend of his youth recalls it differently: "one mile at most." As for swimming, the friend remembers Thant's enthusiasm for it, but not as a competitive sport. The same was true of Thant's attitude toward Burmese cane ball, the object of which is to keep a light wicker ball in the air as long as possible without touching it with the hands.

After school, Thant, sometimes alone, sometimes with a friend or brother (the Burmese word for relative and friend has the same root), would walk out into the countryside. During the planting season he would have to keep to the *bunds,* or earthen dikes, separating the paddy fields, and during the monsoon he would have to sprint, at times, for the nearest *basha* (thatch) hut.

Flat as the Delta is, its vistas are ever-changing. The rice season progresses from the brown dryness of the soil to the spidery green shoots rising from their squares of water which, like mirrors, reflect the sky. (This kind of wet rice farming is said to have been invented in Burma and there, as elsewhere, it has often encouraged an almost fierce localism among its practitioners.) Later the rice turns to gold, and after harvest the ground dries back to brown again. Mountain folk are known to yearn for the dramatic contours of their craggy homelands when separated from them; but the same kind of yearning is felt by a Burmese removed from the Delta (or by an Argentine removed from the pampas): for him an undulating landscape is almost a form of natural impertinence.

Thant's athletic endeavors, beneficial in themselves, also helped him avoid the numerous illnesses that, in Burma, still take an unusually high toll. A well-nourished, well-exercised body was the only form of health insurance, and Thant was never sick, despite the prevalence of dysentery, malaria, tuberculosis, leprosy, and other tropical woes.[4]

Illness and death, as well as birth, are facts of life familiar to an Asian child. As Mi Mi Khaing says:

[4] When U Thant returned to Burma in 1961 after four years in New York, he had lost his immunities and was reduced to taking anti-dysentery medicine like the rawest Western tourist.

Burmese children do not live in a child's world cut off
from reality. . . . They go everywhere with the grown-ups.
. . . They eat and sleep in the same rooms as the elders and
hear most of the conversation. One result is to make Burmese
children more conscious of family ties and responsibilities,
and to prepare them better for any calamities that may befall
them before they are grown up.[5]

Death, to a devout Buddhist, is not the end, but the
prelude to rebirth. When Thant was eleven years old,
everyone he knew was agog over an event that had occurred three miles away. A venerable monk, well versed
in Pali, the dead language—related to Sanskrit—in which
the Buddhist scriptures were brought to Burma, had died
several years before in a local monastery. Subsequently, in
a nearby town a four-year-old boy was discovered who had
never been to school and yet knew Pali. He kept pleading
to be taken to "his" monastery. Once there, he headed for
the old monk's bed, saying it was his. He also inquired
after people, some long dead, whose names he could not
ordinarily have known. That he was the old monk reborn
was not doubted in Pantanaw. Indeed, the boy's accomplishments were so startling that the press in Britain
featured the story. (The boy's later life, Thant admitted,
was something of an anticlimax: he became a monk but
then left the monastery, married, and went into business.)[6]

Thant's religious ideas did not interfere with his primary interest, which was English literature (Burmese
literature was so Buddhist-oriented that its secular development has only recently become notable). He also
began to write, and his first published article in English
appeared in the Boy Scout magazine *Burma Boy,* in November, 1925, when he was fifteen. The career he yearned

[5] Mi Mi Khaing: *Burmese Family,* p. 34.
[6] Interview with U Thant, New York, 1963.

[*35*]

to follow, that of journalist, i.e., columnist, was off to a precocious start.

Perhaps because he was such a model child by Burmese standards, studious, respectful, and handsome, his second brother, Khant, kept trying to embroil him in controversy. But Thant, whose nickname was "Moonface," would sail serenely by. As the spirited U Khant says today, "I always played a rebel or truant vis-à-vis U Thant's moderation." Thant, even at an early age, tried to keep peace, not only between himself and his rambunctious next brother, but between the younger boys and their assorted friends and cousins. One explanation for this proclivity was that in waiting until five minutes after midnight to be born, Thant had come under the astrological sign of the balanced scale—the kind that blindfolded Justice holds in her hand. For many Burmese, including some members of U Thant's family, the credit, dear Brutus, *is* in our stars. . . .

Thant's attitude of eschewing conflict, moreover, was in the Buddhist tradition. Burmese children were not permitted to hit each other or indulge in the kind of rough horseplay taken for granted among Western siblings.[7] Self-control is considered to be of utmost importance, both within onself and as an attribute of other people that one must not provoke them into losing. During the seasonal festivals the children were warned not to be disobedient lest the adults be forced to scold them. And recently an American political scientist noted that in Burma those who are provoked to "commit acts of violence are not severely censured; rather it is the one who does the provoking who is considered something of a fool and probably deserving of uncontrolled violence."[8]

[7] The head is the most sacred part of the body; for example, one never idly pats a child on the head.
[8] Lucian W. Pye: *Politics, Personality, and Nation Building* (New Haven, Conn.: Yale University Press; 1963), p. 139.

An excellent reason not to provoke a Burmese is the terrible rage that may result. The Burmese, like the Spaniards, are famous for the duality of their nature. On the surface they appear peaceable, even passive, yet Mi Mi Khaing in *Burmese Family* casually told of a neighbor whose wife enraged him during a quarrel and who quickly put an end to the quarrel—and to the wife—with his *dah,* a very sharp curved knife. She also described her home town, Ye, much like Pantanaw, as the locus of frequent armed robberies.

In Burma armed robbers in a group are called *dacoits.* Sometimes they acted as self-appointed Robin Hoods against the British overlord; other times simply as criminals. The crime rate in Burma, after the British had conquered her kings, became far higher than that of her neighbor Siam, which had remained independent. As the British historian, G. E. Harvey admitted, "Not only did crime increase under British rule [but] it is even arguable that it was caused by British rule."[9]

To a small, owlish lad, the prevalence of robbery and murder was perplexing. So was the existence of poverty in the midst of plenty. Burma had long been one of the richest countries in Asia, and had never suffered from overpopulation. But after British occupation many peasants lost their land and became tenant farmers, working hard for inadequate returns. The tenants on Thant's family's land, like the two maids in the house, were Karens, members of one of Burma's several minority groups. "We boys," Thant recalls ruefully, "were taught to look down on them."

Thant's family was Burman-Mon. The Burmans constitute the vast majority in Burma today and are staunchly Buddhist. Indeed, according to adage, "to be a Burman

[9] G. E. Harvey: *British Rule in Burma* (London: Faber & Faber; 1946), p. 38.

is to be a Buddhist." Though the Burman kings of old, when establishing their supremacy over the other tribes in Burma, had admired and intermarried with the Mons, they had treated the Karens, according to Dr. Gordon Seagrave, "like scum."[1]

The ethnic conflict between Burmans and Karens was expanded, after the arrival in 1813 of the first American missionary, the Reverend Adoniram Judson, to include a religious conflict as well. For while the Burman Buddhists were impervious to Judson's Baptist teachings, many Karens embraced them. The Karens, according to Seagrave, himself a great-grandson of Judson's missionary followers, were originally "very religious, with a mythology very close to that of the Jews"; and subsequently, he said, "so many Karens have been converted to Christianity that it has become their national religion."

Adoniram Judson's son and biographer suggested in 1883 that "the Karens are related to the Burmans somewhat as the North American Indians are to us . . . being . . . original inhabitants . . . and having been subjugated in the past."[2] U Thant, who later risked his life in the attempt to bring peace between Karens and Burmans, makes a similar comparison: "The Karens are like the American Indians, shy, quiet, refusing to live in towns, and normally poor; some of their leaders, though, have been exceptional men."

Thant's acquaintanceship with the Karens started in childhood when he trudged around the countryside, watching the farmers with their single-share plows and

[1] Gordon Seagrave: *The Life of a Burma Surgeon* (New York: W. W. Norton, Inc.; 1943), p. 39. U Thant was a regular contributor to Dr. Seagrave's hospital in Namkham, Burma, until after Seagrave's death in 1965, when the hospital was taken over by the Burmese Government.
[2] Edward Judson: *Adoniram Judson* (New York: Anson D. F. Randolph & Co.; 1883), p. 61.

talking to those who spoke Burmese (the most common of Burma's 110 languages and dialects). The Karen tenants on his family's land happened to be Buddhists, but they made no secret of their sense of unity with their Christian fellow-Karens.

Soon after Adoniram Judson, came the first two Anglo-Burmese wars of 1824–26 and 1852. From the beginning the British trusted the Karen Christians more than the Burman Buddhists. And many Karens, in turn, trusted the British more than their historic oppressors, the Burmans. After the third Anglo-Burmese War of 1885, there followed five bloody years of pacification during which many Karens, with the encouragement, it is said, of the American Baptists, fought on the British side against the Burmans.[3]

At the end of this period, the British did nothing to minimize ethnic rivalries in Burma. They accepted only members of minority groups into the armed forces, deliberately excluding the Burmans despite their proud history of having defended Burma's frontiers against the Chinese and others. "Divide and conquer" was reputed to be Britain's colonial policy, not solely in Burma, but in neighboring India, as well as in Ireland. Certainly, when independence was finally achieved by these three, it was promptly followed by civil war among the groups that had thus been "divided." (Burma and Ireland then joined the American colonies as the only former British possessions to stay out of the Commonwealth.)

To a boy with a child's natural sense of justice, together with a tendency toward peacefulness, the situation was a puzzlement. On the surface everything was calm, but underneath there were seething forces he did not under-

[3] The British Secretary of State for India at that time was Lord Randolph Churchill, father of Sir Winston.

stand. The British assumed they would rule Burma for a long time; the Burmese assumed the opposite. Some Karens were Burmese nationalists; others, fearing the Burman majority, wanted an independent Karen state. Buddhism taught tolerance of all religions, but many Burman Buddhists looked down on the Christian Karens. Which group had been most at fault, and how far back in history should one go in assessing blame? If he was going to be a journalist, he would have to understand fully the history of his people. At fourteen he started attending the Pantanaw National (read national*ist*) High School and studying in detail his country's historic, geographic, and social roots.

CHAPTER TWO

Social Roots

What heredity is to the individual, geography may be to a country. Burma is one example of C. Northcote Parkinson's theory in *East and West* that "a country's basic interest . . . can be read from the map."

The map shows plainly that Burma is dwarfed by her enormous land neighbor, China. Between them runs a 1500-mile frontier, some of it passable and some of it not. Southward, in the thirteenth century, the Mongols "came down like the wolf on the fold."[1] Originally under Kublai Khan, they stayed for two centuries, were harassed by Burmese guerrillas, and finally withdrew. Again, in the

---

[1] That peripatetic reporter Marco Polo describes the climactic battle in which Burmese elephants played a determining—but unsuccessful—role (see Appendix I).

eighteenth century, the Chinese tried to invade Burma, but three times they were thrown back. The Burmese, moreover, did some invading of their own. "Our kings," said U Kyaw Nyein, formerly the Deputy Prime Minister of Burma, "were small imperialists in their own way," having briefly annexed part of the Chinese province of Yunnan, as well as Assam and Manipur, which were part of India, Burma's other huge neighbor, by sea.[2]

Burma also has three small neighbors, today known as Thailand (formerly Siam), Laos (formerly part of French Indo-China), and East Pakistan (formerly part of British India).

Burma, the size of Texas, with a population (24 million) only twice that of Texas, on the map looks like a diamond-shaped kite with a tail. Down the kite's body flow three rivers: the majestic Irrawaddy, "Burma's Mississippi," which *is* "the Road to Mandalay where the flying fishes play"; and the Salween and Sittang. Burma also has three main seasons (the "cool," the "hot"—when Rangoon's temperature averages 97 degrees—and the "monsoon"), and three main regions. These comprise tropical Lower Burma, the greatest rice-growing area in the world; cooler, drier, cotton- and vegetable-growing Upper Burma, where the kings had their capitals; and the mineral- and jewel-rich, teak-forested Hill Country, where 18,000-foot peaks, torrential streams, and jungle make communication difficult even today. (Burma's chief minerals are tin, tungsten, lead, petroleum, and silver; her jewels include rubies, jade, and pearls.)

Since Burma lay north of the main east-west sea routes and south of the main caravan routes, she had, until the nineteenth century, little contact with the outside world. And since, like pre-modern Japan, she was self-sufficient, she had little interest in it. At the Burmese Court foreign

2 *Atlantic Supplement,* "Perspectives of Burma," 1958.

traders were scornfully characterized as "Black Indians" (natives of India whose skin was darker than that of the Burmese) or "White Indians" (Europeans and Americans). So little desire did the Burmese have to voyage beyond their own frontiers that they never developed the science of navigation. When their ships ventured as far as India, the captains, it is said, were careful to keep in sight of land.[3] The Indians, on the other hand, had started sailing to Burma around 500 B.C. And two hundred years later, when India's great king, Asoka, established Buddhism for a period as the state religion, some of his followers, the Burmese believe, settled in Burma to spread the faith.

From A.D. 500 to 800 other people also migrated to Burma, but by land, not by sea. From the colder, less fertile regions of northern Asia came the Mon branch of the Mon-Khmer people (whose fellows in Cambodia built Angkor Wat), the Karens, and then the Burmans. Subsequently the Kayahs (also called Karenni), the Shans (some of whom also migrated to Siam), the Kachins, and the Chins came down as far as the Hill Country. Their feudal chieftains, under British rule, were given the same autonomy as the Maharajahs in India. The British "divide and conquer" policy that intensified hostility between Karens and Burmans similarly intensified distrust between the Hill peoples and those of "Burma proper."

Also into Burma came South Chinese, who were looked down upon by their own northern brethren and who often suffered from droughts and floods. Today in Burma there is a sizable Chinese minority, largely traders in Rangoon, many but not all of whom approve of the Mainland Communist regime.

Despite Burma's post-independence efforts to indus-

---

[3] The Burmese, into the twentieth century, were so disinterested in emigration that the United States Oriental Exclusion Act of 1924, which inflamed the sensibilities of many Asians, meant nothing to them.

trialize, some 75 per cent of her people still live on the land. In the past the proportion was even higher. Because farmers are dependent on the weather, life in Burma has annually alternated between periods of backbreaking work and periods of relaxation. So adept are the Burmese at profiting from leisure that in 1908 a young American engineer, who later became President of the United States, was much impressed. Said Herbert Hoover: "The Burmese are the only genuinely happy people in all of Asia."

This happiness appears to stem from the people's nature, the precepts of Buddhism, and the fact that there is room and food for all. The Burmese have been accused of being lethargic, but those like U Thant, who are healthy, have great stores of energy and endurance.[4] In Rangoon the pedestrians move along rapidly, while many of the vehicles go too fast for safety (it was from one of the careening, crowded, open-door buses that U Thant's young son was hurled out backward to his death).

Peaceful as today's Burmese appear to be, they are like the peace-loving Scandinavian descendants of the Vikings, proud of the mighty warriors of their past. From the fifth to the eleventh century the tribes in Burma were constantly at war with one another. Finally, at the time England was being forged into a nation at the Battle of Hastings, Burma was forged into a nation by the great Burman, Anawrahta, who conquered the Mons, Karens, and others, and gained control over the internal land and river trade routes.

From Anawrahta's royal capital of Pagan, with the king's blessing, went the saintly monk Shin Arahan and other Buddhist teachers. Throughout the kingdom they established monasteries where the scriptural language of

---

4 "Lack of energy," said the Lord Buddha, "is to be despised."

Pali was taught, where the vernacular Burmese language was first recorded, and where all little boys were required to attend classes. Because of this compulsory education—which also influenced the girls—Burma in the nineteenth century had the highest literacy rate in the world.[5] The first injection of Buddhism into Burma under King Asoka of India had not "taken," but the second, under their own King Anawrahta, became part of the life-blood of the Burmese people.

Buddhism in Burma affected not only individuals but the structure of society. Its rejection of the caste system, for example, encouraged the Burmese to develop a unique degree of social mobility between the vast majority who were peasants and the sprinkling of courtiers, both civilian and military, at the top. Yet the tragic flaw in Burmese society stemmed from this same egalitarianism. Just as any commoner could become a courtier, so any child of royal blood could become king. On the theory that the throne should go to the best-qualified successor, no automatic Crown Prince was provided for. The resulting palace intrigues often brought to the throne not the best, but the craftiest, prince while the other royal children, their mothers, and advisers, were killed or exiled. Not only were there consequent psychological strains on the royal family but also genetic ones. As Dr. Htin Aung says, "To keep the blood as pure as possible, Burmese kings often married their half sisters. This practice . . . was also known in Siam, the East Indies, Peru . . . and Egypt."[6]

Since royal blood was not permitted to be spilled, the manner of execution was to tie up the royal prisoner in a

[5] This estimate was made by G. E. Harvey, a British historian not known for a pro-Burma bias.
[6] Htin Aung: *Burmese Drama* (London: Oxford University Press; 1937), p. 120 n.

red velvet sack to be dumped into the river or trampled by elephants. *Pwés,* or night-long variety shows with loud musical accompaniment, were performed in order to drown out the shrieks. The enlightened mid-nineteenth-century king Mindon tried to prevent this excruciating slaughter by letting it be known beforehand whom he wished to succeed him. But this did not work either: the successor was promptly murdered.

Mindon, however, established many other reforms that have been compared to those of the Meiji Restoration in Japan fifteen years later. He introduced coinage, and paid salaries, instead of a percentage, to the tax collectors, or, as the Burmese called them, the "Eaters." He also maintained the Hlutdaw, or Council of Ministers, one member of which was empowered to talk back to the king. Mindon further established good foreign relations with the British and French and tried to make friends, by letter, with the President of the United States (see Appendix II). During Mindon's reign the Suez Canal was opened (1869) and, in return for Burmese rice and teak, machinery and manufactured goods began to flow to Burma. Mindon sent bright Burmese lads to England and France to study. He also convened the Fifth World Buddhist Council in order to purify the Scriptures.

When Mindon died in 1878, Thibaw, son of one of the forty-five queens, together with a lesser queen and her daughter Suppayalat, succeeded in having the other princes killed or exiled. Thibaw then married this half sister, a beautiful young lady reminiscent of today's Madame Nhu of South Vietnam. Between them they abrogated many of Mindon's reforms and dissipated the good will he had earned abroad.

It was dangerous to bring Thibaw bad news. When an adviser warned him and the queen that the British had a better army and were being provoked by Burma's flirting with the French, the queen accused the man of being a "woman," i.e., a coward, and he was exiled forever from the royal presence. As a result of Thibaw's attitude, the courtiers hesitated to tell him when the British issued an ultimatum in 1885. The British, dissatisfied by the tardiness and content of his answer, attacked. The Burmese fought bravely, but the third Anglo-Burmese War was over in fourteen days. Thibaw and Suppayalat were bundled into a *gharry,* the horse-drawn Burmese vehicle that has been described as a "doghouse on wheels," and driven to the Irrawaddy, where they were taken by boat to exile in India. (Suppayalat, when widowed, was allowed to return to Rangoon, where she lived quietly with a few retainers until her death.)

So sudden and unexpected was the defeat of their king that the Burmese people could not accept it. The British, during the next five years, were forced to bring in 32,000 troops and 8,500 military police to pacify the countryside. Even afterward, there were sporadic small rebellions, such as that of the Pretender for whom Thant was named. And during Thant's boyhood, a quarter century later, the country people had not yet recovered from their shock at the fall of their dynasty. As the British civil servant Maurice Collis observed: "In their dramas they had an imaginary world into which they could retreat and hear the king's voice as he addressed his ministers, a scene repeated over and over again, which they never grew tired of watching."[7]

The yearning of a people for glamour in their national life, past or present, is apparent throughout the world. It may be embodied in ecclesiastical or temporal rulers

[7] Maurice Collis: *Into Hidden Burma* (London: Faber and Faber; 1953), p. 52.

(alive or dead), in mandarins or presidential families, in bemedaled military leaders or movie stars. Whatever this added dimension to humdrum living may be, it is felt to be worth considerable effort and money. From all reports, the Burmese, during the time of royal panoply, felt they were getting their money's worth.

For one thing, money meant little to them. The Burmese, Shway Yoe noted, had no bankers: "In native times there were exceedingly few who would have anything to lodge with such a personage. . . . The Burmese detest hoarding. A miser is threatened with as terrible a hereafter as a parricide."[8]

Second, the needs of the Burmese people were relatively easily satisfied: enough good rice, a few longyis for everyday wear and festivals, and a simple house open to the breeze. The Burmese food, clothes, and houses, moreover, did not vary as glaringly between those of rich and poor as in the West. A rich man would have a few more condiments, but rice would still be the basis of his diet; the material, but not the cut, of his clothing would be more elaborate (silk for the rich, cotton for the poor); and the major furnishings of his house would still be mats, though of a satin-soft quality. Except for women's jewels, conspicuous consumption in Burma has taken the form less of personal indulgence than of generosity to monks, friends, and strangers.

Third, the taxes paid to the royally appointed "Eater" were rarely exorbitant. Except for his annual visit, and that of the occasional conscriptor of boys for military service or of girls for royal concubinage (considered an honor), the Burmese lived unbadgered by their ruler. In return for their contributions they received a court of unexcelled Oriental splendor. As one of the eighteenth-century kings let slip in a letter to the British governor of

8 Shway Yoe: *The Burman*, p. 558.

Bengal, "My palace, as the heaven studded with gold and precious stones, is revered more than any other palace in the universe."[9]

The king was revered, in part, because a lofty position in this life was believed to stem from "merit" achieved during previous lives. The obverse was that ordinary people should be content with their lot, however burdensome, because this too stemmed from behavior in previous lives. In a sense, therefore, Buddhism preserved the royal status quo. On the other hand, Buddhism reinforced the status quo only when the ruler was the official defender of the Buddhist faith. The Burmese king, therefore, spent much time and money building Buddhist shrines and supporting the *Sangha,* or monastic community.

The Sangha leaders had considerable authority. Their ecclesiastical courts, in which a monk could be unfrocked, maintained a high standard of monkly behavior, and if any monk disapproved of the severity of the secular officials he could interfere on the side of mercy. When a monk threw his robe over a prisoner condemned to death the sentence was automatically commuted. As a result, Professor Kyaw Thet of Rangoon University says,

> Where the megalomania of local officials became unbearable, the monks were the only ones who . . . could appeal to a higher authority. Personal good faith and humanitarian ideals have functioned in this fashion through the centuries. This tradition—call it, if you will, the guarantee of civil rights by the spirit of religion—is part of Burma's most precious heritage.[1]

At the royal court there was a group of Brahman *ponnas,* or astrologers, whose power sometimes exceeded even that of the Sangha. When King Mindon, with Sangha

---

[9] King Bodawpaya's letter is quoted in John F. Cady: *A History of Modern Burma* (Ithaca, N. Y.: Cornell University Press; 1958), p. 8.
[1] *Atlantic Supplement,* "Perspectives of Burma," 1958.

support, tried to end the custom of burying people alive under a new royal palace (a practice similar to that in Glendalough in Ireland during the Dark Ages), he was prevented from so radical a departure by the ponnas. (Even in 1948 the hour of Burmese independence was set according to the computations of the astrologers: they chose 4:20 A.M.—a time of day then and on subsequent anniversaries not wholly convenient to the former British rulers.)

It was thus difficult even for the king to revise palace procedures which had continued for centuries, whether the capital was in Tagaung, Pagan, Pegu, Toungoo, Shwebo, Ava, or, finally, Mandalay. Only the king could use the white umbrella, and only the royal family and high courtiers could wear velvet on their persons. If the king chose to leave the palace, which he did rarely, he was carried in a palanquin on the shoulders of his countrymen. The word "golden," a symbol of excellence, could be applied only to the king or to the palace. When the king granted an audience, everyone knelt, head to floor, as the golden sliding doors behind the throne were rolled back and the king came forward in his jeweled surcoat and pagoda-shaped crown.

The few people who refused to shikko were the American missionaries. Adoniram Judson wrote in his diary on January 27, 1820:

The king . . . came forward unattended—in solitary grandeur and exhibiting the proud gait and majesty of an Eastern monarch. . . . Every head except ours was in the dust. We remained kneeling, our hands folded, our eyes fixed on the monarch.

But there were no exceptions to the doffing of shoes in the royal presence (today in the pagodas, visitors must remove not only shoes but socks, stockings, or footlets). Even after the British had conquered Lower Burma and part of Upper Burma, their envoy was refused entrance to the Burmese palace until he had taken off his shoes.

In theory the king owned the persons of his subjects, which meant that they could emigrate only with his permission—but no one wished to emigrate. Also in theory, he owned all land, but in actuality the peasant who farmed it could leave his five- to twenty-five-acre plot to his descendants. Foreigners, on the other hand, could not gain title to any real estate. (Adoniram Judson recorded in his diary on January 8, 1822, the terms upon which a high court official permitted him to establish a small school: "Understand, teacher, that we do not give you the entire owning of this ground. We take no recompense, *lest it become American territory.*") The king also owned all the teak forests, including the elephants that dragged the great logs to the river to be floated to the mills. The rare "white" (actually pink-gray) elephant was deemed so valuable (the Lord Buddha in one life had been a white elephant) that it was kept near the palace and when it died it was given a state funeral.

But the king's power, though formidable in the capital, was diluted in the countryside. With neither a standing army nor a regular police force, he could not risk a rebellion, and he knew that among the five woes from which his people have traditionally prayed to be free one was government (the others being flood, fire, robbers, and "those who hate you"). Actually, under the kings, the governing figure the Burmese knew best was the "headman" of their village or "circle" of villages. This position was sometimes hereditary, sometimes elective, and sometimes held by a woman. If unpopular, a headman could be deposed by his people, while the popular headman remained sensitive to their wishes. "Thus," said the British civil servant J. S. Furnivall, "without the machinery of the ballot box, there was to some extent the substance of democracy."[2]

The headman also administered justice, not by formal court procedures, but by patiently working out a consensus. Public opinion rather than the threat of jail was the source of his effectiveness.[3]

Easygoing and generous, the Burmese refused not only to amass capital for themselves but to help others amass it. A British contemporary of Shway Yoe's pointed out that "the European employer of labour . . . hates the Burmese who prefer freedom to money."[4]

The Burmese love of personal freedom is combined with an equal love of national independence. (These two do not always coexist: in China, for example, personal freedom has long been, and still is, less important than national independence, whereas in American Samoa, the people's desire is to remain part of the United States, partly, perhaps, to be certain of retaining their valued personal freedom.) In Burma, moreover, the yearning for independence from the British was bound up with the dedication to Buddhism. Although Queen Victoria had the title "Defender of the Faith," her faith was not Buddhism. Consequently, there was inner chafing at her rule and, according to the American historian John F. Cady, whom U Thant enjoyed meeting in 1955:

2 Frank N. Trager and Associates: *Burma* (New Haven, Conn.: Human Relations Area Files, Inc., Subcontractor's Monograph; 1956), p. 41.
3 U Thant's patient attempts to negotiate a solution to the UN's long financial crisis of 1964–65 were reminiscent of the headman's reliance on persuasion, rather than power, and on public opinion, to bring about an eventual solution.
4 Fielding Hall: *A People at School* (London: Macmillan & Company; 1906), p. 156.

British efforts to mollify Burmese-Buddhist unrest and to enlist popular support by developing efficient administration and by dispensing impartial justice failed largely because they were more or less beside the point. The cry, "Buddhism in danger," was one of the perennial appeals which political agitators could employ to enlist popular support.[5]

The British ruled the whole of Burma for sixty-three years; their impact upon it was therefore far less than in neighboring India where they ruled large sections for three hundred years (the British arrived in Madras twelve years after their landing at Plymouth Rock). Nor did the British try to win over the intellectuals in Burma as they did in India. Whereas hundreds of bright Indian lads were encouraged each year to go to England to study, the greatest number that ever left Burma in any one year was ten. In Pantanaw the family of U Thant would have had the means to send him abroad, but they had no thought of doing so. Nor did he think beyond the glorious possibility of one day going to Rangoon to attend the brand-new University that was established there, under British auspices, in 1920.

[5] Cady: *A History of Modern Burma*, p. 9.

CHAPTER THREE

An Adolescent
Takes Hold

The Burmese frequently surprised the British, especially on December 4, 1920, when they greeted the establishment of the first university in Burma by going on strike.

The strike spread to the provinces. Forty-seven schools in twenty-six towns, including Pantanaw, were affected. Parents and monks, together with students, marched in protest against British domination of Burmese education. At Rangoon University, it was felt, there were too few Burmese as directors and as teachers; and in the high schools, there were too few courses in Burmese history or in the subjects prerequisite for eventual careers in medicine, engineering, and the administrative echelons of business and government.

U Thant, aged eleven, marched in the school strike, but he did not understand its significance. If anything, he was slightly repelled by the undisciplined behavior of some of the students and adults who appeared to know no more than he did of what they were trying to accomplish. Unknown to him, in the nearby town of Wakema a boy of thirteen, destined to be independent Burma's first Prime Minister, was marching in a similar parade. Said U Nu years later: "The political spark ignited in my breast by the boycott movement gradually developed into a flame."[1]

In Pantanaw, as in Wakema, a new National High School was founded. In contrast to most National Schools that died of financial anemia, the Pantanaw School survived, thanks largely to the efforts of its subsequent headmaster, U Thant.

At the time of the school strike Thant, like Nu, had started middle school. The difference in the reaction of the two boys (who did not meet until University days) may have stemmed from the difference between their fathers. While Nu's father was a politician and a nationalist who knew no English, Thant's father eschewed politics and worked to promote better education. U Thant's father was one of the original shareholders of the *Sun* (Thuriah) newspaper in Rangoon which favored home rule for Burma within the British Empire and supported the efforts of the Young Men's Buddhist Associations to foster Burmese cultural self-awareness. This self-awareness, however, U Po Hnit believed, must not be a form of cultural isolationism. He therefore encouraged young Thant to read the few American books that found their way to Pantanaw. Willa Cather's *Death Comes for the Archbishop* was one; Edna Ferber's *So Big* was another. Yet so thorough was the insulation of a Burmese provincial from the United States that the first American whom Thant heard of was not George Washington or

---

[1] Richard Butwell: *U Nu* (Stanford, Calif.: Stanford University Press; 1963), p. 7.

Abraham Lincoln (who later became one of his heroes) but Adoniram Judson, the missionary who had translated the Bible into Burmese and devised the first English-Burmese dictionary, a later edition of which was used by Thant.

Thant's enthusiasm for literature was so great as to be contagious. U Khant writes in a letter:

I can still vividly remember the evenings at our house when U Thant's classmates would come and listen attentively to what U Thant had to say to them about the story of Lorna Doone, as well as the travels of Stanley in search of Dr. Livingstone. He would tell the story to his friends in Burmese, sometimes quoting suitable excerpts from the English texts. I was two years junior to U Thant in class, and actually I had no business to listen to what U Thant had to tell his classmates from his text-books. But I must say that the way U Thant told the story was so interesting that we younger brothers could not help listening.

U Khant also remembers the only trip he and Thant as boys took outside of Pantanaw township. Thant was fourteen and Khant twelve in 1926 when Edward VIII, then Prince of Wales, was scheduled to visit Rangoon. At five in the afternoon the boys and their mother stepped aboard the two-decker, single-stack steamer owned by the Irrawaddy Flotilla Company.[2] Family members came to the dock to make sure that they had all their necessities, including sleeping mats, mosquito nets, cooking utensils, and food. But no farewell hugs or kisses were exchanged. In Burma there are no demonstrations of affection in public, except to babies.[3]

[2] Elsewhere in the British Empire the same kind of equipment was in use, as was dramatized in the movie *The African Queen*.

[3] Almost forty years later, on July 25, 1964, U Thant's eighty-year-old mother met him at Mingdalon Airport in Rangoon, and they walked hand in hand to the car. Next day, a newspaper photograph in *The Working People's Daily* showed a circle drawn around their clasped hands, to call the readers' attention to them.

The paddle-wheeled boat edged away from the dock, avoiding the multitude of gondola-shaped sampans with double flanges on the stern, and the fishing boats with their single or double oars. The eighty-mile journey took twenty hours. The boys and their mother were met at the large commercial wharf of Rangoon by friends who lived in the Burmese section of the city. At that time Rangoon's population was 60 per cent Indian, which meant that the Burmese were a minority in their own capital. According to Maurice Collis, who lived there for years, Rangoon under the British was less a Burmese city than an Asian *entrepôt*.

To the boys, however, the stunning sight was not the variety of people but the Pagoda. What St. Peter's is to Catholicism, the Shwe Dagon Pagoda is to Theravada Buddhism. Even today, with multi-story buildings growing in Rangoon, the Shwe Dagon's shapely gold-covered, 360-foot spire (regilded every three years) dominates the skyline.

Like many Burmese pagodas, it is *stupa* shaped, resembling an upended bowl, inside of which a sacred relic is buried. From the stupa's center, the Shwe Dagon steeple rises, its tapered top surrounded by seven-tiered golden umbrellas, flat, not humped, and decorated with hundreds of tiny silver bells. The boys climbed one of the four long staircases, one at each point of the compass, that lead to the black and white marble-tiled platform surrounding the base of the stupa. They wandered through the sixty-four open chapels, in many of which a monk was instructing the people sitting cross-legged on the floor. Other people were shikkoing or burning joss sticks or making offerings of fruit or flowers before the many seated, reclining, or standing statues of the Lord Buddha.

But crowded as the Pagoda was, there were no Britons

in sight. The reason for their absence is given by Lady Diana Duff Cooper.[4]

> At tea, conversation was about [the Shwe Dagon Pagoda]. To my surprise, no one had ever been inside. "Footwear," was the explanation: "you have to enter barefoot—and Englishmen can't do that—people do everything there—full of lepers—the stink of the place"—out rolled the excuses. I said one's feet were washable, one did much worse with one's hands, leprosy isn't caught that way, a temple *vaut bien* a whiff. . . . They looked exaggeratedly shocked.

After being driven around Rangoon in a closed car, Lady Diana could stand it no longer. As they returned by way of the pagoda, she said, "I'm going in," and before they could stop her, she had her shoes and stockings off and was climbing one of the great dark staircases:

> It was one of the most repaying sights I have ever seen. . . . On and on you mount . . . faint with the smell of exotic flowers. . . . Little oil-saucers with floating wicks were everywhere being lit. I wished I could have stayed till dark. . . . Even without pausing it took me over an hour.

During the evening in Rangoon young Thant and Khant sat on the banks of the Royal Lake and watched the Prince's barge floating in the middle. They enjoyed the boat races and the fireworks, but they never did see the Prince. The next day they paid their first visit to a zoo and took what U Khant termed "our first train ride" (there were trolleys on tracks in those days).

Back in Pantanaw, they resumed "the even tenor of their ways," studying, playing, and, as a special treat, going to the movies. They saw Rin Tin Tin and Tom Mix. Sometimes their mother accompanied them, but for-

[4] Lord Alfred Duff Cooper quotes his wife in his autobiography, *Old Men Forget* (London: Rupert Hart-Davis; 1953), p. 295.

tunately not when the movies were of a Western romantic variety. Mi Mi Khaing describes her own experience in this regard:

On the screen . . . my mother and my aunts . . . liked the way that love was shown [in Burmese movies], concentrating on sentimentality rather than sex. . . . No wonder the aunts, who once in a while accompanied us to an American film, looked all around during the passionate kissing scenes, with scrutiny of our reaction to such displays of what should not be admitted to exist.[5]

"As an adolescent," U Thaung recalls, "U Thant was meticulously groomed; he dressed carefully and combed his hair neatly; this characteristic, coupled with his sociability and the possession of handsome features, quickly made him extremely popular with the girls and, in later years, with the ladies."

Had it not been for Thant's not always innocent humor, he might have been a goody-goody. His mother remembers no time when he needed to be punished, and U Thaung wistfully adds, "I would like to conjecture scenes where he played truant, where he had rows with bigger boys and beat them up, where he made girls swoon for him, when he went around breaking hearts and such like; but such conjectures would be mere idle fantasy."

Actually, Thant's contemporaries remember him as being shy with girls, mooning over them in private, but not daring to make an advance that might be rebuffed. There are, however, hints that on one occasion he fell in love and the girl returned his affection. When queried about this, the Secretary-General gives neither a yea nor a nay, but only the Burmese equivalent of the Mona Lisa smile.

5 Mi Mi Khaing: *Burmese Family,* p. 178.

In Asia there is no equivalent of the West's tradition of "courtly love," and in Burma there is no "dating" in the Western sense. There is, however, ample opportunity for boys and girls to congregate. The Pantanaw High School was coeducational, and the ready Burmese hospitality meant that friends and relations of all ages and both sexes were in and out of the house. On Sabbath days at the pagoda and during the frequent festivals, groups of boys and girls commingled.

U Thant's easy manner with the opposite sex may also have stemmed from there being girl cousins nearby, and two servant girls in the house who were treated as members of the family. From them he learned the importance of jewelry to young ladies, especially earrings. Each girl looked forward to the day her earlobes would be pierced; this ceremony, like the naming ceremony, involves the foregathering of clan and friends, with the young person the center of attention.

The male equivalent of the girl's ear-piercing is even more impressive. This is the *shin byu,* a Buddhist ceremony comparable in its timing to the confirmation and the bar mitzvah in the West. For the Burmese lad it signals his assumption of self-responsible morality, and he enters the monastery for at least a short stay. He thus, according to an American observer, "becomes a man and not a mere animal; he becomes something which . . . no non-Buddhist, no woman can become; one who may realize Nirvana on passing from this world."[6]

Mi Mi Khaing describes the ceremony which symbolically reproduces the departure of Gautama, the Lord Buddha, from his father's palace to live in self-imposed poverty:

The boy is dressed in princely garments. . . . For him [later] to wash the powder off his face, to doff the turban and show

6 Pye: *Politics, Personality and Nation Building,* p. 100.

the newly shaven head, to change the glittering clothes . . . for a plain yellow robe showing golden on the bare brown skin, this is moving indeed. And when he comes back the next day in procession with other monks, his eyes cast down and his bowl before him, his mother makes obeisance to him for the first time, not as her son now but as one of the priestly order, a *pongyi,* a "great glory."[7]

For some Burmese boys this is a high point. For Thant it was not. Profoundly as he believes in the moral and spiritual teachings of Lord Buddha, he is not attuned to religiosity. And at the time, the fastidious young man could not help noticing that some of the monks had not bathed recently: his nose was offended.[8] He had also, by then, read so widely that in secular matters his education was superior to that of many of the older boys and even of some of the teachers.

U Thant's form of Buddhism has been compared by a friend to the Christianity of a liberal Protestant in a predominantly Catholic country, such as France. Thant compares it to that of a Unitarian in the predominantly Protestant United States. Buddhism, moreover, makes room for the kind of intellectual questing that Thant was beginning to engage in.

As a small child Thant had been influenced by his mother's devoutness; as a youth he was influenced by his father's following of the Buddhist precept, "Test each step with a free will and take nothing on trust." These views were not incompatible since Buddhism is a great umbrella covering an enormous variety of belief and practice.

Every spiritual resource that Thant had developed was put to a bitter test the summer he was fourteen (1923).

[7] Mi Mi Khaing: *Burmese Family,* p. 72.
[8] Ordinarily the Burmese are very clean; indeed cleanliness, according to C. Northcote Parkinson's *East and West,* was imported to post-Renaissance Europe from the Orient.

His father fell ill. For well over a month U Po Hnit suffered, while hope and despair alternated within the hearts of his family, and every resource of medical and monkish skill was brought to bear. And then he died.

It is perhaps a benign distraction to the grief-stricken family that in a tropical country, such as Burma, many things need to be done quickly. As Shway Yoe wrote:

> The body is carried to the side of the central room of the house. . . . Messages are then sent to the monastery, to the friends and neighbors, and a funeral band is summoned. . . . Meanwhile the corpse is closely swathed in new white cotton cloth, and . . . the best clothes put on. The face . . . is left uncovered. . . .
>
> By this time the band has arrived, and commences to play dirges in front of the house. . . . A number of relatives and friends now come to condole and lend their assistance in making and ornamenting the bier and hearse, most of them bringing presents of money or food. . . .
>
> When the day fixed for the funeral arrives the *pongyis* are invited to the house. . . . There is ordinarily an address . . . dwelling mainly on the vanity of human wishes. . . . Then the coffin is brought out. . . . The procession having been formed, a start is made. At the head come the alms intended for the monks and the poor, some carried by men, some by women, and the sexes going in separate lines. . . . Following them comes the band, and often a group of singers. . . . Close upon the musicians comes the bier carried by six or eight young men. Then in a general crowd follow the relations, friends, and neighbors, all on foot. Many passers-by, total strangers, join in the procession from motives of piety.[9]

Thant's mother was so distraught with grief that she was incapable of following the coffin to the cemetery. She remained at home, with her sons trying unavailingly to comfort her. The following day the boys went to pay their

9 Shway Yoe: *The Burman*, pp. 589–92.

last respects to their father, shikkoing at the graveside.

Thant, as the eldest son, was now head of the family. He was already taller than his mother and, in terms of books, better educated. But neither he nor she was equipped to cope with the problem that followed hard on the death of his father. Instead of being well off, as they had been and assumed themselves still to be, they were in straitened circumstances.

In Burma, as in most of Asia, customary law makes no provision for property to be disposed of by will: predetermined shares go to spouse, children of both sexes, and other close descendants. Shortly before the death of U Po Hnit, his uncle and business partner, U Shwe Khin, had also died, leaving an estate of a million rupees (a quarter of a million dollars). U Po Hnit and his family expected to share in this estate with U Shwe Khin's widow.

But in Burma, as elsewhere, there are scoundrels, and one turned out to be the nephew of U Shwe Khin's widow. She herself, sick and bereft, had allowed this nephew to cajole her into turning over to him all her husband's movable properties. "When he was alive," U Khant recalls in a letter, "Father had not the heart to hurt her feelings." The boys' father did, however, consult a Rangoon lawyer, B. N. Burjoree, who recommended serving notices on her and the nephew. Resorting to court action was frequent among the Burmese. "Their passion for litigation," says an American long-time resident of Burma, "is comparable to the passion of Frenchmen for women." But U Po Hnit died before legal action could be initiated.

"The crafty nephew," U Khant recalls, hired a lawyer:

He served Mother with notices for the recovery of sums of money alleged to have been entrusted to Father by U Shwe Khin (before his death) for the purchase of paddy, etc. . . . At the District Court . . . Mother won all the cases, but on appeal by the nephew at the High Court of Judicature at Rangoon, some of the cases were lost by Mother. . . . It is said that the nephew bribed the judge with a new English-made car.

This could well have been the fact. As J. S. Furnivall has written, the substitution of British legal procedures for those of customary law had a corrosive effect on justice in Burma: "As the general belief in judicial corruption grows, the people are more ready to offer bribes, and the judges are less fortified to resist them."[1]

The boys' mother, in order to pay the court judgment, was forced to sell much valuable property and was left without funds for the boys' higher education. What should she do? To the eldest son she turned, not only for emotional support but reasoned advice. He, at the age of fourteen, was thus catapulted for the first, but not the last, time into a position of responsibility which he had never sought. He was also for the first, but not the last, time confronted with evidence of the evil side of man. It is possible that Thant's loathing of deceit stemmed from the experience of being cheated by a man who, under ordinary circumstances, would have been called cousin.

Thant finally decided that he would go to the University, but only for two years, rather than the anticipated four. He could earn the "intermediate degree" and then come home to make money for the younger boys' tuition. His deep deprivation at the death of his father was thus joined to a further deprivation, that of two years of precious education. There was also now no possibility of following his chosen career of journalism, which was too poorly paid and too risky for a young man with a mother and three brothers needing his support.

An alternative career came to mind, partly because of

[1] J. S. Furnivall: *Colonial Policy and Practice* (Cambridge, Mass.: Cambridge University Press; 1948), p. 176.

his friendship with a teacher at the Pantanaw High School. Professor K. Bhattacharya was a bespectacled, warm-hearted Indian with ideas then considered "leftist." Each week the teacher and his star pupil held a public debate on literary subjects; in private they argued politics. Here was Thant's Mark Hopkins. Bhattacharya, Thant says, "was one of the nicest men I ever knew."

To be a teacher was more rewarding in prestige than in money, and many of Burma's future leaders were teachers in National Schools:

The teachers, ill-paid but enthusiastic young men in their late teens and early twenties, lectured their students mainly about the glories of the Burmese past and the contrasting humiliation of imperial domination. The students were encouraged to feel that they were playing a part in the nationalist struggle by their very attendance.[2]

Thant's decision to become a teacher made it even more important that he master his studies. For him, as for many adolescents, reading may also have been a refuge. Perhaps he resorted too much to this refuge, at least from the point of view of his younger brothers. As U Thaung poignantly recalls in a letter:

I'm afraid I can't say that U Thant filled the vacuum caused by the death of my father. He was only fourteen and I was five years his junior. U Thant saw to it that our education was not interrupted. But apart from that, his voracious reading and writing didn't give him the opportunity to fill the role of a father.

And U Tin Maung, the fourth brother, remembers that the few occasions Thant grew impatient with the younger boys were when they disturbed him at his books.

2 Butwell: *U Nu*, p. 8. Besides U Thant and U Nu, other prominent Burmese who were schoolteachers were Sir Paw Tun, Than Tun, U Ba Win, U Win, and U Tin Tut.

Thant, apparently, also became preoccupied at school. A former classmate recalls that "many of us were fond of him but we were not intimate." Another says, "We nicknamed him 'Philosopher.' " And a friend of Thant's later youth, U Bo, writes in a letter:

The image I got of him is that of a person in whom the well-known national traits, subject to ridicule by foreigners, are neither accentuated nor minimized. . . . To illustrate, he is not a hilarious, carefree, happy-go-lucky Burmese of a social club type, nor a serene-seclusive looking Burmese of a meditation-centre type. His non-conformity with the former type does not make him any the less social . . . and his non-conformity with the latter does not make him any . . . the less religious.

Thant says of himself, "I am a nonconformist." By this he means that although outwardly he may go along with what is expected of him, inwardly he may be questioning it. In his teens, he became the Burmese equivalent of "the man from Missouri," with a show-me attitude. For an American youngster today to set everything under the chill light of doubt is not exceptional, but for a Burmese of that day it was quite exceptional. Years later Thant approvingly quoted Geoffrey Gorer's characterization of English people as "shy . . . and consequently very lonely," going on to add, "I think I can say this of most of my Burmese friends." What he did not say was that in a profound sense it may also have been true of himself.

Thant, like many of his Burmese friends, does not appear shy on the surface. But behind the friendly exterior of these attractive and educated people there appear to be moats within moats guarding the inner citadel of the self. One moat is gregariousness: if the person is surrounded by others he need not be intimate with any single one. Another moat is humor, or as Robert Frost characterized it, "the most engaging cowardice": what can be laughed about need not seriously be discussed—and, as Frost continued, "With it myself I have been able to hold some of my enemy in play far out of gunshot." A third moat is simply silence: a Burmese will register what you say but remain quiet in response; there is no "felt need" to keep a conversation going.

On the other hand, what appears to Westerners as a profound reserve may be but the response to communal life in a hot climate where doors, windows, and sometimes the whole front of the house are open to the street. No one could possibly have a family quarrel in a town like Pantanaw without everyone knowing about it; voices, therefore, are rarely raised. Everything one wears or eats, even the number of times a week a woman washes her hair, cannot help but be known to the neighbors. Since outward privacy is rare in the Orient, even in the under-populated countries, inner privacy may be necessary for the sensitive person, especially one like Thant with an intense craving for the freedom to explore various possibilities before making his own judgment.

In Rangoon, at the University, he would find many opportunities to arrive at his own conclusions. His mother was still deeply saddened by his father's death, but three years had passed and Thant was young and hale. As he says today, "I wasn't fully conscious of the implications of my father's death." Perhaps he was able to surmount it precisely because he had loved his father and knew he was loved in return. It was, however, difficult to take leave of his mother, who was further saddened by her son's departure. Thant was grateful both for her stoicism and for the solace her religion provided. For in Buddhism, as in the Biblical religions, to turn the grieving self toward the eternal can be "a refuge and strength, a very present help in trouble."

CHAPTER FOUR

A Faith
Takes Hold

"Buddhism," says a contemporary Burmese, "has shaped the very nature of our inward selves, and has exercised a curbing influence on the natural exhuberances of a virile Mongolian people."[1]

Buddhism has also shaped the profile of the villages of Burma so that the one- or two-story houses are dwarfed by the spire of the pagoda.

Most extraordinary are the more than nine hundred pagodas of Pagan started by King Anawrahta in the eleventh century. Although subject to fierce sun and drenching monsoon, to ants and other monument nibblers, the

[1] U Khin Zaw, Director of Broadcasting, published an article in the only issue of the Burmese magazine *Chinthe*, April, 1951. U Thant at that time was a member of its four-man publication committee.

ruins of these varied and beautiful temples still constitute one of the man-made wonders of the world. G. E.
Harvey says of Anawrahta and his dynasty, "Their rule
was aesthetic and religious rather than political. To them
the world owes in great measure the preservation of
Theravada Buddhism, one of the purest faiths mankind
has ever known."[2]

Theravada, the form of Buddhism prevailing in Burma
and also in nearby Ceylon, Cambodia, Laos, and Thailand, differs in important respects from the Mahayana
Buddhism of China (and Vietnam) and from the many
branches of Japanese Buddhism, one of the smaller of
which is Zen. (All subsequent references to Buddhism in
this book are to the Theravada variety.)

Inwardly Buddhism becomes part of the Burmese
people before the age of memory: infants and toddlers are
welcome at the pagoda, where they view the combination
of awe and bustle from that securest of childhood vantage
points, a parent's arms. Outwardly Buddhism is part of
Burmese life because of the frequent festivals. The more
ebullient of these are said to be essential in channeling,
if not wholly in curbing, the natural exuberances of the
people. An American social scientist states (in a letter)
that "the repressed aggression in Burmese personality
is so great that formalized release of it is necessary to
prevent the more frequent occurrence of individuals 'run-
ning amok.' "

Although "repressed aggression" is not a term familiar
to the Burmese, many would admit to difficulty in controlling their strong emotions. U Nu, the placid-faced devout former premier, whose youth had included periods of
alcoholism and delinquency, was known while in office

---

[2] G. E. Harvey: *History of Burma from the Earliest Times to March
1924* (New York: Longmans, Green & Co., Inc.; 1925), p. 69.

for his temper. And at that time (1951) he attributed a similar problem to his countrymen:

Even before the attainment of independence, I had deeply pondered on the ways and means of relieving the chests of our nationals . . . of pent-up feeling so long suppressed during British and Japanese rules. Such feelings can be dangerous. For example, if a man entertains very strong feelings and has to suppress them against his will, he will not only experience the greatest discomfort but his suppressed feelings are likely to result in uncontrollable outbursts.[3]

The key phrase here is "against his will": controls imposed from the outside are profoundly resented by the Burmese. At the same time, they are capable of imposing, each upon himself, the most stringent and prolonged controls. The Buddhist "Lent" lasts a quarter of a year and is strictly observed. Even though marriage is a civil ceremony it may not be solemnized during this period. In the meditation centers, laymen as well as monks follow the rule of silence for weeks on end. U Nu, after a romantic courtship and happy marriage, with five children, announced in 1948 that in order to be worthy of leading his country he was vowing sexual abstinence for the rest of his life—a monklike act that was highly approved by the Burmese people.

The shaven-headed monks and nuns vow not only to celibacy but to poverty and a form of fasting (they eat nothing after the noonday meal) for as long as they choose to wear the orange robe. These robes—the nuns wear over theirs a persimmon-colored chiffon-like scarf—are reminiscent of ripened rice or gold, yellow being the holy color in Burma, as the yellow *padauk* is the national flower. Just as devout Buddhists are expected to give food

[3] U Nu's "From Peace to Stability" is quoted by Pye: *Politics, Personality and Nation Building,* p. 140.

to the monks at dawn, the monks, to symbolize their indifference to worldly things, are expected to eat whatever
is given.[4] In practice, two boys from each monastery carry
a wooden or lacquer tray with separate dishes for condiments and sweets so that the gifts for the monks will be
appetizing, whereas the larger monasteries maintain their
own kitchens. Still, the food for these kitchens is a gift
from the people, either in the form of rice or money with
which to buy it.

Today the number of monks in Burma is estimated
at 100,000. From a purely economic point of view, those
who do not teach or administer are nonproductive members of society: they sow not, neither do they reap. Yet
from a spiritual point of view, the good monks are the
living embodiment of those values for which the sowing
and reaping of this world are but the preliminaries.

He who taught these values, Siddhartha Gautama,
lived between 563 and 483 B.C. Born the son of a local
king on the southern border of present-day Nepal, he
married a beautiful and loving princess whose favor
he had won by demonstrating his varied skills. Had he
docilely gone along with high-caste Hindu tradition, he
would have inherited precisely the kind of worldly power
and riches with which Satan tried to tempt Jesus five
hundred years later. But Siddhartha's father, warned by
an astrologer that the prince would have a most unusual
destiny, had preserved him from contact with the uglier
realities of life; and perhaps because the young man had
thus been insulated, his inner peace was shattered when
he saw in quick succession an old man, a sick man, a dead
man, and, in contrast, a monk.

[4] The Oxford don Edward Conze, in *Buddhism: Its Essence and Development* (New York: Harper Torchbook; 1959), p. 62, refers to the respect
in which the Venerable Pindola is held for having calmly eaten the
thumb of a leper that had fallen into his bowl.

So great was his questioning and self-questioning that even after his son was born, he could no longer enjoy the love and beauty with which he was surrounded. In the dark of night, with a loyal companion, he left his home, resolved not to return until he had solved the problem of human suffering: "Only one thing do I teach: suffering —its cause and cure."

For six years he wandered, penniless, sometimes with a friend or disciple, sometimes alone. He tried out mortification of the flesh, but found it an impediment rather than an aid to truth:

The emaciated devotee produces confusion and sickly thoughts in his mind. Mortification is not conducive even to worldly knowledge; how much less to a triumph over the senses! . . . To keep the body in good health is a duty, for otherwise we shall not be able to trim the lamp of wisdom. . . . Water surrounds the lotus-flower, but does not wet its petals.

After a variety of spiritual and physical adventures, Siddhartha sat meditating under a pipal tree (the sacred Bo tree), and there enlightenment came to him. This enlightenment he summed up in the Four Noble Truths, first, that suffering is built into man's condition; second, that its cause is craving for personal, selfish gratification; third, that suffering will cease once the craving is stilled; and fourth, that this result can be achieved by treading the Noble Eightfold Path. This path of moderation is also called "The Middle Way" and it has three main components: ethical conduct or morality, mental discipline or meditation, and knowledge or wisdom (see Appendix III).

In Burma one of the most influential of Buddha's teachings is the basic equality of all persons: "The priest is

---

THE MIDDLE WAY

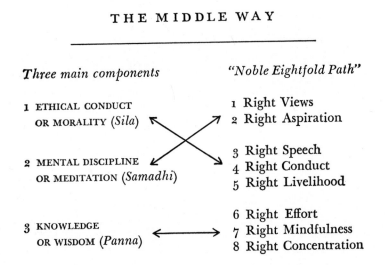

Three main components   *"Noble Eightfold Path"*

1 ETHICAL CONDUCT
  OR MORALITY (*Sila*)

2 MENTAL DISCIPLINE
  OR MEDITATION (*Samadhi*)

3 KNOWLEDGE
  OR WISDOM (*Panna*)

1 Right Views
2 Right Aspiration

3 Right Speech
4 Right Conduct
5 Right Livelihood

6 Right Effort
7 Right Mindfulness
8 Right Concentration

born of woman; so is the outcaste. My law is a law of grace for all . . . without exception, men, women, boys, girls, poor and rich."

An aspect of this equality is the wheel of rebirth to which all creatures are subject. Yet rebirth is not the same as transmigration of souls. Instead, according to the scholar-diplomat U Mya Sein, "It is the ceaseless transformation of life force along the infinite chains of existence."[5] This transformation, in turn, implies that every creature that has lived and does live and will live is kin. Such egalitarianism, including by inference the animal world, goes beyond that of the West, and may have stemmed in part from Siddhartha's reaction against the cruelty to outcastes and animals in his native India. In any event, Buddhism, like Christianity, finally had its greatest influence outside the area where it began. A

5 The *Guardian* magazine, August, 1961.

prophet being not without honor, save in his own country, might well be a Buddhist dictum too.[6]

If human beings are basically equal, all should be treated with equal consideration. In the Buddhist *Udana*, as in *Leviticus*, self-centered man is warned against doing unto others what he would not want done unto himself:

I have never yet met with anything that was dearer to anyone than his own self. Since to others . . . the self is dear, therefore let him who desires his own advantage not harm another.

The question of what is, and what is not, to a person's true advantage is a central one in Buddhism. The kind of craving to be avoided, says U Mya Sein, is "desire which grows into attachment and multiples into craving or lust." For, from craving comes hatred against those who frustrate its satisfaction. The three cardinal vices of Buddhism, therefore, are craving or greed, hatred or anger, and illusion or ignorance.

On the other hand, satisfaction of basic human needs, intellectual as well as physical, is not frowned upon. There is nothing grim about Buddhism—or the Burmese people. But the satisfaction of these needs is viewed as a means rather than as an end. The end to be sought is self-improvement through meditation, wisdom, and good works. Many Burmese heads of family labor no longer than they must in order to provide responsibly for their dependents, and then they retire in order to prepare themselves spiritually for the next rebirth.

[6] Although, two hundred years later, King Asoka made Buddhism the state religion of India, his successors went back to the Hinduism that had preceded it. A millennium later the Moslem religion was introduced in India, where it too has flourished. Moreover, just as post-Reformation Catholicism cleansed itself of many of the abuses that had led to the growth of Protestantism, so post-Buddhist Hinduism cleansed itself of many of the abuses that had led to the growth of Buddhism, and in both instances the new religion went on to thrive in foreign lands.

Although good works in Buddhism are a means of obtaining "merit," the essential prerequisite is correct inner feeling. This merit may be credited to the person himself, his family, or his friends. (U Thant, on a visit to Rangoon in July, 1964, was reported by the local press as hoping that the merit he gained by feeding fifty-five monks—his age being then fifty-five—and by various cash donations might bring wealth and happiness to the people of Burma.)[7] Some Burmese build small pagodas—one orthodox sect says there is more merit to be gained by building a new one than by repairing an old one—or they establish near the road a resting place or water tank for travelers. Or they buy back from the slaughterhouse doomed animals and set them free. Or they enter for a period a monastery or nunnery.

Merit is also achieved by obeying the five precepts for laymen (there are five further ones for monks). These, reminiscent of the Bible's Ten Commandments, are: neither to destroy life, nor to rob, nor to commit adultery, nor to lie, nor to become intoxicated (when intoxicated one loses certain forms of awareness and may lose self-control). Conversely, merit is achieved by cultivating the four cardinal virtues: equanimity, charity, compassion, and joy. Compassion or loving kindness, moreover, is enjoined in the *Dhammapada* in terms comparable to turning the other cheek:

> *Never in this world is hate*
> *Appeased by hatred;*
> *It is appeased by love—*
> *This is an eternal law.*

The love extolled in Buddhism is selfless love (*metta*). Its value is compounded of the merit achieved for the

[7] *Guardian* newspaper, Rangoon, July 27, 1964.

person who feels it, of the joy that accompanies it, and of its providing the precondition for equanimity or peace of mind. That such love may arouse positive feelings in others is not emphasized. Buddhism is not primarily a way to make friends and influence people. Instead, it is a form of spiritual self-help; desirable as its by-products may be, these are not its purpose. Its purpose is the spiritual purification of the person by the person: "Though the Buddha can point the path, he cannot walk it for us."[8]

Because of its emphasis on the individual and his inner life, Buddhism has been criticized by some Western theologians as a form of otherworldliness that leads to ignoring the pressing economic, social, and political problems of the day. To many Burmese, on the other hand, an activist country like the United States puts too much stress on material things and thus whets the wrong kind of "want," the kind that leads to suffering. As one of them says, "Your fear of wasting time strikes us as the greatest waste of time." Thant, characteristically, tries to bridge the two viewpoints:

In my very conservative Buddhist family, moral and spiritual power was thought more important than material or intellectual power. In the West, or the non-Oriental regions, the development of "intellect" means more doctors, more engineers, more trips to the moon. I believe that moral and spiritual values must be kept in mind and developed together with the intellectual ones. Otherwise one crisis will lead to another. On the other hand, mere moral and spiritual development at the expense of the intellect is an anachronism. I think the development of man must be in all three fields.[9]

8 Bhikku U Thittila: *Atlantic Supplement,* "Perspectives of Burma," 1958.
9 He spoke extemporaneously before the Riverdale AAUN on May 24, 1963.

Though all of human life is encompassed within Buddhism, Buddhism has rarely attempted to encompass all of human life, in the sense of all people. Despite Asoka and Anawrahta, it is not a proselytizing religion; over the millennia, it has relied on preachment more than force, and on example more than preachment, to extend its influence.

Theologically, the difference between Buddhism and the biblical religions is especially important in regard to God and the self. In Buddhism there is ultimate reality but no supreme deity; Siddhartha Gautama demonstrated how life should be lived so as to avoid suffering and achieve "the peace that passeth understanding," or Nirvana. But Siddhartha did not worship any God. And although he eventually became the Buddha, this is not the same as being God. In Buddhism there is no personal God and not even necessarily a Prime Mover. U Mya Sein restates this ancient world view in modern terms:

> In the circle of casual links there is no First Cause. The universe could not have been created out of a nothingness because in a condition of void, empty of phenomena and events, there could be no pre-existence of Time. As a concept Time can only exist in relation to physical bodies and their movements in space; this is the basis of Einstein's "space-time continuum."
>
> It is apparent, therefore, that Time could not have existed prior to the existence of the physical universe on which it depends. . . . All human reasoning ends in a paradox because it follows the periphery of a circle, the sphere embracing time, space and phenomena. . . . There is no answer to the problem, but that the problem never existed.[1]

Once this basic paradox is accepted, Buddhists utilize logical, cause-and-effect reasoning in an attempt to ex-

[1] *Guardian* magazine, August, 1961.

plain the apparent terrible injustices that many Jews
since Job, many Christians since Jesus, and many Moslems
since Mohammed have stated are mysteries to be explained only by the will of God. U Khant, a more devout
Buddhist than his elder brother, provides an explanation:

> The history of an individual does not begin with his birth:
> it does not end with his death. He has been endless ages in
> the making. In all this incalculable series, there is no chance,
> no accident, no caprice. According to Buddhism, the law of
> Karma is the law of cause and effect: as we sow, so do we
> reap. A man's character and situation are largely determined
> by what he had done or left undone in previous lives. But he
> is no fettered slave. He can alter the consequences of his past
> deeds by deliberate acts in the present, by his energy and
> determination. Karma, or action, is a continuous process. A
> man's future entirely depends on what he makes of the pres-
> ent. In Buddhism, man is master of his destiny.

The way to become master of one's destiny was shown
by the Lord Buddha in his life as well as his teachings.
For this contribution he is deeply revered. On the altar
before his statue, sanctified by the monks, daily offerings
are laid by the devout. (U Thant, when presented with a
statue of Buddha in New York, refused to bring it home
to his devout wife because, in the United States, it could
not be properly sanctified by the monks. In his upstairs
study, there is a small Buddha shrine with a statue sanctified before they left Burma. Behind it is a window with a
sweeping view of the Hudson River; in front of it is a
figured rug upon which no one steps with shoes on. Daw
Thein Tin keeps fresh flowers and filled water goblets
beneath the statue.)

As for the self, this is not, in Buddhism, a true entity.
Buddhists believe that there is nothing inherently lasting
about anything on earth, including the "I." As U Thant

says, "Permanence and continuity are two different things."[2] And U Mya Sein points out that nuclear energy, newly discovered, is but one aspect of the eternally changing character of the universe. In some forms of Buddhist meditation, a major focus is upon the process of change itself. An Australian writer describes her experience in a Burmese meditation center:

There followed a short sermon on the technique we were to adopt . . . "Phyit-pyet," literally "In-out," creation and destruction, or coming to be and ceasing to be. We were to start by applying this conception . . . at the tip of the nose, extending it to the top of the head and thence all through the body until we became conscious of the body and mind as consisting entirely of particles in creation and destruction.[3]

Such meditation can be carried on while walking or lying down as well as when sitting. A difficulty encountered by Westerners who try to sit in the traditional "lotus position" is that their legs go to sleep, whereas if they lie down *they* go to sleep.[4] U Nu, a long-time devotee of meditation, has never, despite the extreme tensions of his political life, needed a sleeping pill. And U Thant is thus described by U Khant in a letter:

He is one of the fortunate men who have the capacity to cast aside care and relax, however anxious the situation. He has that power of detachment in a most remarkable degree. After a heavy day's work, he would go to bed, whether at a regular hour or at a late hour, and would sink into sleep the moment that his head touched the pillows. This happy inter-

[2] Interview with U Thant, New York, 1963.
[3] Marie B. Byles: *Journey into Burmese Silence* (London: George Allen & Unwin Ltd.; 1962), p. 47.
[4] When I asked U Thant whether, on a trip to Burma, I should spend time in a meditation center, he responded, like my husband, with an immediate and wholehearted laugh. In Burma, as elsewhere, apparently one can't make a silk purse . . .

lude would enable him to return to his task like a giant refreshed.

As essential and refreshing as sleep to U Thant is meditation. It involves, he says, a temporary closing off of the senses, a concentration on inner realities. "You could set off a firecracker next to a person really meditating and he would not hear it; you could wave Chanel Number Five under his nose and he would not smell it."

The result is comparable to the action of the lungs on the blood: impurities and fatigue are removed, and the person feels energized, ready to tackle an old problem with new perspective, or a new problem without undue ego involvement. Instead of holding a grudge against someone who has injured you, you may feel objective curiosity about what you might have done to make him want to injure you. You emerge from a successful experience of meditation, U Thant says, with a feeling of "give my love to everybody" (metta-pura). Or, as U Mya Sein says, "A living man or woman may foretaste salvation any number of times."[5]

U Nu, who has often retired into meditation centers, as U Thant has not, describes the "spiritual exercises" of meditation as the building of a "massive wall of awareness." By this he means an exorcism of both "attachment and revulsion," comparable to the effort of Hercules when lifting Antaeus on high:

Not being able to derive any strength from the earth . . . Antaeus became weaker . . . and was destroyed. In the same way by completely preventing the mind-defiling passions and thoughts from arising, through a constant application of the

5 Edward Conze (in *Buddhism*, p. 59) goes so far as to compare the serenity and well-being that follow meditation to those that follow good sex. He suggests therefore that the celibacy of the monks is expected partly because a higher purification and peace can come through meditation.

sense of awareness, mental states that produce defiling passions and thoughts, wither and disappear.[6]

In this sense Buddhist meditation is the opposite of Oscar Wilde's dictum that "the only way to get rid of a temptation is to yield to it." It is the opposite, too, of the psychoanalytic practice of bringing to consciousness the person's repressed urges. Rather, it is reminiscent of the "perfectionist ethic" of Jesus when he warned that the man who committed adultery in his heart was as culpable as the man who acted it out. Although no human being, presumably, can voluntarily prevent a forbidden thought from arising, he can, to some extent, determine whether or not he dwells on it in fantasy. Or, as C. S. Lewis says in *Letters to Malcolm,* "If the imagination were obedient, the appetites would give us very little trouble." In Buddhist meditation the imagination is, through discipline and habit, diverted to matters beyond the self and its desires. In the process the person may be aided by what some psychiatrists call unconscious sublimation, and some theologians call grace.[7]

For Marie Byles, "names do not matter, but the psychological attitude of relaxing and trusting in a Power not oneself, matters very much indeed."[8] This turning to a power, or, more accurately, to a universal principle, is for some Buddhists the essence of prayer. When they tell you they will pray for you, this implies a devout remembrance of the Buddha who taught the efficacy of sending out loving and health-bringing thoughts. If, it might be argued, the sticking of pins into an effigy can bring about a person's downfall, then the mobilizing of loving con-

6 U Nu: *An Asian Speaks,* p. 43.
7 "It is the fruit of grace," says Protestant theologian Reinhold Niebuhr, "that frees us from the prison-house of self-concern."
8 Byles: *Journey into Burmese Silence,* p. 37.

cern can contribute to a person's health and well-being.

As for meditation, like other endeavors, it is not invariably successful. U Thant believes that, in addition to the arid periods experienced by all practitioners, there are some persons who because of their nature or their youth are not suited to its rigors. He did not, for example, teach its techniques to his young daughter, son, and foster son. On the other hand, there are many Burmese, uninterested in meditation in their youth, who turn to it in middle age or after. Indeed the natural turning away from material concerns in later life is one reason older people are held in high regard in Burma.

U Nu is more optimistic than Thant about meditation being for everyone at all ages. In 1955 he recommended it to the American people:

I earnestly plead with the people of the United States . . . to put the truth of Buddhism to the test, in the same way as a scientific theory is put to the test.

In regard to the testing of scientific theory, brain research on animals at Western Reserve University and the University of California has uncovered evidence that the brain of mammals contains a "consciousness switch," an arrangement of interconnected nerve cells that convey a special pattern of electrochemical impulses to the centers of consciousness.

This "consciousness switch" can be disconnected from some stimuli by concentration on other stimuli. As Dean E. Woolridge reports:

. . . if a cat . . . is exposed to a . . . sequence of musical tones, measuring equipment will detect a corresponding sequence of electric impulses in the nerve leading from ear to brain. If then, with no change in the tone sequence . . . an object of great feline interest is displayed to the cat—mice, let us say— the measurements will show a great decrease. . . . The appearance of an object of overriding interest generates a new electric signal that serves to turn down the "volume control" of the nerve system registering the object of lesser interest.[9]

What the cat's brain does instinctively, man's can be trained to do by discipline. Buddhist awareness, according to *Saya* (the Burmese equivalent of the Indian *Guru*) U Ba Khin, involves learning to "put a ring through the nose of the bull of consciousness." So convinced is U Nu of the value of this kind of mental discipline that in 1955 he suggested that ten Americans come to Burma, expenses paid, to try it out for themselves and then report on its success to their own people. For the values of Buddhism are often such that they must be experienced before they can be understood. Thus Buddhism is both more and less than a religion; it is a way of life. And while it may involve a rigorous discipline of the self, its attitude toward other persons is one of tolerance. Seeing a person act in a manner that the Buddhist neither understands nor condones, he is likely to shrug, saying, "That is his way," and go about his own. Indeed, with the person's future rebirths dependent on his behavior in this life, the woe he may cause others is as nothing to the woe he may ultimately cause to himself.

Buddhist tolerance, furthermore, appears to be grounded in a spiritual sense of security. The Burmese view was described by Fielding Hall in somewhat idealized terms:

Each person is responsible for himself, the foreigner no less than the Burmese. If a foreigner has no respect for what is good, that is his business. It can hurt no one but himself if he is blatant, ignorant, contemptuous. No one is insulted by it, or requires revenge for it. You might as well try and insult

[9] *The New York Times Magazine,* October 4, 1964.

gravity by jeering at Newton . . . as to injure the laws of
righteousness by jeering at the Buddha.[1]

Yet, in actuality, many Burmese were offended by the
attitude of those British individuals who refused to visit
pagodas or observe the rules of the "footwear-prohibited
places." Also, the British rulers abolished the Sangha
courts and put monks under civil law. And the attitude
of the first English Nobel Prize-winning poet, Rudyard
Kipling, was anathema to educated Burmese such as
Thant. In the second stanza of "Mandalay," for example,
Kipling described the British soldier's view of the Lord
Buddha as a "Bloomin' idol made o' mud."[2]

Before Thant went to Rangoon University in 1926, he
had been insulated from the British rulers. In Pantanaw
his conservative Buddhist family was highly respected.
They were Burman-Mon, which is comparable in the
United States to being "wasp" (White Anglo-Saxon Protestant). He was the eldest child of parents who loved
each other and their children. Altogether he had enjoyed
what is variously called good luck or reward for merit
in previous existences.

Burmese clothes being simple, his luggage was light as
he stepped aboard the boat; and being seventeen years
old, his heart was light too. He was on his way to the
capital of his world, Rangoon.

1 Hall: *The Soul of a People*, p. 142.
2 Although the American publishers of Rudyard Kipling, Doubleday
& Company, Inc., granted permission to quote the second stanza in full,
Kipling's daughter in England first asked to see the context, and then
refused permission. Even today a well-meaning British author may un-
intentionally inflame Buddhist sensibilities. In *The Land and People
of Burma*, C. Maxwell-Lefroy (1963), for example, thus describes the
awe-inspiring Shwe Dagon Pagoda (p. 30): "Around the base . . . small
pagodas cluster like ducklings around Mother Duck."

CHAPTER FIVE

British Impact
on a Man

A Burmese student coming to live in Rangoon was comparable to a young Italian Catholic coming to Rome or a French artist coming to Paris or a British banker coming to London. For Rangoon, like Rome and Paris and London, had become the religious and cultural and commercial hub of the country.

In another sense, Thant's coming to Rangoon was like a Midwesterner's coming to New York: the two great ports, being host to large numbers of foreigners, are atypical of the rest of the country. For the Burmese, Mandalay, rich in monuments and historic tradition, is the city that is most their own, as perhaps Boston is for Americans.

For Thant it was stimulating to wander through Rangoon, jostled by Indians in dhotis and saris, or Chinese of both sexes in trousers and long jackets, and to hear the honk of British automobiles. And one of his chief joys was to browse in the few bookshops where volumes in English crowded those in Burmese and where British newspapers and periodicals were available.

Although the Burmese were encouraged to visit British bookstores, few were invited to visit British homes. And the British clubs were wholly "restricted": the famous sign alleged to have been posted in a park in Shanghai, "Dogs and natives not allowed," had its unspoken counterpart at Rangoon's Kokine Swimming Club, Gymkana Club, and Pegu Club. Young Thant had neither the funds nor the desire to join a club, so this made no difference in his life.

His interest was centered in the University, which then had a student body of 1,500, with the boys outnumbering the girls four to one and the classes averaging forty students. The first year he lived in Tagaung Hall, a two-story wooden hostel named for the first dynasty of Burma; the second year, in a hostel named Penhurst. From the Burmese Tagaung to the British Penhurst was itself a small parable of his country's history.

The British had worked hard and thoughtfully in setting up Rangoon University. But its full professors and top administrators were, despite the school strike of 1920, primarily British with a few Indians or Anglo-Indians. It was not until the mid-thirties, ten years after Thant's entrance, that a Burmese was finally made a full professor.

This professor, Dr. Htin Aung, was two years ahead of U Thant, as was U Nu. Nu had been told by mutual distant relatives to look up Thant. He did so and the two young men found many intellectual and literary interests in common. One of the teachers they shared was the British historian D. G. E. Hall. When interviewed in

1961, Hall remembered Nu and Thant as "good boys and good students" in his European History course, but said that because of the inadequacies in their National High School preparation neither was "good enough to take honors degrees in history."[1]

In addition to history, which was an optional subject, Thant took English and Burmese (both compulsory), mathematics (including logic), and additional Burmese (literature). One of his classmates, U Myo Min, today Professor of English at Rangoon University, remembers him as "studious, quiet, tidy, neat, well but not expensively dressed."[2] Although, as U Myo Min explained, it is easy to look crumpled in a longyi, Thant "always looked fresh." Thant, moreover, washed his own clothes, and used the weight of his mattress on the folded damp longyi to keep it pressed. The only items that went to the launderer were his dress shirts, of which the cuffs and neckband (shirts were collarless) had to be starched.

U Myo Min's first impression of Thant was not entirely favorable:

I thought him a little effeminate because he applied liquid velvet to his face. His behavior was always gentlemanly. He didn't care for pranks or dirty jokes.

But later U Myo Min grew fond of Thant:

He wasn't really meek or mild. He just didn't like taking part in quarrels or rough horseplay. He would be the observer rather than the participant. He never spoke ill of people. Everyone knew he would do well in his studies but he didn't make a show of brilliance. He hated to be conspicuous.

Thant, however, began to be conspicuous in his extracurricular activities. He was elected joint secretary of the

[1] Butwell: *U Nu*, p. 13.
[2] Interview with U Myo Min, Rangoon, 1964.

University Philosophical Association and secretary of the Literary and Debating Society. Also, according to Dr. Maung Maung:

> Thant began to bombard . . . the press with many letters and articles. He applied his mind to all subjects, found solutions to all problems, passed down his sermons to political leaders and sages alike, commented on everything. It was a fertile mind served by a facile pen.[3]

It was also a mind that let itself go in print as it did not in personal confrontation. As Thant wrote about issues he often gave rein to the strong feelings that otherwise were held back. Unminced words flew from his pen. His description of the leading Burmese politicians of the day, for example, was as "England-returned barristers (some of them quite scatterbrained) . . . towering over the scene in their tails and bow ties, striking poses, speaking bad English at political meetings to people who understood no English and therefore liked the speeches very much."

Young Thant was also not averse to taking an unequivocal stand on complex and debatable issues. One was the issue of "separation," whether or not the British should administratively separate their "province" of Burma from their "colony" of India. Burmese proponents of both sides were primarily interested in hastening home rule for Burma, but they differed sharply as to the means. Their disagreement was heightened by the announcement that a British "Indian Statutory Commission," led by Sir John Simon, was coming from London on a fact-finding mission. The Anti-Separatists wanted the Burmese to boycott the Simon Commission meetings. Young

[3] Dr. Maung Maung, today Chief Judge of the Chief Court in Rangoon, wrote a series of profiles of important Burmese for the *Guardian* magazine in 1956. The one on U Thant appeared in the August issue.

British Impact on a Man

Thant, in a letter to the Rangoon *Times,* January 3, 1928, thought the opposite:

The Statutory Commission is coming to Burma and the feeling . . . that is being manufactured against it will undoubtedly stand in the way of its successful working. To avoid sitting at an examination speaks of the ignorance of the examinee; to avoid a battle denotes the weakness of the combatant; and to try to boycott an enquiry as to the fitness or otherwise of the ruled to hold the reins of government shows either the prejudice of the ruled against the rulers or their incapacity of undergoing an enquiry.

It is not to our advantage to refuse to make the best use of what is given to us and to blame the rulers for not giving us more. It is earnestly expected that better sense will prevail among our so-called leaders and that they will . . . then prove to the entire satisfaction of the Commission that the Burmese are fit to govern.

"So-called leaders" indeed. Thant, with the temporary omniscience of the nineteen-year-old, was as ready to criticize the British-appointed Burmese officials as the Burmese nationalists who permitted themselves "the prejudice of the ruled against the rulers." Thant, like his father before him, favored eventual autonomy for Burma, but refused to couple this aim with a wholesale denigration of the cultural and economic improvements brought by the British to Burma. As Dr. Maung Maung later wrote in the *Guardian,* "Thant was . . . not an Anglophile, not by a long shot." At the same time Thant was not an Anglophobe, although he had the type of experience that turned some of his fellow Asians against the British for life. Thant was on his way from the University to the other side of the Rangoon River. When he reached the jetty, a bit early, a steamboat was tied up at the dock. He stepped aboard. No one was around. On the deck there was a bench with arm rests. He sat down and began to think. Suddenly he felt himself being poked from behind with a stick. He turned. There stood an elderly Briton with his wife and dog. The man said no word, merely gesturing to Thant to leave the bench. The wife tried to smile away the insult. With dignity Thant rose and left the bench—and the boat.[4]

The Briton probably never gave the episode another thought. "In my young days," says Mr. Macgregor, a British colonial in George Orwell's early novel *Burmese Days*, "when one's [native] butler was disrespectful, one sent him along to the jail with a chit saying 'Please give the bearer fifteen lashes.' "[5] And British parents in the colonies brought up their children to assume an attitude of superiority. As one of these children recalls:

The native! A person with whom one did not mix, and whose children were shunned by nice little boys and girls. One might catch all manner of diseases from them; their English accent was all wrong; they would teach us things it was not nice to know.[6]

The person toward whom such an attitude is directed may, if very young, feel not only injury but deep confusion. Mi Mi Khaing, a Mon, never forgot the suffering inflicted on herself and her sister when they went to an English-run school:

The nuns . . . with sincere conviction and fervor . . . condemned everything in us that was different from the great mass of Anglo-Burmese who filled the school. A good portion of these were the children of Englishmen who, not having

4 Interview with U Thant, Geneva, 1963, and only in response to a specific question.
5 George Orwell: *Burmese Days* (New York: Harper & Brothers; 1934), p. 34.
6 Foucar: *I Lived in Burma*, p. 14.

entered into a legal marriage with the Burmese mothers, had now left mother and child with a sum of money which the kind nuns stretched to cover as much schooling as was possible. These and other Anglo-Burmese children were encouraged to swank over us with childish cruelty about our darker skins, flat noses, and uncurling hair. They did this to such an extent that many of us in our minority and our helpless misery branded our distinguished parents as . . . "half-Burmese and half-English," in order to gain their good opinion. . . . We shrank from telling [our parents] about it, however. My father and mother never knew how different our life at school was from the world at home.[7]

This shrinking from telling, this secret bleeding, is characteristic of a racial wound. Mi Mi Khaing was in her thirties before she wrote about her experience; U Thant was in his fifties before he spoke about his own.

One result of racial prejudice is that the hatred aroused by the insult may turn inward, against the self and the self's own kind, rather than outward against the one who insulted him. John Hersey, while researching for *The Wall,* said that he could scarcely believe the disunity that had persisted among the Jews incarcerated in the Warsaw ghetto even when their mutual danger from the Nazis and anti-Semitic Poles was mortal for them all. And U Nu, who pondered the disunity among the Burmese people during World War II, tried to explain it on a similar ground:

When people have long been enslaved very few can retain self-respect. . . . They place little value on the strength they might derive from social unity with their own folk.[8]

The British rationale for their attitude of superiority was its necessity in ruling a country where the British

[7] Mi Mi Khaing: *Burmese Family,* pp. 143–44.
[8] Thakin Nu: *Burma under the Japanese* (New York: The Macmillan Company; 1954), p. 35.

were such a tiny minority. They had achieved what the Burmese call *hpone,* or prestige, by conquering the Burmese king, who himself was the embodiment of hpone. Had they then dealt with the Burmese on an equal basis, it was argued, their hpone would be reduced and more overt power would be necessary to keep the "natives" in line.

Some Britons, however, defied the prevailing mores. One was a retired Indian Civil Service (ICS) officer who had come to Burma in 1902, married a Burmese girl, and, domestically speaking, lived happily ever after. J. S. Furnivall was over fifty when Thant met him. "Furnivall looked," according to Thant's contemporary U Nyun, "like Abraham Lincoln, tall, with a slight stoop, but without the beard." A less reverent observer (American) says that Furnivall looked like Ichabod Crane. In 1922, Furnivall had established his own bookshop near the University, The Burma Book Club, Ltd. One of the many students who flocked to see him and his wares was Thant.

Furnivall was a Fabian. He was also a skilled and original writer. He had great faith in Burma's future, but in the meantime, he felt, there was much educational work to be done. He established for the first time public libraries and reading rooms; he founded the Burmese Education Extension Association, and The Burma Book Club, and published a bilingual, bimonthly magazine, *The World of Books* (which became, in the 1930s, Thant's major outlet for his writings). Furnivall, in his conversations with the University students, U Nyun recalls, "sowed the seeds of nationalism among the younger group."[9]

Thant appeared to Furnivall a young man of such

[9] Interview with U Nyun, Geneva, 1963. Furnivall in 1909 had also founded the Burma Research Society, an event, he himself said, not politically but "morally and potentially of great significance."

promise that Furnivall tried to persuade him to enter the Civil Service, and offered his own not inconsiderable backing to ensure that Thant would get a good post. The pay would be better than that of a National High School teacher, but Thant was not seriously tempted. For one thing, it would have meant two more years at the University, which he could not afford; for another, his teacher's salary, though small, would be adequate for his family's needs; third, as a National High School teacher he would have more freedom to write than as a civil servant; and lastly, his ultimate aim of becoming a journalist might be jeopardized if he had once worked directly for the British overlord.

Thant, moreover, has the natural-born teacher's gift of being able to renew his enthusiasm over familiar material to the point of presenting it as if it were new also to him. "I enjoy putting my ideas across," he says. And his rapport with young people has remained to this day. At an American Thanksgiving dinner in New York in 1961, U Thant turned away from the adult distinguished guests and spent most of his time with the family's teen-agers. These youngsters, varying from the "beat" to the "square," were spellbound, first by Thant's exposition of Buddhism and then by his puns and jokes.

In 1928, Thant passed his Intermediate Examination with the expected high marks. It was a wrench for him to leave the University, but it was U Khant's turn now (U Khant also did well in his Intermediate Examinations and stayed on to help Furnivall in the bookstore and later as editor of *The World of Books*).

Thant went back to Pantanaw, a high school "Senior Master" at the age of nineteen, but he kept his ties with Rangoon by visits and frequent correspondence with Furnivall, Nu, and others. Shortly after his return to Pantanaw, *The World of Books*, August, 1928, announced a prize of fifteen rupees (less than four dollars) for the best translation into Burmese of the English version of La Fontaine's "The Fox and the Raven." When the prize was awarded, Furnivall wrote in *The World of Books* with typical outspokenness:

Apparently the clarity and grace of La Fontaine baffled our translators, for the attempts . . . were few in number and poor in execution. . . . Thilawa was much too florid in his language, but succeeded in retaining the poetry though not the simplicity of the original, and we have no hestitation in awarding him the prize.

"Thilawa" was Thant's pen name, chosen in memory of a seventeenth-century Burmese noble who was reputed to have smiled only three times in his life. To Thant he symbolized the serenity he himself was striving to attain. But it must also have made Thant smile to sign the name of a non-smiler to some of the translations he later submitted, including, as he recalls, "several naughty little stories by de Maupassant." Translating and writing were sports young Thant enjoyed, and he was happy to take on all comers. Literarily the young boxer was dancing in his corner.

A few months after the La Fontaine competition, *The World of Books* announced a more substantial prize of 150 rupees (almost forty dollars) for the best Burmese translation of a poem in any standard English anthology. Thilawa chose Browning's *The Pied Piper of Hamelin*, which combines a clear sermonic moral with delicious humor, rollicking rhythm, and, in places, complicated language and rhyme:[1]

---

[1] The moral of the poem, to beware of Pied Pipers, was later also emphasized by U Nu in *Burma under the Japanese*.

British Impact on a Man

"So munch on, crunch on, take your nuncheon,
Breakfast, supper, dinner, luncheon!"
And just as a bulky sugar puncheon,
Already staved, like a great sun shone.

This time, when Furnivall awarded the prize, he found no need to criticize the winner:

Thilawa ... has achieved a wholly admirable piece of work which gives a faithful rendering of the English poem in verse strongly reminiscent of the Burmese classics, and he has produced a poem which will stand comparison with the classical narrative *pyos* [verses] of Burma. . . . In awarding him the prize . . . we must congratulate him on having thoroughly deserved it.

Later Thant won another competition with a translation of a scene from Oliver Goldsmith's *She Stoops to Conquer*. At Furnivall's request he went on to translate more of the play, but then decided that it was too foreign for the Burmese. For one thing, its action centered around the innkeeper's beautiful daughter, and in Burma there were no inns; travelers stayed out of doors or took shelter in a monastery where, by definition, there were no daughters, beautiful or otherwise. Also there was a climactic tavern scene dependent on intoxication, forbidden by Buddhist precept. Thant explained his reasons to Furnivall who, though disappointed, agreed that the project should be dropped. The future Secretary-General was learning to call a halt when an enterprise no longer seemed realistic.

Not only did Thant see Furnivall when he went to Rangoon, but Furnivall tried to see Thant when he came to the Pantanaw district headquarters, Maubin. One time Furnivall was scheduled to deliver a lecture there on the Public Library Movement. According to U Khant, in a letter, "about fifty town elders, and most of the government officials were present. . . . U Thant was the only person who did not wear the traditional *gaung-baung"* (Burmese headgear for men: a cloth turban with a tie at the side).

Here was an outward example of Thant's nonconformity. Although he always wore Burmese dress, he hated wearing anything on his head. He would cheerfully don his gaung-baung to accompany his mother to the Sabbath ceremonials because she might be hurt if he refused. But in going hatless on other occasions, he felt, no one could be hurt but himself. He therefore indulged his idiosyncrasy and later recommended that others do the same. In *The World of Books,* April, 1935, he wrote:

Clothes are one way in which individuality can be preserved. I am writing these lines under the blazing hot March sun, dressed in an open shirt and a cotton longyi, with legs bare; it is a pre-sabbath day, and only by a strong effort of imagination can I bring myself to realize that some of my colleagues in other schools are at this moment sweating horribly in gaung-baungs and thick jackets. I put on a gaung-baung on school days, as my job requires me to do so, and what a burden it is.

Thant knew that Furnivall, himself a nonconformist, would be pleased to see him whether he wore no hat or three. Nor was he wrong. According to U Khant, "The distinguished visitor . . . clasped the young schoolteacher's hands, and introduced him to all others present there, hinting at the promising talents of Maung Thant as a good translator well imbued in the literature of the land."

Thant's fields of teaching were history, English, mathematics, and civics. His fields of learning—the completion of his formal education meant but the beginning of his informal one—were political theory, history, biography, and philosophy. He read with deep interest about the life and thought of the two Asian national leaders who have most influenced him, Sun Yat-sen and Gandhi, and of the Irish nationalist, Eamon de Valera. Thant also answered an advertisement in a British magazine and thus became the first Burmese member of the Left Book Club of London. Strange shelf-fellows began to join the Victorian poets and novelists collected by his father: There were books by Sidney and Beatrice Webb, John Strachey, Abraham Lincoln, Gogol, D. H. Lawrence, Marx, Hegel, H. G. Wells, Nietzsche, Harold Laski, Bertrand Russell ("I liked his independent thinking"), and Emil Ludwig whose *Genius and Character* impressed Thant. From faraway America came books by Theodore Dreiser, Sinclair Lewis, and Upton Sinclair.

Thant read and pondered and wrote, either for publication or privately in the diary he has kept for twenty-five years. His mother, who did not share his intellectual interests (or his knowledge of English), nonetheless liked seeing him with his nose in a book. This was a posture suitable for a Burmese Buddhist gentleman (even if some of his ideas were not), and besides she knew he was busy preparing himself for the nation-wide Teachership Examination of 1931.

The day the results of the examination were announced was one of jubilation in Pantanaw. It was as if the town had won the Daily Double. First place in the whole country was won by Thant, and second place by his current colleague in the Pantanaw High School, K. Bhattacharya. So proud was Bhattacharya of his former pupil that whatever annoyance he might have felt at being outdone was dissolved in his excited boasting about Thant, and, of course, about how well taught Thant had been.

Bhattacharya was then posted as headmaster in another town while Thant was made headmaster in Pantanaw. He continued teaching despite his new administrative duties. In both roles, however, he found the hand of the British overlord heavy upon his students, who were repeatedly required to take examinations in order to qualify for the next round of education or for jobs. These examinations, he felt, were not only too rigid in the material covered, but they were assigned too much importance in judging the student's future capabilities. "The headmaster's assessment of the student's whole career should have been taken into account," he says in retrospect.

The students, he felt, should be given more freedom of time to work on projects of their own devising, and also more freedom of space in which to do it. The Burmese Buddhists had long relied on examinations as stepping-stones to higher degrees of monkhood. Then the British had installed their own examination-based educational system. The result was a too narrow sieve which prevented many Burmese youngsters from going on to prepare for fruitful careers. As U Thant wrote in his monthly column, "From My School Window":

We should be as content to turn out a good mechanic . . . as a mathematician, if the society into which these students go were adapted to permit of our doing this.[2]

The society into which Thant's students went provided few good openings for the intelligent Burmese. The corrosive effect of this lack of opportunity was noted not only by the Burmese but by Furnivall:

With no openings for doctors or engineers there was no incentive to study the elements of natural science or to

[2] This and the following quotations from U Thant's column appeared between 1935 and 1939 in *The World of Books*, a magazine not available in the United States.

acquire the mental discipline on which the modern world was based.[3]

Thant worried both about the few who could afford the University and the many who could not:

A large percentage of students each year fail in their High School Examinations and the small number . . . who pass fail to get any employment. And then University education is too expensive, and it is not too difficult to see what a source of trouble such half-informed and immature products of the schools might prove.

He devoted his days to making the students at the Pantanaw High School as well informed and mature as possible. Many of them came from lower-income groups, the poorest being the Karens. "Most of the pupils had to do house chores," Thant recalls. "It was hard for them to study while tending the kettle or caring for the younger ones."[4]

While recognizing the problems faced by his students, Thant maintained strictness toward those who breached the rules. "There should be some fear in the minds of the children toward their teachers and parents," he says. On occasion he administered a smart rap with a stick across the palm of a recalcitrant older boy. On the other hand, the smaller children, according to Thida Maw Sturtevant, knew that if they had no pennies to buy a sweet they could always go to the Headmaster who would fish some out of his pocket.[5]

As for classroom discipline, Thant had relatively "progressive" ideas. The teacher, he said, should keep order

---

[3] Furnivall: *Colonial Policy and Practice*, p. 130.
[4] Interview with U Thant, New York, 1963.
[5] Thida Maw Sturtevant (daughter of Dr. Ba Maw, a former Premier of Burma under the British) was interviewed by telephone in Washington in 1962.

not by punitiveness but by engaging the interest of his students: "if [he] deals out harsh punishment he only succeeds in making the class despise both himself and the work and no good is done to anybody." Student interest, Thant further stated, should be engaged by problems outside the school as well as those in books. He encouraged study, by teachers and students, of the problems of clean water, public health, and improved veterinarian and agricultural services. His job, as he saw it, was to prepare good citizens for all the nation-building roles.

When the position of Pantanaw School Superintendent, above that of Headmaster, became vacant, Thant wrote to his friend Nu. U Nu's biographer quotes one Burmese as saying, "Nu took the teaching position in Pantanaw because this was the only job he could get." The biographer goes on to comment: "This may be so, but there is evidence that Nu expected to like the work. Moreover, his friend Thant was there and urging him to come."[6]

Among the subjects the two young men spent many warm evenings discussing were life, love, and the pursuit of happiness, which in Burma at that time included the pursuit of nationalist goals.

[6] Butwell: *U Nu*, p. 15.

CHAPTER SIX

British Impact
on a Country

Although both the United States and Burma once belonged to Great Britain, their colonial experience was different in many respects.

First, the American colonies were annexed early, and Burma late. By the time the whole of Burma came under British control, the American colonies had been independent for over a century.

Second, while the colonizers in the temperate zones came to settle, those in the tropics came to extract, or, as Furnivall said, "The tropics have been colonized with capital rather than with men."[1]

Third, when the British arrived, the American continent was virtually empty and its few disparate Indian

[1] Furnivall: *Colonial Policy and Practice*, p. 3.

tribes were driven from the land wanted by the British. Burma, on the other hand, was settled throughout by indigenous people who were organically knit together by the slow-growing, tensile strands of race and religion, language and education, custom and a common history of self-rule.

Visibly, from the British point of view, there was much to be built in Burma, but invisibly, from the Burmese point of view, there was much to be destroyed. If the road to hell is, indeed, paved with good intentions, some of its foundation stones must have been laid by British colonial administrators. Certainly the good intentions of some were unmistakable. As Sir Thomas Munro had written from Madras to the officials of the East India Company in the early nineteenth century:

You are not here to turn India into England or Scotland. Work through, not in spite of, native systems and native ways . . . and when in the fullness of time your subjects can frame and maintain a worthy Government for themselves, get out and take the glory of achievement and the sense of having done your duty as the chief reward for your exertions.[2]

A spiritual descendant of Sir Thomas Munro was J. S. Furnivall. The Indian Civil Service had superb esprit de corps and was generally recognized as the best organization of its kind in history. But for a full century after the British began annexing Burma, no Burmese were permitted to join its British, Anglo-Indian, and Indian ranks.

In Burma, moreover, the ICS was outnumbered four to one by the British business community, the head of which, Furnivall said, was "the uncrowned king of Burma." Starting in 1852, the British had established monopolies in ocean and river shipping, railways, rice

[2] Quoted in Lord Radcliffe of Werneth: *The Problem of Power* (London: Martin Secker & Warburg, Ltd.; 1952), p. 76.

exports, teak and other timber, and subsequently in tin and copper mines and oil wells. Their profits were enormous and mostly remitted abroad.

For business to flourish in Burma law and order had to be maintained. This was the responsibility of the ICS. Unfortunately there were too few Sir Thomas Munros and Furnivalls to go around. Instead there were plenty of road-company Procrustes' who, sometimes with good intentions and sometimes with impatient arrogance, chopped or stretched the Burmese way of life to fit British purposes. (While U Thant generally had good luck in his British contacts, one of his Burmese contemporaries reports having never seen a Briton he could like or admire until he went to England.)

An unintended result of British hard work in Burma was to create havoc where once there had been stability. In place of Burmese customary law, the British imposed a centrally administered system of government. From the logical point of view they may have been right, but from the psychological point of view they could scarcely have been more wrong.

Trouble started promptly over the basic question of land ownership. Under the kings, no one had legally owned land, but everyone knew to the nearest centimeter which family had the right to farm which plot. The British insisted on registering land, not in the name of a family but of an individual. With one stroke they undermined the Burmese tradition of family responsibility for all its members and left the way open for unscrupulous individuals to grab land tilled at one time by their family or even village common land. If the family sought legal redress, the British-instituted court system tended to back the new individual owner. "Thus," says an American economist, "British rule broke down the basis of family life, and for individuals who were landless, the basis of community life."[3]

The British, furthermore, insisted on tidying up the traditional village boundaries. In Rangoon the map divisions were rational, but in the countryside many family, ethnic, social, and linguistic unities were sundered. The old villages and "circles" of villages not only lost people they wanted to keep, but were forced to accept people they did not want (or who did not want to join them). As a result, Furnivall said, the formerly close-knit Burmese villagers became "a crowd of strangers." Unrest followed and there was little compunction about disobeying what seemed to the Burmese arbitrary rulings of an alien group. Lawlessness began to move from the dacoits to the dignified, from the unusual to the usual.

Deeply upsetting also to the Burmese was the British interference with the prestige and power of the monks. Part of this interference was unintentional: the newly installed British schools provided a more up-to-date education than did the monks' schools and attracted bright boys like Thant. But part of the interference was deliberate: in 1891 the British had extended civil law to cover all monks. In defense of the British, it must be pointed out that, up till then, any Burmese rebel or dacoit or criminal could easily take refuge in a monastery and don the orange robe. Under the Burmese kings the monks had been kept in line, first by their own abbots, then by the courts of the Sangha. But under the British a monk had to be judged, not by his spiritual peers, but by an uninitiated non-Buddhist foreigner. No self-respecting Burmese, therefore, would testify against a monk in court. In Burmese eyes the British brought into disrepute, not

[3] Everett E. Hagen: *On the Theory of Social Change* (Homewood, Ill.: Dorsey Press; 1962), p. 463.

the occasional unruly monk, but the whole British system of justice.

Sadly too, as U Thant's mother discovered, there were judges, including some Burmese appointed by the British, who were subject to bribery. Corruption proliferated not only in the courts but in the police, hospitals, and other government services. This corruption, Furnivall said, was less a characteristic of the Burmese than of the system under which they were being ruled. He pointed out that there was *more* corruption in those departments where *few* Burmese were employed than in those where "they are chiefly employed, and the people understand and value their activities."[4]

Even when the British, belatedly, gave back some self-government to the Burmese, the cancer of corruption had metastasized, and when officials were finally elected by the Burmese, rather than appointed by the British, the corruption spread to the election process itself. Said Furnivall:

> There was no organic connection between the people and their representatives; villagers did not look beyond their village or care twopence who represented them, so that votes went for less than two a penny paid in promissory notes.[5]

This was the kind of "democracy" that U Thant witnessed when he moved back to Pantanaw and for the first time saw local politics through the eyes of an adult.

The British interference with the power of the Sangha, combined with their grant of the vote to the adult Burmese populace, opened the way for monks to enter the political scene. Some of these monks were self-sacrificing

[4] A committee of Burmese Ministers in the 1930s found, on investigation, that 70 per cent of the two lower judicial grades were dishonest and not less than two-thirds of the police were corrupt (Furnivall: *Colonial Policy and Practice*, p. 174).
[5] Furnivall: *Colonial Policy and Practice*, p. 169.

heroes; others were not. The British felt forced at times to jail both types, and when it was a hero who was jailed, the feelings of the Buddhist population churned.

Burmese laymen too began moving toward the political arena. A key date in Asian history is 1905, the year the Japanese conquered the Russians, thus proving to Asians that they were not inferior to Europeans. Within a few months, in Burma, the first of many Young Men's Buddhist Associations was formed (support for them came from the *Thuriah* newspaper U Thant's father had helped to found).[6] These groups, modeled on the YMCAs, consisted of students meeting to discuss religion. Before long, however, their branches expanded in numbers and agenda: Burmese art and literature joined religion, and through the discussions a sense of national identity was formed.

Burmese employees of the government were forbidden to join the YMBAs, but three years later another group, The Burma Research Society, was founded by Furnivall on the understanding that it would eschew politics and economics (U Thant joined it as a "life member" in 1931). This group, which Burmese employees of the government were finally permitted to join, discussed Burmese literature, language, archaeology, religion, art, music, folklore, and customs. Innocent sounding as the Society was, the British Financial Commissioner at first refused his approval lest it be, as he said, " a deep-laid scheme to encourage nationalism . . . and subversive tendencies."[7] And in a sense the Commissioner was right.

At the same time, his timorous and censorious attitude was an example of the colonial experience corroding the

[6] Among the YMBA songs, according to Dr. Maung Maung in *Burma's Constitution*, was "God Save Buddha," sung to the tune of "God Save the King."

[7] Quoted in Furnivall: *Colonial Policy and Practice*, p. 173.

overlord as well as the subject people. The British at home, more perhaps than any people, have protected the right of groups to foregather to discuss bad as well as good ideas. Yet until the middle of the twentieth century the British were denying this right not only to the Burmese but to the Indians.

In 1915 a middle-aged lawyer, Mohandas K. Gandhi, had returned to India from South Africa with ideas for "a new kind of revolution." In 1921 one of Burma's monk-heroes, U Ottama, joined Gandhi in the National Congress Party and brought back to Burma the concept of peaceful non-cooperation as a political weapon. The British responded by jailing him for "sedition." This action caused many Burmese monks to travel the countryside preaching against the British (there are few groups more mobile than those living under rules of poverty and chastity).

Also in 1921 the YMBAs joined with various non-Buddhist groups to form the General Council of Burmese Associations. Its members were mostly middle class, and the Union of Burma magazine, *Chinthe,* recalled in 1951 that "they took to the masses, though somewhat nervously." Nervous or no, they swelled the organization's membership, while the political activities of the monks increased. In 1929 another hero-monk, U Wisara, was jailed by the British. Because they forbade him his priestly robes and the observation of his clerical vows at a properly consecrated place, he undertook a fast unto death, and died in a British-administered jail. Buddhism and nationalism thus jointly had their first martyr.

The following year, 1930, Gandhi led his Salt March to the sea, and more than 100,000 Indians were imprisoned. From the British point of view, government by the few over the many was growing more complicated, while

from the Burmese point of view, frustration was compounded by the sibling relationship that the British had
imposed on India and Burma despite their vast historic
differences in race, religion, and social structure. (While
the Burmese word for Chinese is "cousin," their word for
Indian is "foreigner".)

This sibling relationship was further poisoned for the
Burmese by evidences of parental favoritism. India, where
the British had succeeded over the centuries in establishing Western techniques of government and business, was
treated like the eldest child, while Burma, in Furnivall's
phrase, "was the Cinderella of the provinces." (A similar
sibling relationship might be said to have existed between
Algeria and Tunisia, with the French treating Tunisia
as the stepchild.)

The year Furnivall founded his "Burma Research Society," 1909, saw an early example of this favoritism.
The Indians were permitted to elect officials of their own
choosing to the Governing Council while the Burmese
were permitted to vote only for people "nominated," i.e.,
appointed, by the British Governor.

A decade later an even more galling example of favoritism occurred. In 1917 India was promised "dyarchy"—
a system of joint indigenous and British rule—partly as
a reward for the service by her troops on behalf of England during World War I, partly to forestall further successes by Gandhi. News of this reform was greeted with
joy in Burma as well as in India. But two years later the
British made it clear that the reform would apply solely
to India. The British writer Hugh Tinker says in retrospect that the British denial to Burma of what was granted
to India "did more than anything else to direct [Burmese]
pride towards a demand for political freedom."[8]

8 Hugh Tinker: *The Union of Burma* (London: Oxford University Press;
1961), p. 86.

Finally, in 1923, six years after India, Burma was given dyarchy (Thant, for one, was delighted). But dyarchy in Burma was better on paper than in reality. First, the key powers of foreign affairs, of the police, and of the purse were "reserved" for British Ministers; second, although Burmese Ministers were assigned various local government portfolios, they themselves were appointed by the British Governor; third, the senior civil servants were still British and had access, socially as well as politically, to the Governor, as even the Burmese Ministers did not; and, lastly, a Burmese Minister could not discharge a British civil servant.

On the other hand, the Burmese Ministers were paid the same salary as their British counterparts ($20,000 a year, in contrast to the national average of $50). This left them open to suspicion by their countrymen of having been bribed to toady to the conqueror. Here was an example of the apparently insoluble problems inherent in the colonial situation. For had the British paid the Burmese Ministers less than their British counterparts, there would have been an outcry against such discrimination. Yet by paying them equally, the British caused the Burmese Ministers to be despised. As Frank Trager says of that period, "To be trusted by the British meant *not* to be trusted by the Burmese."[9]

Furthermore, as Fielding Hall had noted before the turn of the century, many of the best Burmese refused to consider working for the alien conqueror, while many of least worth were willing, if not eager, to do so. Actually, with a few exceptions, the Burmese Ministers in the twenties were of poor caliber, as young Thant was not alone in pointing out.

Though all Burmese were frustrated with dyarchy, the Burmans were the most frustrated of all. Under any ordi-

[9] Trager and Associates: *Burma*, Vol. III, p. 1015.

nary democratic system they, the majority, would have had the dominant voice. But under Britain's 1923 arrangements, the Burman voice in the new Legislative Council was easily drowned out by many other voices. Of the Council's 103 members, a quarter were "nominated" by the Governor, while a further fifth represented Europeans, Indians, Anglo-Indians, and non-Burman "communal" minorities living in Burma proper (the Hill Areas were still separately ruled). The result was either log-rolling or legislative inaction, while political parties proliferated, demarked less by differences of ideas than by personality clashes between their leaders.

As U Thaung, U Thant's third brother, recalls in a letter, "Politics in British-held Burma meant cliques, disruptions, power-craze." As a result, U Thaung says, "U Thant detested politics, although it would not be wrong to say that there could not have been more than a handful in Burma who studied as much politics and public affairs as he."

It was in part U Thant's study of public affairs in Great Britain that made him so impatient with politics in Burma. "I didn't hate politics," he explains, "I hated politicians." Compared to some British statesmen, the Burmese "so-called leaders" appeared to him as "a pretty sorry lot."[1]

Burmese rivalry with India extended also to the civil service. In 1923 when Burmese applicants were finally accepted by the ICS, these were kept to a minimum. That same year a Burma Civil Service (BCS) was established, but it was kept as a Class II service (with the ICS remaining Class I). The business community also continued utilizing Britons, Anglo-Indians, and Indians rather than Burmese in responsible positions. As U Kyaw Nyein

[1] Interview with U Thant, New York, 1964.

recalled in 1958, "The country presented the picture of a social pyramid which had the millions of poor, ignorant, exploited Burmese at its base, and a few outsiders— British, Indian, and Chinese—as its apex."[2]

Capital investment in Burma was primarily British, secondly Indian, and thirdly Chinese. Many of the Indians were *Chettyars,* a Hindu caste of moneylenders, from Madras. In a sense the Burmese had permitted moneylending to go to foreigners by default, having neither saved money themselves nor respected those who saved it to lend it out at interest. Eventually a few Burmese-owned banks were established in the large towns, but these did not make a practice of offering individual loans to farmers. The farmers, meanwhile, never adapted their lackadaisical attitude toward money to the exigencies of growing a cash crop such as rice. When time to pay taxes or buy seed came around, they simply borrowed. By the 1930's more than three quarters of the farming population were in debt.

Rates of interest were as high as 400 per cent and did nothing to endear the Indian Chettyars or the Chinese moneylenders to the Burmese. Some Burmese still write of the Chettyars with loathing, yet G. E. Harvey calls them the most moderate of moneylenders, going on to describe as vicious those Chinese and Burmese who led their victims to drink or opium and deliberately ruined them.

In all events, the Chettyars played an integral role in the development of the Burmese Delta. And this development was, in the long run, beneficial to many Burmese. For families such as U Thant's, it meant a higher standard of living and hence of education; for the country as a whole it meant for the first time the growth of a middle

2 *Atlantic Supplement:* "Perspectives of Burma," 1958.

class. But during the world depression of the 1930's, when the price of paddy dropped by three quarters, the combination of the British system of land ownership with the Chettyar system of moneylending spelled disaster for most of the Burmese peasants.

Dispossessed, these peasants drifted to Rangoon where the lowest-paid work, that of loading rice bales onto the dockside ships, had long attracted Indian "coolies" mostly from Madras. The British had deliberately encouraged unlimited immigration from overpopulated India into lightly populated Burma of these poor undernourished men who accepted wages that even the most unskilled Burmese rejected. (From 1926 to 1929 the Indian immigrants averaged 400,000 a year.) But after the start of the depression, the unemployed Burmese became desperate.

The stage was set for an explosion—and it occurred in May of 1930. Some coolies, encouraged by Indian Congress Party agitators, struck against the British shipowners for higher pay. Immediately they found their jobs filled by hungry Burmese. The untrained Burmese, however, did not handle the cargo expeditiously, and the owners quickly settled the strike. The reinstated Indians proceeded to taunt the Burmese for having been unable to hold on to either their jobs or their women. The Burmese responded to this intolerable provocation by reaching for their dahs.

For two days and nights the battle lasted, with hundreds, including by-standers, killed or wounded. It was the first serious "communal" riot in Burma, and its economic, sexual, and religious overtones were to recur. The Burmese men were fearful that their daughters or sisters might marry the muscular, industrious Indians.[3]

[3] A cosmopolitan Burmese woman today says that if the Frenchmen are the most prone to make a woman aware of her femininity, the Burmese men are the least prone to do so: "They act platonic even if they don't

Especially did they fear marriage to the Indian Moslems, who reputedly demanded that the wife adopt the husband's religion. That the Burmese had grounds for fear is indicated by the existence in 1931 of 122,705 offspring of Indian-Burmese unions. When the violence was finally quelled, several Burmese Ministers pleaded with the British to restrict immigration from India, but even the achievement of "separation" from India did not stem the influx into Burma of the low-paid labor so eagerly sought by the European entrepeneurs.

Less than a year after the dock riots came a second uprising of impoverished Burmese, this time against the flourishing Chinese merchants and moneylenders.

The third uprising occurred in the Tharrawaddy District, not far from Thant's Maubin. Saya San, a former Buddhist monk and self-styled "doctor," a man with great charisma but little education, had persuaded local peasants that his magic tattooing would guard them against the foreigners' bullets. As a result, brave men raced into deadly close-range fire. So dramatic was the courage of Saya San's followers that it was commented upon by the far-away *New York Times*.

The Tharrawaddy Rebellion lasted almost two years. Finally the British, with the aid of two combat divisions sent from India, together with local forces consisting of Karens and other minorities, encircled Saya San's jungle "palace" and captured him. He was tried for treason and hanged. The majority of educated Burmese, according to an American historian, had considered his rebellion at

---

feel that way." When a Burmese couple, for example, are reunited after a long absence, they make no public show of their intense inner feeling: this is simply "their way." On the other hand, the Burmese are not shy about discussing intimate parts of the body with a member of the opposite sex: a uterus, or a hemorrhoid, for example, is mentioned as casually as a foot or a blister.

best quixotic and at worst "sheer madness."[4] (Thant agreed.) Yet the memory of Saya San's bravery lingered on despite the British efforts to discredit him after his death by circulating photographs of him cowering before the gallows.

Saya San's rebellion had several results. One was to heighten Burmese nationalist feelings against the British. Another was to increase Burman dislike for the Karens, who had helped the British capture Saya San. A third was to provide a steppingstone to prominence of two of Saya San's defense lawyers, Dr. Ba Maw, a Ph.D. from the University of Bordeaux—a volatile, vain, and patriotic man with great oratorical gifts; and U Saw, a "lower-grade pleader," far less educated but a shrewd operator with right-wing tendencies. (Thant's connection with both appears in the following chapter.) Although, as lawyers, they lost Saya San's case their impassioned handling of it served them politically so well that both, in time, became Prime Ministers of Burma—each, during the other's term of office, landing in jail.

The final by-product of Saya San's rebellion was the use of his tiny legacy, 300 rupees of royalties from his book *Signs of Diseases,* to establish a small library in Rangoon. The only books on its shelves were those recommended in Pandit Nehru's *Impressions of Soviet Russia,* one being Marx's *Das Kapital* (in English). These books had a great influence on some of the young nationalists. As an American, E. Oliver Clubb, Jr., wrote, "Although capitalism in the West had long since begun to reform itself, in Burma, as elsewhere in Asia, colonial capitalism supported by government riot sticks had advanced but little beyond the predatory state described almost a century earlier by Karl Marx."[5] The injustices

[4] Cady: *A History of Modern Burma,* p. 317.
[5] The younger Dr. Clubb's Ph.D. thesis, 1963, was entitled "The Dynamics of Burmese Independence."

of this "extractive" capitalism included huge profits going abroad while the steadily poorer Burmese peasants were taxed for the costs of administering the country.

To the Burmese beholder, there was an Alice-in-Wonderland quality of nothing being quite what it seemed. Burma was a rich country, but most of her people were poor; Burmese self-government had increased, but the real locus of power had not shifted to the Burmese. The consequence, Furnivall later said, was that "the constitutional reforms of 1923 onward were in practice an education in political corruption . . . the corruption that office without power naturally engenders."[6]

In 1930 the Simon Commission had recommended that Burma be separated from India. But many Burmese, formerly in favor of this move, began to wonder if, after all, it would be in Burma's interest. Their suspicions were aroused by the enthusiasm for it on the part of the British Government of Burma, big business, and the European press. The anti-separation feeling, moreover, was whetted by Indians in Burma whose Congress Party at home, under the leadership of Gandhi and the young Jawaharlal Nehru, wanted Burmese support. "The view rapidly gained ground," Furnivall said, "that the real object [of separation] was to make Burma safe for Capital."

This view, furthermore, has persisted. Twenty years later, in 1950, U Nu, then Prime Minister of independent Burma, said that capitalism and Western colonial imperialism were so thoroughly linked in the minds of the Burmese that "it has been impossible to view the two in isolation."[7]

In the vacuum created by Burmese indecision about separation, the British decided to go ahead with it, and

[6] Furnivall: *Colonial Policy and Practice,* p. 167.
[7] Butwell: *U Nu,* p. 73.

the Parliament in London passed the "Government of Burma Act" of 1935. Thus Burma, fifty years after being fully absorbed into Britain's Indian Empire, regained her identity. But identity was a far cry from independence. Although the Burmese people were now empowered to elect all the members of the lower House and half the members of the upper House, the rest were still "nominated" by the British Governor. And the British still "reserved" for themselves the control of foreign affairs, defense, and monetary policy. A general election was scheduled for 1936.

These steps by the British, though progressive, were grudging and late. (In fairness to the British it must be recalled that during this period they were faced with more substantial problems both in India and the Middle East.) The British writer, Maurice Collis, says that "if Burma had been granted a free parliament some years before we gave it to her, she would have remained within the Commonwealth."[8] As it was, political restiveness increased during the thirties while the economy remained stagnant.

Yet the British, often described as the most enlightened imperial power in history, had made many visible contributions to Burma. They improved communication, transportation, and education; they reduced disease through vaccination and clean water. They established a competent Forest Service which prevented timbering from denuding the forests as the Burmese kings had done; they promoted the development of the Delta and built Rangoon into a major Asian port.

The British had also made many invisible contributions. Through sponsoring elections they gave the Burmese some training in the techniques of democracy. After 1923, through the ICS and BCS, they gave the Burmese some training in administration. Through the court sys-

8 Collis: *Into Hidden Burma*, p. 49.

tem they proclaimed the worth of each person's freedom and the equality of all persons before the law. Partly because these values reinforced those of Buddhism, they were welcomed.

Three decades later, U Thant listed many of the "material accomplishments" of colonialism, such as better schools, hospitals, etc. "Nevertheless," he said, "against these substantial benefits must be reckoned many features. . . . Chief among them is the fact that, in the past at any rate, the primary motive of the colonial power . . . was its own commercial profit." For that reason, U Thant added, the colonies were kept "essentially as primary producers, with little industrial development."⁹

But the indictment by Thant that, although generally felt, had the poignancy of personal involvement was that "the colonizers often kept themselves aloof from native society. Very few of them bothered to learn the language . . . or made a real effort to understand the indigenous culture. . . . This aloofness and cultural exclusiveness created resentment, particularly in the minds of the educated subject peoples."

He was one of these "educated subject people" who watched with fascination as his friends and acquaintances took charge of the independence movement in the mid-thirties. At the same time he felt the need known by young men the world over, to establish his own personal independence. The time had come for U Thant to found his own home.

9 U Thant's speech was in response to his being granted an honorary Doctor of Laws degree by Williams College, June 10, 1962. By the end of 1965, U Thant had fourteen such degrees—eleven American, two Canadian, one Russian (and a medal from Czechoslovakia). With Harvard, Yale, and Princeton all having honored him, the one-time Burmese drop-out has been teased about his Ivy League connections. Because of the pressure of work, however, Thant now limits acceptance of honorary degrees to three a year.

CHAPTER SEVEN

A Young Man
Presses for Independence

Thant, in his early twenties, was a precocious patriarch. Khant, the only brother who ever challenged his authority, was off in Rangoon, and Thaung and Tin Maung were still adolescents. By the time their stint at the University came around Thant was able to pay their tuition for the full four years. Each later joined the Burma Civil Service and was posted away from Pantanaw. Thant was left alone with his mother.

Theirs was a relationship of mutual respect. Thant dutifully accompanied her to the pagoda on the Sabbath and festival days, and she, in turn, sought his counsel, as did other relatives and friends. His opinion was valued because he was educated and responsible, and because he relished keeping secrets.

Even Nu, Thant's superior at the National High School,

shared a secret with him. As Dr. Maung Maung recalled of Nu and Thant: "It was a happy partnership. Both loved the same things—fortunately not the same women, or maybe they did."

U Nu's secret was his love for Mya Yee, daughter of a rich rice miller who served as Chairman of the Pantanaw School Committee. Nu, however, was too outspoken and radical to get along well with the man who, in effect, was President of the School Board. Also, Nu was penniless. There was therefore no chance of Mya Yee persuading her father to approve the match.

In Burma, then as now, most marriages were arranged. This means that the young people were acceptable to, but not necessarily in love with, one another (Burmese connubial endearments include "Big Brother" and "Little Sister"). On the other hand, with characteristic Burmese dualism, elopements were not uncommon. An example is described by Mi Mi Khaing:

> There is always a confidant of the girl's or man's or both to help with the arrangements for the flight, or for the refuge. ... The disappearance of the girl is soon discovered, the alarm is given, people rush about with the exciting news. ... Mother and father make a crying visit to the house of the ... young man's family, and beat their breasts at the shamelessness of the girl. The hidden couple are soon tracked down, and a reconcilation takes place and a proper wedding feast is held. ... Then the whole disgrace is completely forgotten, until about seventeen years later, when perhaps the daughter of the bride elopes, and her friends, commiserating with her tears, shake their heads sadly and say that this is ... the punishment for her own sin of seventeen years before.[1]

Thant, however, was not in love with Mya Yee. When Dr. Maung Maung was later asked (by letter) why he had

[1] Mi Mi Khaing: *Burmese Family*, p. 106.

implied that "maybe" U Thant and U Nu "loved the same woman," he replied:

That is what I heard from their mutual friends, but perhaps it was in a lighter vein that they said it. It would not be an entirely unheard of thing; in fact we have a stock joke in our society about the go-between walking away with the girl. But U Thant has denied it, and Mrs. Thant also, only more stoutly.

Although many people in Burma still think of Thant as the go-between for U Nu and Daw Mya Yee, two factors militate against believing this. One is that Thant himself denies it, and his mother also, "only more stoutly"; the other is that if Thant had managed the elopement, he would presumably have done at least an adequate job. According to Nu's biographer, the job done was anything but adequate.

Daw Mya Yee . . . fled her family household. She rushed to Nu's residence only to discover that he had gone home to visit his parents. Her father, meanwhile, had gone to the police, charging that she had absconded with some of his possessions, the almost ritualistic response of the Burmese father in what was not an uncommon situation. Daw Mya Yee was hidden in a local fishery while a motorboat was dispatched to Wakema to bring back Nu. The returning school superintendent and his beloved then eloped across the Irrawaddy and went off to Rangoon for their honeymoon.[2]

Although Daw Mya Yee's parents ultimately became reconciled to their daughter's marriage, U Nu did not return to Pantanaw. His place as superintendent was taken by U Thant, who also retained the job as headmaster. The difference between the two young men is captured, with typical Burmese humor, by Dr. Maung Maung:

2 Butwell: *U Nu*, pp. 15 and 16.

When Nu fell in love, he wrote poetry aflame with emotion and dedicated them, one and all, to the dear lady. When Thant fell in love he wrote letters to the editor, and articles, and a new book.

The book was a translation, at Furnivall's suggestion, of *Cities and Their Stories,* portraying the glories of ancient Athens and Rome for the high school student.

In addition to his writing and translating, Thant had a multitude of administrative duties. As one of his then fellow National High School superintendents, U Ba Myint, now Director of Education in Rangoon, says:

It was a difficut job needing lots of diplomatic skill. There were lots of different types of people to keep happy, parents, teachers, students, often with conflicting interests. It was good training for a future Secretary-General.[3]

Thant's sense of the significance of his job was similar to that of Oliver Wendell Holmes when he said that "all education is moral." Thant, when asked today about his former students, says that "not a single old boy has become a robber or a murderer or an alcoholic; this is very gratifying."

While Thant believed in encouraging each student to develop his own potential, he was well aware that human nature has potentialities for evil as well as good. In Burma, he said, freedom needed to be combined with education, or else the people, on attaining self-government, would not be able to manage their own affairs constructively. For his students, therefore, he included a thorough study of their country's history. As he wrote in his regular column, "Apparently paradoxical, it is nonetheless true that nations are borne forward by looking backward."

[3] Conversation with U Ba Myint, Rangoon, 1964, at a luncheon given by U Khant.

His portrayal of Burmese history, however, was not a patriotic whitewash: "The past must prove a warning and a lesson rather than an ideal for imitation and emulation. A blind worship of the past is a decisive impediment . . . to progress."

He therefore tried to use history as a training ground for the development of the student's critical powers:

Burmese chronicles are peculiarly incredible for the simple fact that they were mostly written during the time of autocratic Burmese kings when freedom of speech or of expression were undreamt of. Burmese kings, like other mortals, had their likes and dislikes. It is quite natural that they wished to see only one side of the picture; the valour of their ancestors, superhuman powers of the forefathers, etc. I do not believe that Anawrahta had over fifty million soldiers. . . . It is surprising that many educated Burmese are even now hugging these beliefs or have no courage of their convictions [if these be otherwise].

Thant, who tried to show the mistakes as well as the contributions of the Burmese kings, tried also to show the contributions as well as the mistakes of the British rulers. To do so he needed the "courage of his convictions," for his views were satisfying neither to the intense Burmese nationalists (whose ranks Nu had joined after leaving Pantanaw) nor to the British-dominated Education Ministry of Burma from which the Pantanaw school received part of its funds. Thant was learning to cope with the loneliness that sometimes goes with the middle position of the balanced scale.

Besides having the courage of his convictions, Thant encouraged his teachers to have the courage of theirs. He was not only willing to forgive an honest mistake, but on occasion would jeopardize his own position by supporting their freedom to make an honest mistake.

One such occasion involved a Pantanaw teacher much older than himself. The teacher had included in a test for students a passage from an antigovernment newspaper ridiculing the then Education Minister, Dr. Ba Maw (one of Saya San's defense lawyers). The article pointed to Dr. Ba Maw's vanity and poked fun at the rakish angle at which he wore his headgear (made of velvet like those of the royal court, rather than the usual cotton or silk gaung-baung) and the fact that he visibly used powder on his face. (Thanakha is often used by the Burmese to prevent perspiration from making the skin greasy, but its use by men is expected to be discreet: unlike the "French shave" in the West, the use of powder by men in Burma could not leave telltale traces and still be acceptable. Burmese children, on the other hand, still have their faces and ears rubbed with thanakha and no one minds what appears to an American as a Halloween look.)

Incensed as Dr. Ba Maw was when the article appeared, there was no action he could take against the newspaper. But when a teacher in one of the schools under his jurisdiction used the same article, as he thought, to defame him in the eyes of school children, he was furious.

He demanded that Superintendent Thant dismiss the teacher. Thant politely refused. This was the first of many times that Thant would stand firm against an angry official in the name of freedom. For Thant believed not only that education was essential for the growth of freedom, but that freedom was essential for the growth of education. As he wrote in *World of Books:*

Freedom of speech and of opinion are of course not dreamt of in our schools, since they are held to be much too dangerous. Dangerous they certainly are, so dangerous that they would find fault with our school system itself, and clamour for the removal of some of its defects.

Thant's refusal to dismiss the teacher caused Dr. Ba
Maw's anger to shift from the teacher to the superintendent. The high school, unlike the newspaper, did lie
within Dr. Ba Maw's power. In order to punish, if not
destroy it, he decided to "disregister" it, i.e., deny it government funds. But U Thant secretly got word of this
decision and went for help to the leader of the legislative
opposition, U Saw (the other of Saya San's defense
lawyers). U Saw, for his own reasons, apparently welcomed the opportunity to embarrass his rival, Dr. Ba
Maw, and prepared a list of searching questions about the
reasons for disregistering the Pantanaw school. Since Dr.
Ba Maw did not care to expose these in the legislature,
the funds for the school remained intact.

The first round of the battle had gone to U Thant, but
the second one, several years later, went to Dr. Ba Maw.
When appointments of Divisional Inspectors of Schools
were being considered in 1942 U Thant's name was proposed as an obvious candidate. For a High School headmaster the Divisional Inspectorship was, as U Khant says,
"a most coveted post." The name of U Thant was passed
over by Dr. Ba Maw, and to this day the two men have
not spoken except to exchange a formal greeting once
when Dr. Ba Maw made an official inspection trip to
Pantanaw. Thant bears no resentment. "He knows I'm
difficult; I know he's different," he once told a Burmese
teacher. And Dr. Ba Maw, who appears to have forgotten
the episode, speaks favorably, if somewhat condescend-
ingly, of Thant.[4] He also still wears his velvet headgear.

Thant remained in Pantanaw throughout the thirties,
teaching, writing, administering, and helping the School
Committee to raise the funds essential to supplement the
government grant. Once a year, there was a fair with

[4] Conversation with Dr. Ba Maw at a dinner in Rangoon, 1964.

booths and games which U Thant, by then known to everyone in town, attended with his mother. The future Secretary-General was learning about fund raising at the rice-paddy level.

At the same time, he was continuing his own informal education. A few American novels, among them Hemingway's *For Whom the Bell Tolls,* came his way and he enjoyed them. He also read biographies of British statesmen, past and present, and subscribed to numerous British periodicals. In the process, he became devoted, in absentia, to Sir Stafford Cripps: "I tried to model myself on him." Cripps was a "politician" of the highest caliber, who came, as did Thant, from a conservative, middle-class family, yet had no hesitation in breaking with its traditions in order to improve society. "Failure is not the test of right or wrong," Cripps had said; "of that there is but one test—your conscience and reasoning powers."[5]

Thant's reasoning powers were leading him in the direction of the same kind of democratic socialism Cripps espoused. As with Cripps, Thant's socialism had a religious basis; while that of Cripps was based on Christian compassion, Thant's was based on Buddhist compassion. Thant could agree wholly with Cripps's friend Clement Attlee, who said that "many men and women have drawn from the [Scriptures] the support which they needed for their instinctive revolt against the inhuman conditions which Capitalism brings."[6]

Thant also agreed with Cripps in regard to international affairs. To him, as to Cripps, Lord Palmerston's statement rang true, that nations have no permanent friends or permanent enemies, only permanent interests. Thant too was interested in the League of Nations, and

5 Eric Estorick: *Stafford Cripps* (New York: John Day; 1941), p. 4.
6 Estorick: *Stafford Cripps,* p. 7.

translated a book by that name for high school students. The main difference between Cripps and Thant was in regard to humor. "It's not that Cripps can't see a joke," a friend once said; "he saw one not long ago—but it was by appointment." Thant, on the other hand, was often observed laughing out loud at the puns and earthy jokes which alternated with scenes of royal splendor in the *pwés* which, in those days, he still had time to attend.

Thant's studies of history made him realize the ramifications not only of past events but of their chroniclers:

History written without bias is inconceivable, since it is written by human beings, and not by machines; and human beings are not only individuals with idiosyncrasies, but belong to a race and a time: their writings must be coloured however oblivious they may be of the tinge.

Even if history is not unduly tinged with the writer's biases it is still falsified in part because of the need for selectivity. Said Thant: "A history must be a work of art, and once you have art, you have distortion."

Thant wanted his students trained to make independent judgments, not only in regard to intellectual matters but to practical ones. No subject was too small to start with. In his column in April, 1935, he opposed the idea that Burmese students wear uniforms to school. While recognizing arguments on the other side, such as that "the students, rich and poor, can drown their social inequalities in these uniforms," he insisted that the harm done would be greater than the good:

I hold that freedom in the matter of clothes is extremely important in a school, not so much for what this would in itself mean in practice, but . . . as a symbol of a free atmosphere. The hardest fight our schools should wage is the fight against standardization in human life. If this standardization is allowed to grow, it will destroy much of the variety of human society.

An answer to this column was written the following month by a leading young nationalist, Aung San, later to become "the George Washington of Burma." Aung San, apparently under the influence of Gandhi, argued in favor of native-cloth uniforms for teachers as well as students:

We then feel like one fraternity pledged for the service of our Motherland, especially because the presence of homespun materials . . . adds to its significance. And with that, freedom as our national goal becomes dearer to our bosom. Freedom of dress on the other hand, only helps to whet and pamper our taste for vanity instead of making us feel the atmosphere of freedom.

For Aung San national freedom (or independence) was of far greater importance than individual freedom (or liberty). "Standardization of human life" in the cause of national freedom, he said, "is to me inevitable and desirable." As for Superintendent Thant's credentials as a nationalist, Aung San was not wholly convinced of these:

Will U Thant . . . complain of the discomfort of donning of thick *Pinni* clothes? I hope not, for he, for all I know, is a nationalist.

Thant's rebuttal, the following month, questioned Aung San's credentials in the field of education: "Ko Aung San put forth a layman's point of view. . . . I look at the problem from the viewpoint of an educationist." (Thant, at twenty-six, could refer to a student six years younger as "Ko," while Aung San, appropriately, had referred to Thant as "U.")

Neither young man ended up persuading the other; but as Dr. Maung Maung recalls, "A wordy war waged between them, in the course of which a lasting friendship was struck."[7]

The next time Thant went to Rangoon he was introduced by U Nu to Aung San. Nu, by then, had gone back to the University to study law, but he was devoting the major part of his time to the activities of the Student Union of which he was President and Aung San Vice President. Aung San impressed Thant as "boyish, quiet, almost shy—not yet wholly mature." A fuller portrait of the young Aung San is provided by Bo Let Ya:

He had the look of a man of mixed Chinese blood, an undernourished one at that. His manners were crude, and he was not a sociable person. He would often sit for hours, deep in his own thoughts. Talk to him and he might not respond. He did not wear his clothes well, and add to this his stern appearance, and who would find it easy to get on with him? But if one could but get to know him, one would find many lovable traits in his character. All in all he was an unforgettable person. . . .[8]

Thant's increasingly frequent trips to Rangoon were to attend meetings of the Burma Text Book Committee, the Council of National Education, and the Executive Committee of the Heads of Schools Association ("our headmasters' labor union"). Thus, more and more, he was able to rub mental horns with other young bucks and discuss his evolving theories with his elders. Even at home he enjoyed stimulating conversation. U Hla, then Deputy Commissioner of the Maubin District, recalls (in a letter) that he always looked up Thant on his monthly visits to Pantanaw:

We had discussions in the evenings either in the Dak Bungalow [government-run hostel] or on my House Boat on

7 *Guardian* magazine, August, 1956.
8 Dr. Maung Maung (compiler): *Aung San of Burma* (The Hague: N. V. Martinus Nijhoff; 1962).

matters of general topic. Then I realized that he has read a great deal and has become an exception in a nation where learning for learning's sake has not yet crystallized into a tradition. During the school strike [of 1936] . . . he gave me several pieces of unbiased advice, to temper justice with mercy and to be firm in controlling the situation. . . . It appears to me he gets inspiration from Bacon's dictum, "Reading maketh a full man, conference a ready man, and writing an exact man."

Thant's writings in the middle and later thirties were full of "unbiased advice," some of which, in later years, he was to reverse. He was, at that time, frankly an elitist, although he wished the elite which governed his country to be Burmese rather than British. After witnessing local elections in the Pantanaw District he had little faith in the average uneducated voter: "Democracy is lovelier at a distance; seen at close quarters it is nothing to write hymns about." With his own eyes he had seen ignorant farmers and villagers being manipulated or bribed by the politicians to vote for the green or yellow ticket. With irony he described his disillusionment:

We found a number of queer fish among the candidates. Whether they were conversant with District Council problems or not, they were certainly familiar with all the odd electioneering tricks. The West has nothing to teach us in this respect. The election day itself was marked by the usual miracles. The dead came back to life, the absent were present, and many an individual assumed sundry personalities.

Thant himself never joined a political party. And he publicly deplored the way a new party would arise in Burma each time there was a new candidate or a new issue:

That in the domain of politics, parties have got their special value is admitted on all hands. They unmistakably demonstrate a healthy current in the political life of a people. But a multiple party system instead of doing any good, spoils the onward march of progress . . . just as too many cooks spoil the dinner. It is all the more true in the case of a dependent country like Burma.

In addition to criticizing the politicians, he also criticized the press. Here again he was in favor of its freedom, but against abuse of its freedom. "The purpose of journalism," he wrote, is to "make for an instructed democracy," and Burmese journalism is "betraying its trust." In his attempt to dramatize its malfeasance, he relied on the Burmese proclivity for punning:

One of the most depressing features of modern life is our amazing susceptibility to [journalistic] stunts. . . . Unless we are careful, our intellects will be "stunted" out of existence.

Thant worried about the intellects, not only of the educated Burmese, but of the less educated economic and social groups, such as those who had involved themselves in the dock riots, the hounding of the Chinese merchants, and the Saya San rebellion:

We already have had sufficient experience of the baneful effects which newspapers can produce by stimulating mobpassion. . . . As there is the need of penetrating to the thousands in the lowest strata of society, the journalist has to write down to their level. The tendency of the news column is to undermine our sense of values by referring every question to the standard of the mob. . . . The effects of the journalistic methods of today on the herd-mind are profound, and may be very dangerous. The tendency to popular hysteria is undoubtedly greater now than when newspapers were unknown.

Yet, like many a moralist, it was precisely those whom Thant most valued that he most castigated. The "herd" or "mob" included the tenant farmers of the Delta whose

children he taught and worried over; the journalists were
the men whose ranks he one day hoped to join; the politicians were the people whose behavior most fascinated him
("I am a very political animal," he told a visitor in 1964).
He, therefore, often combined his castigations with a
stress on the value of the group he was attacking. In regard to the press, for example, he wrote:

We ought to give credit for the special articles written by
distinguished people. . . . These often make a real contribution to the formation of a sane public opinion, but, unfortunately, their appeal is very limited, and any good they
do is counterbalanced by the general tone of the rest of the
paper. After all, it is the irritation element in public opinion
that counts, and it is to this element that the newspaper di-
rects its main appeal. . . . It is no excuse to say that ever since
the press has been in existence, it has worked this way and
no great harm has been done. The answer is obvious. First,
the press in highly educated countries displays more sense of
responsibility than that of Burma, and secondly, whereas a
couple of decades ago there was a reading public of a few
hundreds in Burma, it is now almost co-existent with the
literate public.

"Highly educated countries" presumably meant Great
Britain. In Burma, with no comparable democratic tradition, Thant feared that the voters would be swayed by
political demagogues and a sensationalist press to support
persons and issues against their own interest. In his fear
that through the democratic process the country he loved
would suffer, he lashed out at the democratic process
itself:

Democracy means nothing less than despair of finding any
fit to govern. Democracy professes to believe all men are equal
in their mental capacities. This absurd dogma of human
equality results in the suppression of the superior, reducing

all to a common level of dull mediocrity. The consequence is that humanity is without leadership.

This was, after all, the period when Germany's Weimar Republic had given way, through the democratic vote of 1932, to Hitler; when the Italians had abandoned the untidiness of democracy for Mussolini; when the Fascists were winning over the democrats and others in Spain; when voices such as Oswald Moseley's in England and Father Coughlin's in the United States were arousing prejudice among the desperate millions whose employment had vanished during the Depression; when Europe, the seat of democracies, seemed headed, against the expressed wishes of its people, for war. Thant sounded the tocsin:

> It is not only in Burma and India that representative government has failed. It has failed everywhere. So far from being able to produce a government of the best, the democratic states have not been able to solve the primary problem of making the elected bodies faithful mirrors of public opinion.[9]

Although Thant could denounce with passion, his mind was not a closed one. Assuming that democracy was a failure, how were the nations faring under "the leadership principle"? Thant began reading about Germany, Italy, and Japan. And the more he read the more appalled he became. There, the freedoms he treasured were being violently and cruelly destroyed. If lack of power was bad, dictatorial power was worse. Thant's appreciation of democratic procedures, starting in the latter thirties, became so profound that he actually forgot having ever advised any alternative. When the passage about "this absurd dogma of human equality" was read to him twenty-

[9] *The World of Books*, September, 1939.

five years later, he asked with interest, "Who wrote that?" And when told that it was himself, he sighed: "Young men are apt to be fiery."

Yet even when he was at his most fiery, he always held out hope for improvement. His best-known pre-war article, "Oh! We Burmans," attacked not only Burmese politicians and journalists but—most daringly—some Buddhist monks, yet it ends on a hopeful note (Appendix IV): "This is a picture of the Burmans as one of them sees them, but we need not despair. Recognition and detection of the causes of a malady are half the cure."

He was not, in short, a journalistic *enfant terrible,* applying verbal shock treatment in order to watch his countrymen jump; he was an idealistic reformer with the long-term goal of education for all his people so that, in time, they could take responsible charge of their own affairs.

In his own affairs he had previously come to a point where progress was imperative. His mother had never been in the slightest hurry for her sons to marry. When U Khant fell in love with a girl slightly older than himself, from a neighboring village, his mother wanted him to give her up. Thant sided with his mother, even delivering a small sermon to U Khant on the advantages of the wife's being younger than the husband. U Khant took care of the situation—and the sermon—by eloping, and he and Daw Saw Yin have been happily married for thirty-five years (and have five children).

A year after U Khant's marriage—family harmony having been re-established—U Thant found himself in the interesting position of having to eat his own words and also go against his mother's wishes. Nor was elopement an option for a school superintendent who believed in the importance of example. Instead, he engaged in long-term diplomatic persuasion of his mother to agree to his marrying a young lady older than himself. U Thaung, then at the University, remembers the family drama well. "Actually Mother had nothing against the girl, who was the only daughter of a well-to-do family in Pantanaw and who was also a distant relative [the young lady's aunt was married to Thant's uncle]. In deference to my mother's wishes, U Thant waited till I graduated from Rangoon University and joined semi-government service."

The young woman was Daw Thein Tin, the only child of a lawyer, U Khinn; she had been born and brought up near Mandalay. When her father died she was in her late teens. She and her mother, Daw Kyè, moved back to Pantanaw to live with Daw Kyè's parents. After graduating from high school she went on to learn some Pali in order to study Buddhist scriptures in the original. As U Thaung says, "She was and is extremely religious; a rumor had it that before she met U Thant she had decided to become a nun." Such an attitude was considered a factor more in a bride's favor in Burma than it might be in the United States. In Burma, according to Mi Mi Khaing, "They want a girl with wealth, a meek nature, good looks, religious piety and education." And Thant himself, by then, had learned the techniques of Buddhist meditation and practiced them daily.

Daw Thein Tin not only had "wealth,[1] a meek nature," etc., but a passion for the domestic arts. Her greatest joy comes from nurturing others. Today her serious, serene face lights up when a small child enters the room, and she registers a true hostess's delight when a guest reaches for a second portion. She also enjoys sharing family jokes with a guest, even at her own expense. She says, for ex-

[1] Wealth, says Mi Mi Khaing, "means not merely money, property or jewels, but an absence of younger brothers and sisters." *Burmese Family*, p. 139.

ample, that when word went around Pantanaw that she was to marry U Thant, her friends congratulated her on "having won the sweepstakes."[2]

Thant's reaction to this story is a broad grin. "Well, there weren't that many young men in Pantanaw who had won the All Burma Headmastership Examination." In a way, this typifies his lack of false modesty. If he has done something well, he refers to it objectively, yet at the same time he is aware that no one can be fully objective about himself. Referring to an article about himself in an American magazine, he said, "I think it's too adulatory, but I can't really tell." Most people considered the article by no means adulatory.

When American youngsters ask about his courtship, he says that the growing devotion between himself and his future wife was not "what you in the West call romantic love." But this, he explains, is in no way denigrating the relationship. To Asians, the Western emphasis on romance and the physical manifestations of love often appears in bad taste. "When I first came to the United States," Thant remarked in a speech in Madison, Wisconsin, July 6, 1961, "I was rather shocked by the public embracing in city parks [and by] the American habit of using a parked car as a bedroom. Such behavior would be inconceivable in Burma."

In Burma, perhaps because of Buddhist emphasis on control of the senses, the marriages appear more stable than in the United States; and although divorce is easy for either side to obtain, it is rarely resorted to. Extramarital affairs apparently occur, but relatively rarely, in part perhaps because people find out and discuss them at length. The privacy based upon mobility and ano-

[2] Lunch with Daw Thein Tin in Riverdale, 1962, Aye Aye acting as interpreter.

nymity that is taken for granted in the urban centers of the industrialized West does not exist even in Rangoon. And although some Burmese men openly take on a second wife, the behavior of the average Burmese woman is decorous. As U Khant said, "Her greatest quality which has been ingrained in her through centuries of her national culture is her modesty," and U Thant agrees "in general" with the estimate by a contemporary, U Tin Tut:

> The woman of the West with all her fascination, glamour, charm, and beauty, appears to be too masculine in her deportment. The *purdah* woman of some of the Oriental countries, though beautiful and full of grace, lacks the charm and bonhomie which only freedom can give. The Burmese woman is friendly without immodesty: she welcomes friendship, but repels liberty.[3]

In the nineteenth century the Burmese women were the freest in all Asia and may still be so today. The majority of Burmese small traders are women, the name of a typical enterprise being "Daw X and Daughter." Burmese women, moreover, are consulted on every major decision affecting the family. Yet they also remain aware of the concept of hpone, the prestige epitomized by the Burmese king and shared, to some extent, by every male. A woman would never think, for example, of carelessly throwing her longyi across her husband's bed. In this attitude there is an element of Buddhist teaching, according to which a man, if he has once been accepted by the monks and thereafter practices the Buddhist virtues, may obtain Nirvana, whereas a woman cannot do so until reborn as a man. In any event, Mi Mi Khaing, a Burmese wife with plenty of gumption, feels no sense of oppression:

> In the all-important matters of money, of divorce, of inheritance, of freedom of movement, the right of giving advice,

[3] Quoted in a letter from U Khant, 1965.

of transacting business or of putting one's own name along-
side a husband's on the shop-front, women admit no inferiority. Thus they serve without shackles, and are equal without
impairing the pride of masculinity.[4]

Some men, particularly perhaps in the West, want a
wife who challenges them: they like to play intellectual
tennis in the evening. Other men, particularly perhaps
in the East, want a wife who safeguards their serenity. U
Thant's mind has always been a self-generating one. An
equally probing mind on the part of his wife might not
permit the relaxation at home which may be part of his
quiet strength. It is possible, for example, that Daw Thein
Tin's lack of interest in UN problems is a source of relief
to her husband. Sometimes when a man is troubled by
an apparently insoluble problem, a woman's genuine dis-
interest in it can remove some of its power to cause
anxiety. For a man it may be a blessing, after a long day of
wrestling with world crises, to return to a home where the
chief concern is whether he has a good appetite for
supper. Also, for U Thant, who today must spend so much
of his time conversing, it must be a true respite to spend
the few hours between dinner and bedtime quietly reading a book, with his wife nearby.

As an engaged couple, U Thant and Daw Thein Tin
had to wait, not only until U Thaung had graduated
from the University, but until the Burmese Lent had
passed. After that they had to wait for a day, in November,
1934, deemed suitable by the astrologers for the marriage
of a Friday-born groom and a Saturday-born bride. (The
only time Daw Thein Tin showed surprise while being
interviewed was after she had asked me on which day of
the week my husband and I had been born, and I had
not the slightest idea. Fortunately, research involving old

4 Mi Mi Khaing: *Burmese Family*, p. 189.

calendars, since neither of our mothers had any recollection, revealed that both of us are Friday-born and our wedding had been on a Wednesday. This, Daw Thein said, was seemly. Subsequently when my husband ran for public office, Daw Thein Tin computed numerologically that he would win. The Secretary-General conveyed this prediction by phone the night before the election. Since most of the newspapers were predicting the opposite, the message was a comforting one. It also turned out to be correct.)

In Burma there is a proverb that says, "Monks and hermits are beautiful when they are lean; four-footed animals when they are fat; men when they are learned; and women when they are married."

Daw Thein Tin, on her wedding day, wore a new yellow longyi, a dazzling white *aingyi* (blouse) with a white silk stole over it, and velvet sandals (in the days of the kings, only royalty was permitted to wear velvet). The aingyi was sufficiently décolleté to display her lovely diamond choker and string of pearls. On her arm she wore a diamond bracelet; her hair was piled high over and around a small raffia basket, with one long dark mane rippling down over her shoulder, and in it she wore a diamond-studded comb.

U Thant was dressed in a yellow longyi, a white silk collarless *pa-so* (jacket) fastened with Chinese ties, velvet sandals, and a yellow gaung-baung. He sat on the right, Daw Thein Tin on the left, and both listened respectfully to the speaker, who gave a eulogy not only of them, but of their parents and grandparents. As the speaker went on, there was some chatter and laughter among those of the guests who were more interested in exchanging views about the young couple than in listening.

The speaker then gave to the bride and groom a small

branch of *thabye* (eugenia) leaves. They bowed low, offering their first shikko to the Buddha. After bowing they placed the thabye leaves in a large silver bowl. Six times they repeated the ritual, honoring, in order, the *Dhamma* (the Way), the ponghis (the monkhood), the parents, the teachers and elders, and, lastly, the guests who had come to the wedding (the monks themselves do not appear at a marriage since it is a civil contract with no religious significance).

Then an elderly and happily married couple known to both families placed the hands of bride and groom in the silver bowl. This symbolized the actual marriage, but to make it official the master of ceremonies repeated three times in a triumphal voice, *"Aung Bye,"* which translated, means roughly "it is successful." The bride, groom, and guests were then showered with colored rice, newly minted coins, and confetti.

The bridal chamber, richly adorned, was in the home of the bride. After the ceremony, the guests trooped about admiring the wedding presents and inspecting the bridal chamber to which the women were freely admitted, but not the men unless they paid a gold coin. Some women lifted the coverlet of the bed to see if the blankets of velvet were present, some prodded the mattresses, others estimated the bride's taste in the choice of fine linen and lace hangings.

After the guests were done satisfying their curiosity and their appetite for food and drink (nonalcoholic), the bride retired to her chamber. But the bridegroom's friends guarded the door, and when the bridegroom tried to enter, he was forced to pay off each one of them (one can imagine U Khant, by then back with the family, laughing and making his brother pay double). This token, Reba Lewis writes, "is known as 'stone money,' for in ancient times if the groom refused to pay, the house was stoned. Having placated his friends he is then allowed to enter the room where his beloved waits. . . ."[5]

U Thant's mother went home—as mothers of newly-married children must, the world over—to rooms echoing with loneliness. A tie with the past had irrevocably been cut. Her first born had now established his own independent home, just as, in fewer years than the British feared and the Burmese hoped, the Burmese people would similarly be able to do.

[5] *The Burman,* September 10, 1958: "Burmese Marriage Through Western Eyes."

CHAPTER EIGHT

A Country
Presses for Independence

A people's yearning for independence may operate on
every level of the personality, unconscious as well as conscious. Alex Quaison-Sackey, former President of the UN
General Assembly and now Ghana's foreign minister,
describes, in *Africa Unbound,* his country's flag being
raised for the first time in place of the Union Jack: "For
myself, I felt that I had suddenly become a different person, that I had broken free from some shell or casing that
had been preventing me from growing to full stature."[1]

In Burma the yearning for independence had started
the day the British sent King Thibaw into exile, and was
accentuated by the forces of anticolonialism already stir-

[1] Alex Quaison-Sackey: *Africa Unbound* (New York: Frederick A. Praeger, Inc.; 1963), p. 6.

ring in the world. "The Burmese," says Furnivall, "never accepted foreign rule with more than passive acquiescence, broken intermittently by futile peasant uprisings."[2]

Yet most of the British, whether in Rangoon or London, remained oblivious to the restlessness of the Burmese. Sir Edwin Montagu, later British Secretary of State for India, did not even bother to visit Burma when he went to India in 1917. In his published diary he described the Burmese leaders (including the President of the YMBA) who came to India to see him as "nice simpleminded people with beautiful clothes. Complete loyalty; no sign of political unrest."

Sir Edwin's feeling was mirrored in the official Montagu-Chelmsford report (written after President Woodrow Wilson's Fourteen Points had further encouraged Burmese hopes for self-determination): "The desire for elective institutions has not developed in Burma."

There were, however, some Britons with an unusual degree of knowledge about Burma, like Furnivall, or an unusual degree of artistic empathy, like George Orwell. Indeed Orwell's 1934 novel, *Burmese Days*, revealed the subsurface of British Burma much as E. M. Forster's *A Passage to India* had, a decade previously, of British India. In *Burmese Days* the tragic protagonist is Flory, an Englishman working for a British teak company. The only real friend he can make is neither a fellow British colonist nor a Burmese, but an Indian doctor. To him Flory complains that he and his British colleagues are all living a lie:

"But, my dear friend, what lie are you living?"
"Why, of course, the lie that we're here to uplift our poor black brothers instead of to rob them. . . . There's an everlasting sense of being a sneak and a liar that torments us and drives us to justify ourselves night and day. It's at the bottom

[2] Trager and Associates: *Burma*, p. 56.

[*142*]

of half our beastliness to the natives. We . . . could be almost bearable if we'd only admit that we're thieves and go on thieving without any humbug.''³

The desire to trumpet the truth is perhaps a British— or American—characteristic. In Burma it is not widespread. Perhaps the need to keep secrets stems from the days of the kings when only those courtiers who machinated unobserved were likely to survive the bloodbath at the time of succession. Perhaps it stems from the experience of living under foreign rule. Or perhaps, as suggested by Lucian W. Pye, it predates the British and even the kings:

Deep in Burmese thinking is the belief that to have secrets is to be on the side of power. . . . In nature it is the invisible not the obvious that dominates life, and for most Burmese the world of *nats*, or spirits, is a very real world. . . . The conviction that power operates out of the public view is coupled with a feeling that power is likely to act in unexpected and often malicious . . . ways. Similarly . . . the Burmese . . . appear to derive a great deal of . . . enjoyment out of being able to arrange a completely unexpected development. . . . To be able to surprise the unsuspecting is more than just an indication of cleverness; it suggests . . . that one has real power.⁴

The failure of communication between the British and the Burmese can thus also be attributed to the Burmese. If the British were unseeing, the Burmese were opaque. ("The British," Dr. Htin Aung wrote in *Asia*, Spring, 1965, "could not understand the Burmese . . . character or behavior; the poor British—after having been harassed . . . and mystified by the Irish for five centuries—found themselves harassed by the Burmese and in despair . . . dubbed

³ Orwell: *Burmese Days*, pp. 46–47.
⁴ Pye: *Politics, Personality, and Nation Building*, pp. 134–35.

[them] 'The Irish of the East.' ") On the other hand, by the mid-thirties, there were two groups of young Burmese whose battle for independence was out in the open, and whose importance was nonetheless underestimated by the British.

One group was the Rangoon University Student Union (RUSU), founded in 1928 while U Thant was still at the University. He knew its leaders, not only U Nu and Aung San, but also M. A. Raschid, the tactful and pragmatic son of Indian parents domiciled in Burma, and Kyaw Nyein, a young man whose intellectual agility impressed his friends but whose ambition caused his enemies to say, "Yond Cassius has a lean and hungry look."

The Student Union was forbidden by the University to ally itself with any of the political parties; instead, in effect, it became one. As the University's Principal, D. J. Sloss, said later, "We realized, of course, that the students would be swept up in the nationalist movement, but we hoped that it would be a more gradual thing."[5]

One cause of the students' discontent was the rigid curriculum, which they described as "slave education" fitting the Burmese graduates for nothing higher than jobs as "clerks or menials" in Burma's British-dominated bureaucracy or commercial or industrial establishments. Said the RUSU in an open letter to Principal Sloss in 1936: "The whole University is nothing but an engine for the destruction of the spirit of independence of the hand-picked youth of Burma on whom the country has high hopes of relying for its independence."[6]

That year the University officials recommended Nu for a scholarship to England. This, Thant saw as "a means of getting him out of the country." Nu rejected the offer de-

[5] Quoted in Butwell: *U Nu*, p. 17.
[6] Quoted by E. Oliver Clubb, Jr., in his Ph.D thesis.

spite his father's wish that he take it. As he wrote to Thant, he was not going to be bribed by the colonial authorities.[7]

The second group of young Burmese actively battling for independence were the Thakins. The word "thakin" was the Burmese equivalent of the Indian "sahib" or "master." Up to 1931 it was the form of address used by the Burmese for the British. That year the Burmese saw fit to apply it to themselves; their new organization was a none-too-subtle signal of wanting to be masters in their own house.

In 1934 the structure of the Thakin movement was formalized and some Thakins were elected to the RUSU Executive Council.

Estimates of how many later became Communists vary strikingly according to the political predilection of the estimator and his definition of Communist. Foucar says of the Thakins, "Mostly they adhered to the principles of communism," and Tinker says "the Thakin movement contained a strong Communist element"; yet their fellow Briton, Maurice Collis, says that only two Thakins were real Communists, and the American, Frank Trager, says that Burma was the last country in all Southeast Asia to be appreciably influenced by Marxist thinking, and that its Communist Party was not founded until 1943.[8] U Thant agrees with Trager, though he believes there were more than two Communists among the Thakins.

Burmese resistance to all-out Marxism had several causes. One was the traditional Burmese isolationism and distrust of foreign concepts. Another was that Marxist materialism went against the Buddhist grain; still another was that the Marxist class-war concept was inapplicable

[7] Quoted in Butwell: *U Nu*, p. 20.
[8] Trager and Associates: *Burma*, Vol. III, pp. 1006 and 1076.

to classless Burma. A possible fourth cause is that some Burmese, like many Asians, suspected Stalin of caring more about the white proletariat of Europe than about the yellow peasants of Asia. (This same race issue is currently being used by the Chinese Communists to woo Asians and Africans from Russia's brand of communism.)

Lastly, most Burmese were unenthusiastic about the Indian Communist Party. When several nationalists, including Aung San, traveled to India during the latter thirties, they returned disenchanted. The Indian Communists' theory of violence did not appeal to them, yet the Congress Party's theory of mass nonviolence did not appeal to them either. They feared that the deliberate exposure of large crowds to death, that might be effective in a teeming country like India, would be ruinous in a sparsely populated country like Burma.

On the other hand, the Marxist analysis of imperialism as the final stage of decadent capitalism, together with its pattern for revolution against existing evils, dovetailed with the hopes of some of the young nationalists. According to the journalist, U Tun Pe, "They delighted in using Marxist terminology." They also studied Fabian and Socialist writings and joined the British Left Wing Book Club.

U Thant, the first Burmese to join the Left Wing Book Club, became a charter member of U Nu's Red Dragon Book Club in 1937. This enterprise issued seventy titles in the next few years. Among the books Nu himself translated into Burmese were Edgar Snow's *Red Star Over China* and Dale Carnegie's *How to Win Friends and Influence People* (Nu felt that some of Carnegie's techniques, devised for the American business world, could be adapted to the Burmese political scene). Other authors studied by the young nationalists included Sun Yat-sen,

Nehru, Upton Sinclair, John Strachey, John Reed, and various writers of Ireland's Sinn Fein movement.

Although the Burmese nationalists were influenced by the British liberals, they did not wholly trust them either. For the liberals rarely pointed up the discrepancy between Britain's policy of self-determination for white Europeans (after World War I) and her stand-pat policy for the Asian colonies.

Some of the Burmese nationalists were reading on the other end of the political spectrum too, authors such as Nietzsche, Mussolini, and Hitler. Germany, in their view, had several strikes in her favor, one being her lack of colonies (she had been stripped of them after World War I); another being her apparent national unity; the third being her economic renascence through her own efforts. "Germany," says Trager, "did not appear to be so much of an enemy to Asia as to Europe."[9]

An occasional swastika made its appearance among the many flags carried by the Thakins as they marched (their song, "Doh Bama," later became Burma's national anthem). And some RUSU leaders sided with Germany in her growing conflict with Great Britain: as Aung San said, "We looked upon those who opposed our foes as our friends." Yet, like Thant, the more he studied Fascist methods, the more he disliked them.[1]

Gradually, the young nationalists realized, they would have to improvise methods of their own. The most effective of these evolved almost by accident in 1936 and constituted, Clubb says, "the political watershed in modern Burmese history."

It was a student strike combined with taking refuge on the sacrosanct grounds of the Shwe Dagon Pagoda. It

[9] Frank N. Trager, editor: *Marxism in Southeast Asia* (Stanford, Calif.: Stanford University Press; 1951), p. 246.
[1] Dr. Maung Maung: *Aung San of Burma*, p. 34.

started with one of U Nu's speeches attacking the staff of the University. The President, D. J. Sloss, suspended him and demanded an explanation. This Nu refused to give, and the Student Union marched out on strike. Co-incidentally, *Oway,* the student magazine of which Aung San was an editor, came out with an anonymous article defaming an easily identified faculty member.

The article, entitled "Hell-hound at Large," was written by Nyo Mya, who later became a courageous journalist in Rangoon and a friend of U Thant. Young Nyo Mya was jealous of a Burmese teacher for paying attention to his girl. In the text the teacher was ticked off as a "pimping knave with avuncular pretensions to some cheap wiggling wenches from a well-known hostel."

When Aung San was asked by the University authorities for the name of the author of the article he refused to divulge it and was expelled for three years. (The authorities are said to have known the name all along.) This time not only the Student Union but the entire resident body, some 700 strong, went out on strike. For three months they camped at the Shwe Dagon Pagoda. Final examinations had to be postponed. Finally the University readmitted both Nu and Aung San.

In that same year of 1936 the first general election was held under the Government of Burma Act of 1935. Dr. Ba Maw formed a coalition cabinet and became Burma's first Prime Minister. On the day he took office U Nu and two colleagues burned a copy of the 1935 Constitution and the Union Jack in front of Rangoon's High Court Building. The British and Dr. Ba Maw, chary of making Nu a martyr, took no action against him.

Shortly afterward, Nu resigned from the University to become a journalist, and was succeeded as president of the Student Union first by M. A. Raschid and then by Aung

San. In 1937, Nu and Aung San, together with an intelligent and charming former schoolteacher, Than Tun, joined the Thakins. Nu became its treasurer, "a treasurer without a treasure," as he termed it.

The Thakin program was in three parts: first, struggle; then mobilization; and lastly, revolt. U Thant, still in Pantanaw, agreed with their attempts to organize the people for "struggle" but not with the violence in which they shortly became involved. Some of what appeared to the Thakins as improvization appeared to him as recklessness.

The first episode of violence came in 1938. It was a sequel to the Dock Riots of 1930, with the same economic base, the British refusal to restrict immigration from India. (By 1938, two-thirds of the employees of Burma's factories, mines, oil fields, railroads, tramways, docks, and plantations were Indian.)

As in the Student Strike, the precipitating event was a minor one: a book unfriendly to Buddhism had been published years earlier by a Moslem and largely ignored. But on July 19, 1938, *The Sun,* the newspaper in which U Thant's father had had an interest but which had since been taken over by U Saw, ran an article by a monk asking all Buddhists to take "urgent action" against the book. Other parts of the press made misleading accusations that Moslem men who had married Burmese women were outraging their religion. This was precisely the kind of irresponsible journalism that was arousing U Thant's jeremiads.

One week later 10,000 people, among them 1,500 monks, gathered at the Shwe Dagon. A march following the meeting got out of hand and 200 people were killed and 936 wounded. The British Governor declared a state of emergency in Rangoon. Even after the violence was quelled, many Burmese continued to picket Indian shops.

The second serious upheaval occurred late in 1938. This was the Oil Field Workers' Strike, which culminated in a workers' march of 400 miles from Yenangyaung to Rangoon. As the workers marched they were joined by Thakins and other nationalists organized for the purpose. In Rangoon the students congregated as evidence of solidarity with the workers. This time the British and Indian police did not wait for violence to break out, but actually precipitated it on December 20 by riding with their heavy *lathis* through the streets where the students were about to disperse. A Burmese boy, Aung Gyaw, later died of head wounds. A decade after the monk, U Wisara, had died in a British-run jail, thus giving the Burmese their first martyr in the name of Buddhism, Aung Gyaw died in a British-run hospital, thus giving the Burmese their first martyr in the name of the worker and student movements.

The Oil Field Workers' Strike did not result in materially improved wages, but it provided impetus for the formation of the first Burmese national federation of labor. A leader in this endeavor was another acquaintance of U Thant, Ba Swe, whose nickname was "Tiger" and whose enjoyment of the pleasures of life did not prevent his courting—and receiving—a jail sentence during the workers' strike.

Peasants as well as workers were growing more restive. They were no better off in the latter thirties than at the time of the Saya San Rebellion. The leader of their new organization, Thakin Mya, was a friend of U Thant who later described him as "a balanced and cautious person— very shy—and in a sense an intellectual."[2]

[2] Interview with U Thant, New York, 1964.

Thakin Mya, together with student leaders Kyaw Nyein and Ba Swe, also founded the Burma Revolutionary Party, which later became the Socialist Party. At the same time, an intense young man described by U Thant as "an outstanding stylist as a novelist and pamphleteer," Thakin Thein Pe, gathered a tiny Communist group which included Thakin Soe, and, later, Thakin Than Tun.

This was the time when war, in a slow pincer movement, was closing in on Burma. In 1937, at the Marco Polo Bridge outside Peking, the Japanese had attacked the Chinese, and Britain and the United States hurried to build the Burma Road in order to send supplies to Chiang Kai-shek. This road from Rangoon to the inland Chinese capital, Chungking, covered 2,000 miles. To guard it, a hundred American planes were poised on southwest China airfields, together with American pilots under the command of General Claire Chennault.

Dr. Gordon Seagrave's Namkham Hospital is near the border. Seagrave watched some of the 300,000 workers—mostly Chinese men and women coolies—building the Burma Road, as he said, with "little loving pats":

[It was] just a mud road and was only usable six months of the year, and not always then. The bridges were all of bamboo and had to be replaced after every rainy season. Bamboo makes quite nice bridges. You break through them very frequently, but they very seldom collapse en masse.[3]

Despite his Burmese-type levity, he was well aware of the road's hazards. By the end of World War II, 13,000 American Lend-Lease trucks had careened off it into the gorges. Yet its contribution to the eventual Allied victory was unquestionable. An American historian says that "the legendary Burma Road was at once the most dangerous, the most confused and the most important highway in the

[3] Seagrave: *Burma Surgeon*, p. 100.

world. . . . It was Free China's lifeline until December 7, 1941, when it became also the American Road."[4]

The building of the road called forth countermeasures by the Japanese. As the first Asian conquerors of a European nation (in 1905), they were highly regarded in Burma as elsewhere in Asia. Their slogan, "Asia for the Asians" (with its corollary, "Burma for the Burmese"), and their promise to build an Asian "co-prosperity sphere," conformed to the hopes of the Burmese nationalists. The Japanese were not slow to take advantage of Burmese friendliness. Members of the Japanese armed forces, including a Colonel Minami Suzuki, entered Burma incognito in order to gather information about the Burma Road and to recruit Burmese secret allies.

Meanwhile, on September 1, 1939, 170,000 German soldiers had smashed into Poland, and Poland's allies, Britain and France, declared war on Germany. As a province of Great Britain, Burma, without even a motion in her own legislature, found herself at war with Germany. Earlier in that momentous year of 1939, Dr. Ba Maw had lost his Premiership to one of his Ministers, the quiet, conservative U Pu. On October 6, 1939, Dr. Ba Maw, in his capacity as head of the Sinyetha Party, publicly stated that the Burmese could not be asked to fight for Poland's freedom from Germany unless the Burmese were themselves offered freedom from Great Britain. Thakins Aung San, Nu, and Than Tun began negotiations with Dr. Ba Maw as to how, together, they could take advantage of Britain's involvement in World War II to gain Burma's independence. Said Aung San, "Colonialism's difficulty is Freedom's opportunity."

Sir Winston Churchill, England's great wartime Prime

[4] John Leroy Christian: *Burma* (London: William Collins & Co., Ltd.; 1945), p. 102.

Minister, continued to have a blind spot on the question of promising ultimate self-government to Burma. As U Thant said later, unquestionably Churchill was "a big man," but in regard to Asian nationalism "he was a small man."[5]

Even after Churchill and Roosevelt signed the Atlantic Charter on August 14, 1941, Churchill (though not Roosevelt) insisted it would not apply to Burma. In part, Churchill's conviction may have been based on the indispensability of the Burma Road to the Allied war effort. "As a strategic object," he cabled to General Ismay on January 20, 1942, "I regard keeping the Burma Road open as more important than the retention of Singapore."[6]

In Burma, the British were clamping down on articles and speeches by the nationalists. Starting in January, 1940, large blank spaces began to appear in the newspapers, and nationalist spokesmen, such as Dr. Ba Maw, were jailed. "With Britain at war," Clubb says, "opposition in the colonies took on a treasonous aspect." At the same time, anti-British feeling was spreading throughout Burma. Even so gentle an observer as Mi Mi Khaing reported reading with feelings of surprise and amusement about the face-slapping and stuffing of passports into the mouth to which the Japanese were subjecting Englishmen in the ports of China.[7]

In September, 1940, the Premier, U Pu, was succeeded by U Saw. Now both of Saya San's lawyers had achieved the top government position open to a Burmese. By then Dr. Ba Maw was in jail, but when his term expired U Saw was happy to extend it for another year. On the surface U Saw, like U Pu, got along well with the natty, jovial,

5 Interview with U Thant, New York, 1962.
6 Winston Churchill: *The Hinge of Fate* (Boston: Houghton Mifflin Company; 1950), p. 53.
7 Mi Mi Khaing: *Burmese Family*, p. 163.

Conservative Governor, Sir Reginald Dorman-Smith, but behind the scenes U Saw, according to Colonel Suzuki, was in contact with the Japanese.[8] The leading Thakins, on the other hand, continued denouncing British policies. Under the new "Defense of Burma Rules" the British jailed Nu and issued a warrant for the arrest of Aung San. Disguised as a Chinese coolie, he sailed to Amoy, off the coast of China, on August 8, 1940. As he wrote later in *The Resistance Movement:*

> I had come out to seek aid for Burma and whether that aid was offered by China or Japan mattered little to me. . . . I had faith in the East and all Easterners and my conviction was that no Easterner would betray or exploit another Easterner.[9]

For two months he and his only Burmese companion almost starved. Finally an offer of aid from Japan was transmitted to them. Exultant, Aung San traveled to Japan and was met by Colonel Suzuki who, however, had not studied the social mores of Burma as thoroughly as its political scene, and promptly offended Aung San, self-described as "a hundred per cent bachelor," by casually offering him a woman. Also shocking to Aung San was Suzuki's attitude toward the non-Japanese Asians, such as the Koreans, and toward the whites. After relating how he had killed a group of Russian civilians during World War I, Suzuki said to Aung San, "Similarly you must kill all British, including women and children."

"Though I was very anti-British at the time," Aung San wrote, "I must confess I was not prepared for such barbarity."

After three months in Tokyo, Aung San, wearing a set

[8] After the war Suzuki wrote a chapter for Maung Maung's *Aung San of Burma.*
[9] Quoted by Clubb in his Ph.D. thesis.

of false teeth to make him look more Japanese, sailed back to Burma. Since, unlike most of his countrymen, he had never learned to swim, the arrangements for putting him ashore involved a diving suit and a special float. But the British guards at the dock at Bassein were not alert and he was able to walk off the ship on March 3, 1941. U Nu and Ba Maw were still in jail but Aung San was able to meet secretly with Kyaw Nyein, Thakin Mya, Bo Let Ya and others, and bring some thirty young men, including Thakin Shu Maung (today General Ne Win), back to Japan with him. Maurice Collis, with typical British fair play, later wrote that "the attitude of the Burmese to the war in general and to the possibility of a Japanese invasion was determined by the fact that they conceived of their country as already occupied by foreigners."[1]

The last Burmese attempt to win British agreement to a measure of independence was the trip by Premier U Saw to London in 1941. The mission was not a success. On the way home he was halted in Hawaii by the outbreak of war on December 7. He therefore had to go back around the world. In Lisbon, the British detected him communicating with Japanese legation officials. He was arrested by the British on his arrival in Egypt, and spent the next four years in detention in British Uganda. According to British intercepts of cables from Lisbon, U Saw had promised the Japanese that the Burmese would aid their invading army against the British.

It was a time of extreme confusion and danger. No one in Burma knew what to expect, including an avid listener to the foreign news over his short-wave radio in Pantanaw.

---

[1] Maurice Collis: *Last and First in Burma* (London: Faber & Faber, Ltd.; 1956), p. 21.

CHAPTER NINE

World War II
Engulfs a Man

U Thant had spent much of his first thirty years with his eyes focused on the printed page. As World War II continued, his ears were focused on the short-wave radio. From December, 1941, onward the news he heard was nigh unbelievable.

First there were the attacks by the Japanese on December 7 and 8 on Pearl Harbor and the Philippines which brought the United States into the war. As the Americans reeled from these surprise attacks, the British in the Pacific were reeling from a series of unprecedented reverses. On the Malay Peninsula the Japanese began landing the army that was soon to capture the supposedly impregnable fortress-city of Singapore, and in Asian waters the Japanese sunk the supposedly unsinkable British battle cruisers, the *Prince of Wales* and *The Repulse,* thus crippling the British fleet that guarded

Burma. On December 15 the Japanese landed at the southernmost town in Burma, Victoria Point, and started northward toward Rangoon. Marching with them were Aung San, Ne Win, and the rest of the Thirty Comrades who now formed the core of the "Burma Independence Army" or BIA.

This BIA was promptly and vastly expanded by volunteers who flocked to it en route. The volunteers varied from heroes to what the Burmese call "Bad Hats," from idealists who believed in the Japanese promise of national independence for Burma to cynics who suspected that in the chaos of wartime they could loot their way to financial independence for themselves. Whoever they were, according to Dr. Ba Maw, "the boys were jubilant at the thought of having 'drawn white blood' so cheaply."[1]

The "white blood" was primarily British. British-led troops fought valiantly but were unable to stem the Japanese advance. The same kind of heroism against hopeless odds was exhibited by the RAF and by the American Volunteer Group that Chiang Kai-shek had generously sent down to guard Rangoon. As Churchill reported, "All through January and February the Japanese air attack was held in check and paid its price for every raid."[2]

Into the north of Burma came several Kuomintang divisions under the American Commander in Chief of the China-Burma-India Theater, General Joseph W. Stilwell.

Throughout Burma the people grew confused and panicky. As Mi Mi Khaing recalls:

Even those who had been expecting war . . . did not know how to feel when it came upon them. . . . People ran here

[1] Dr. Ba Maw permitted me to quote from the typescript of the first part of his memoirs.
[2] Churchill: *The Hinge of Fate*, p. 53.

and there, from one set of relatives to another, not always welcoming; setting out with foolish encumbrances . . . and being forced to shed them. . . . The people who thought reasonably in the face of the quick Japanese onrush, that the British would probably have to get out but would prepare, perhaps in India . . . to return one day, expected to spend the next few years in quiet and hiding from danger.[3]

U Thant was and is not prone to panic. He was, moreover, a responsible civic figure in Pantanaw who could not run out on the people who relied on him; and besides, by then he had a sizable family.

His firstborn had been a boy, Maung Boh. A fine, healthy baby, Boh was that source of repeated wonder, almost awe, that the first baby is likely to be to both parents. Having started out healthy, Boh suddenly developed a fever. A Saya was called in but could not ease the cough which developed. Then the medical officer was summoned, who said that Boh had bronchial pneumonia. (These medical officers had neither the full training nor the title of M.D.) U Thant wrote to U Khant (April 22, 1935): "People say that Maung Boh will be better after the customary naming ceremony. So it was performed yesterday . . . and about four hundred people were invited."

The baby *was* better after the ceremony, but within the year he sickened again. A note from U Thant to U Khant (September 22, 1936) revealed the family heartbreak:

Maung Boh died at 3:30 P.M. yesterday after a somewhat long illness. The loss shocks us immensely. The loss is all the more keen as he was exceptionally clever child. He had been ailing for the last ten days, but we had never thought that he would be cut off from us so soon. The burial took place on the same evening at 5 P.M. Ma Thein Tin is so

3 Mi Mi Khaing: *Burmese Family,* p. 194.

much afflicted that her health is a matter of anxiety. I also feel like a man in a dream—and of course life is but a long, long dream.

In order to try to console Daw Thein Tin and U Thant, friends brought them a four-month-old boy whose parents could not keep him. "We both fell in love with the baby," U Thant recalls. He and Daw Thein Tin did not bother to adopt him legally, but in their hearts, Maung Saw Lwin was their own. Not long after the arrival of their foster son, their daughter, Aye Aye, was born and then their son, Maung Tin Maung. With three tiny children, as well as a wife and mother to take care of, Thant never even considered flight when the Japanese arrived.

His two younger brothers were married and had been assigned by the Burma Civil Service to posts in other towns, while U Khant was in Rangoon, having briefly published his own magazine, *The Literary World,* and then become Librarian of the British-established Bernard Free Library. Rangoon had no anti-aircraft guns and in the early months of 1942 the Japanese attacked by air. Maurice Collis describes the first of the bombings:

The streets were crowded with people. . . . They did not at once realize their danger. . . . In a moment the pavements were strewn with the dead and dying. There followed a terrible panic.

The defending two squadrons, however, managed to shoot down eleven Japanese planes for the loss of three Americans. . . . Indeed the losses inflicted on the enemy were so heartening that the real seriousness of the raid was not immediately apparent. This [lay] in the flight of the labouring population, particularly the Indians.[4]

The plight of the fleeing Indians was even worse, because of terrain and weather, than that of the refugees

[4] Collis: *Last and First in Burma,* p. 55.

from the Low Countries had been the previous year, when the Nazi dive-bombing began. The Burmese roads became clogged with old people, children, and overladen adults. As a British observer told Collis, "It was pitiful to see the persistence with which they clung to their little property."

The multitude was estimated at 100,000, and soon they were joined on their way to India by Burmese loyal to the British and by minorities fearful of the Burmans or the Japanese or both. As the refugees progressed on their 600-mile journey, they found the roads dwindling to paths and the paths encroached upon by jungle. This jungle, almost impassable during the dry season, was even worse when the monsoon downpours began. Food became unavailable, and the mud reached to the knees. Uncounted thousands perished. Nobody could afford the time or energy to bury them.

The flight of labor from Rangoon, together with the cumulative bombing by the Japanese, finally crippled the nation's port. Starting in March, 1942, the British blew up its remaining valuable installations and fought a rearguard action up the peninsula—freeing prison inmates as they went. One of these, Dr. Ba Maw, misunderstood the purpose of the British scorched-earth tactics. In his memoirs he stated that they had destroyed "steamboats and industrial installations . . . which had nothing whatsoever to do with the war but . . . in sheer anger against the Burmese."

U Nu, who was also freed from jail—after almost starving and dying of cholera there—showed a greater understanding of the desperate measures of the British. He also apparently could understand the Burmese leaders and civil servants who fled together with the British and set up a Burmese government-in-exile in Simla, India, headed by Governor Dorman Smith and Premier U Saw's successor, Acting Premier Sir Paw Tun. (James Barrington of the ICS got to Simla just in time: since he and his wife are Anglo-Burmese, they would have been marked for especially restrictive measures by the Japanese.)

The British, in their flight, were subsequently joined by General Joseph Stilwell, his American aides, and some of the Chinese troops under his command. To radio listeners like U Thant, Stilwell's remarks to the Associated Press in New Delhi on May 25, 1942, were refreshingly pungent: "I claim we got a hell of a beating. We got run out of Burma and it is humiliating as hell. I think we ought to find out what caused it, go back and retake it."

The Japanese meanwhile succeeded in cutting the Burma Road. The Chinese forces guarding it fell back through the Shan States in order to escape into Yunnan. But they were trapped there by the Japanese motorized forces, and, according to Dr. Ba Maw's memoirs, the Chinese "disintegrated into open bandit gangs who roamed the countryside. . . . For someone with a sense of history, it was like the old Tartar hordes back in Burma again."

For Dr. Ba Maw, with his romantic sense of history, driving the British out of Burma constituted "the Fourth and Final Anglo-Burmese War" and it "symbolized for a short period the recovery of those lost dreams . . . and memories which traveled far back into the past, of kings and conquerors who had once built a great Burmese empire."

For U Thant, whose view of history was critical rather than romantic, the cure appeared worse than the disease: "I never had any hopes of the Japanese giving us real freedom. The situation was difficult to assess—but my mood was pessimistic."[5]

Gradually it became clear that the Japanese occupation of Burma was part of a larger Nipponese plan. Burma to

[5] Interview with U Thant, New York, 1963.

them was a potential springboard for the conquest of India and the eventual union with German forces in Iran; for, poised in the Libyan desert, ready to strike for the Near East, was General Rommel and his Afrika Korps.

This was truly a World War. Indeed, Parkinson says in *East and West* that "the First World War" was a misnomer, since only the second one involved Asia and Africa as well as Europe, and the United States as a Pacific as well as an Atlantic Power.

By May, 1942, Burma was in Japanese hands. Yet, just as in 1885, when the British had conquered the whole of the country, there followed years of covert and overt rebellion. Aung San later reported that he had first considered organizing this rebellion into a Resistance Movement as early as March, 1942, when the Japanese entered Rangoon. But this, he decided, would be premature, and he bided his time.

One of the first questions facing Aung San as well as the Japanese was how to curb the unruliness of the Burma Independence Army. This loose organization had mushroomed in quantity but not quality of men. While the Japanese army was driving the British northward, the BIA was left in control of large sections of the Irrawaddy Delta. Burman elements in the BIA attacked the Karens, and the Karens, bereft now of their British protectors, fought back desperately. As Dr. Ba Maw recalled in his memoirs:

Of all the conflicts, the most savage and also most revealing of the difficulties ahead for the peoples of Burma was the one that broke out in the southern delta region. . . . It lasted for weeks and culminated in a cold-blooded mass slaughter. . . . In a sense the fight still goes on.

U Thant, as one of Pantanaw's leading citizens, was a member of the local administrative committee that dealt first with the BIA and then with the Japanese. U Thant's main contact among the Karens was Saw Hunter Tha Hmwe. Because of their mutual respect, a small personal bridge was thrown across the bloody chasm of group conflict.

On July 24, 1942, the Japanese disbanded the BIA. In its place they established a smaller and better disciplined Burma Defense Army, headed by Aung San, but with Suzuki and other Japanese "advisers" attached to it at every level.

The next step was the establishment—at least on paper—of a "Burma Central Government" under Dr. Ba Maw, but here, too, at every level, were Japanese advisers who, in effect, gave the orders and, when these were not obeyed, called in the dread Japanese Secret Police or Kempeitai.

Thakin Than Tun, in his anonymous *Under Duress* published in 1945, gives a firsthand report of the Kempeitai, a report jibing with that of U Nu, U Thant, and others:

The horrors of Belsen and Auschwitz are being brought to light but are Kempeitai's brutality and inhumanity to be forgotten? Three of my friends, two Burmans and the other an Indian, who had been taken by Kempeitai have never been their old selves again. They had left the camp as physical wrecks. . . . Peeling off fingernails and pouring hot water down the throat were nothing compared with keeping the victim under a water tap and allowing drops of water to fall on his forehead. This often caused large dents in the foreheads and ugly ulcers in some.

For all these crimes, the Kempeitai alone were not responsible. The worst offenders were the informers. . . .

Burmese who informed on fellow Burmese existed throughout the country. An old-time politician living in a small town like Pantanaw summed up for Dr. Ba Maw what was happening in his neighborhood:

The BIA who passed through our town were [bad]. . . . The party men who composed their administrative bodies were even worse. So we had to think of a way to protect ourselves against them. We naturally thought of the Japanese. This made us carry to the Japanese every sort of tale . . . about the BIA misdeeds. . . . The Kempeitai in our town turned against the BIA. . . . The common criminals were also rounded up. But when the Burmese terror was checked that way the Japanese terror appeared. . . . A lot of people played off one side against the other.

Before the Japanese occupation was more than a few months old, Dr. Ba Maw recalls, "the Japanese, the Chinese, the Indians, the Burmans, together with all other indigenous peoples, all were fighting against one another, all finding the enemy in the nearest stranger." To those with a sense of history, Burma, socially, was back in the days before King Anawrahta, when it was unsafe to travel unarmed among groups other than one's own.

U Thant, nonetheless, decided to travel. In May, 1942, he had received word that Aung San and U Nu wanted him to become Secretary of Burma's Educational Reorganizing Committee in Rangoon. Its purpose was to make structural recommendations for the improvement of Burmese education. By that time, public transportation was impossible. For a boat or train, one had to line up for more than twenty-four hours to obtain a Japanese-issued ticket, and if one left the line in order to attend the needs of nature (about which the Burmese are more modest than the Japanese) one lost one's place. Thant was fortunate in having means sufficient to hire a private boat. It was difficult for him to leave his family, and, as he waved good-by to his wife, mother, and the three babies, he was by no means certain he would see them again.

Rangoon was chaotic. Installations destroyed by the British had not been rebuilt and the American B-29s were roaring over from India to destroy what was left. Yet despite the bombing, refugees from the countryside were streaming into the capital. Housing was unobtainable. U Thant moved in with U Khant, whose library job had terminated when the British left and who had not yet been able to find another.

For Thant life in Rangoon was a nightmare. He worried about U Khant's family and his own; he dodged the bombs as best he could; he agonized at the sight of his once proud countrymen doing things of which no one could be proud; and to top everything he too had a Japanese adviser:

I was not happy at all. It was much worse than the British system. There were too many advisers. They called themselves advisers but really they ruled. Life in Rangoon grew pretty hot. Not only the bombing. I was a target of Japanese suspicion. I was thought to be pro-British.[6]

He stuck it out, however, and finished his report, "A New Education Policy for Burma," in late July, 1942. On August 1 the new Burma Executive Administration was officially established by the Japanese. At the same time an "Independence Preparatory Committee" was formed to draw up a draft constitution. U Thant handed in his report but it was shelved. Whether this shelving was the result of Dr. Ba Maw's old antagonism, or disapproval by the Japanese advisers, or simple bureaucratic inefficiency, Thant did not stay to find out. It did not matter much anyway since the new Burmese "government" would have so little power. U Nu, one of its top Ministers, recorded his frustration in *Burma under the Japanese*:[7]

[6] Interview with U Thant, New York, 1963.
[7] Because of rampant inflation, the Ministers and other Burmese officials with a set salary had less money in the end than some trishaw drivers. This situation had been the other way about under the British.

Men who did not understand the situation thought that
we could set everything right with a mere stroke of the pen.
And when I saw how little I could do I was so ashamed to
meet them that I used to go up to my room in the office by
the back stairs and come down again by the back stairs. The
whole time since I took up politics, I have never felt so miserable. Before then I might be thirsty but I was happy; I might
be hungry but I was happy; in jail or out of jail, I was quite
happy. But now it was a case of a golden palace and an
empty belly, as the saying goes. I had a fine house to live in,
a car to drive about in, but what with worrying for myself
and worrying for my people, I never had a moment's peace.

Members of the Thirty Comrades were miserable too.
Nothing they had fought for, except the expulsion of the
British, had come to pass. Indeed Burma's situation was
worse than under the British and daily deteriorating.
Aung San, as Bo Let Ya recalls in *Aung San of Burma,*
continued telling his followers that "they must fight on,
like George Washington, against long odds and if necessary for long years until independence was won."[8]

Before the Burmese could fight for real independence
the Burmese leaders were forced to go along with a sham
independence devised by the Japanese. On August 1, 1943,
exactly a year after the establishment of the Ba Maw
executive government, Burma was declared an independent state and was so recognized by the Axis Powers.

---

[8] Washington's diary, as quoted from Thomas J. Fleming: *Beat the Last
Drum* (New York: St. Martin's Press; 1963), gives a picture of the American colonies which is a parallel to Burma in 1942: "Instead of having
magazines filled with provisions, we have a scant pittance. . . . Instead
of having our arsenals filled with military stores, they are poorly provided. . . . And instead of having the prospect of a glorious offensive
campaign before us, we have a gloomy and bewildered prospect of a
defensive one. Chimney corner patriots abound; venality, corruption,
prostitution of office for selfish ends, abuse of trust, perversion of funds
. . . and speculations upon the necessities of the times pervade all interests."

Secretary-General U Thant tunes in on the English translation at a United Nations Headquarters press conference.

U Thant in 1927, age 18, at Rangoon University, where he was reading Byron, among other things.

U Thant and his family, July, 1957, before leaving for New York. Left to right: Tin Maung, U Thant, Daw Thein Tin, Aye Aye.

U Nu presenting a check for $5,000, to President Eisenhower for the families of Americans who fell in Burma in World War II. Looking on are John Foster Dulles and U Thant. BELOW U Thant with his family, July, 1964. Standing, left to right: U Tin Maung, Dr. Tin Myint U, Aye Aye, U Thaung; seated, left to right: U Thant, Daw Nan Thaung, U Khant.

President Kennedy bidding farewell to U Thant after a visit to U. N. Headquarters in 1961. Behind them is Ambassador Adlai E. Stevenson.

One of its first acts was to declare war on Great Britain and the United States. This caused consternation among some Burmese, particularly those who had heard by clandestine radio that the Philippine Government, also under Japanese domination, had refused to take this step. Other Burmese are said by Collis to have delighted in declaring war on the enemies of Japan while secretly hoping for Japan's defeat: "That the Japanese did not see this was a cover-up seemed the height of comedy."[9]

Reasons for Burmese hatred of the Japanese kept multiplying. There were, of course, some fine officers in the Japanese army, and some of them—in Tokyo as well as in Burma—did what they could to counter the extreme militarism of the dominant group. But they could not control the cruelty of the Kempeitai any more than the German officers who eventually rebelled against Hitler in 1944 had been able to control the Gestapo. Nor could the conscientious Japanese control the arrogance and stupidity of those Japanese soldiers who slapped the faces of the Burmese elders, requisitioned rice, wantonly slaughtered cattle, used the monasteries as latrines for themselves and as stables for their animals, destroyed scriptural scrolls, and bathed naked (as they were accustomed to do at home) in front of Burmese maidens and matrons. Particularly offensive to the Burmese was the Japanese low view of women and the many cases of rape. "I couldn't have believed," U Thant said later, "that anyone could be as cruel as the Japanese were in Burma."[1]

Yet Thant went on to add what other people too have observed, that the Japanese in their home islands can be the most courteous and hospitable of people. Also, in fairness to the Japanese, it must be pointed out that some

[9] Collis: *Last and First in Burma*, p. 206.
[1] Interview with U Thant, New York, 1962.

of their cruelty was in support of their own war effort. In order to facilitate the flow of war matériel overland, for example, they used 269,948 Burmese forced laborers and 61,806 British, Canadian, and Australian prisoners of war to build a railway between Thailand and Burma. Said U Khant, "The railway was constructed at the expense of lives of tens of thousands of people who died by Japanese callous brutality and naked bestiality." This was the background for *The Bridge Over the River Kwai,* a movie that, curiously, has been a big success in postwar Japan.

By the time U Thant returned to Pantanaw in late July, 1942, travel was impossible without a permit, and no word against the Japanese could be spoken or written. The Japanese controlled the broadcasting station in Rangoon and demanded that all radios be turned over to them to have their short-wave apparatus removed. The penalty for neglecting to do this was death.

U Thant had spent his life preaching freedom, and was determined to practice it. He and four Pantanaw friends retained one short-wave set. Every night at nine o'clock they went to the house of U Khin Maung and listened upstairs while the family played records loudly in the living room below. They knew the risk. Even Thant's friend Nu, who was high in the government, would not have been able to save him if he were caught. For the Japanese ran the jails without "interference" from the Burmese officials.

Thant did not burden his wife with having to keep secret the information he gleaned, such as the Italian surrender to the Allies weeks before announcement was made on the Japanese radio. To guard one's tongue around the Japanese was a constant strain and not always possible. As Nu wrote:

When you are looking at their stolid round faces, my friend, don't go thinking you are clever enough to deceive them. . . . There is always a chance of making a slip . . . and any scrap of conversation with a Japanese spy who scrapes up an acquaintance with you . . . is reported to the police station. And the officer in charge compares it with all other reports to check what you have said.[2]

Thant was often in conversation with the Japanese. His behavior toward them remained "correct." He knew he was suspected of pro-British leanings, and in order not to be suspected also of leftist views, he removed from his library all books that either were, or that the Japanese might assume were, anti-Fascist. As Than Tun later wrote in *Under Duress:*

In "independent" Burma there was no such thing as personal liberty or the sanctity of your home. Any Japanese just walked in and out of your house and took anything he fancied.

Thant gave the appearance of being happy to lend books to the Japanese. A Lieutenant Oyama and a member of the military police named Oka came often to borrow books and to talk[3] Thant was receiving valuable training in keeping his face impassive and his hands relaxed in time of strain.

Another item of news that Thant could not legally have known as early as he did was the appointment, in November, 1943, of Lord Louis, Admiral Mountbatten, as supreme Allied commander of Southeast Asia. Here was a personage, forceful and understanding, who could both drive the Japanese off the Asian mainland and be sympathetic toward Burma's hopes of true independence. U Thant began to cherish small hidden hopes. Even today

[2] Thakin Nu: *Burma under the Japanese,* p. 48.
[3] In 1955, when Thant visited Japan, he tried to trace these two but without success.

his face lights up at the mention of Mountbatten. And in May, 1965, when Mountbatten visited the UN, Thant reported that "we had a very good time. He is very interested in UN peace-keeping—and of course we reminisced about Burma."

Under Mountbatten's command were the Allied military forces, the civilian organizations, such as the Burmese government-in-exile, and the secret intelligence units such as the British Force 136 and the American OSS (Office of Strategic Services) Detachment 101, both of which were contacted by the Burmese underground Resistance as soon as it was formed.

Thant's first assignment from the Resistance came in 1944 when, as a leader of the Pantanaw Administrative Council, he was secretly asked to help supply rice to be hidden against the time of national uprising. As Thant rightly suspected, the Resistance had already been hiding arms. Thant provided the rice, although he was under further suspicion for refusing, in effect, to follow the edict about making the Japanese language compulsory in the schools. Thant had never argued against this; he simply remained unable to locate suitable teachers. (Aye Aye Doliner, who as a child in Burma was forced to learn Japanese at school, reports that every word of Japanese was blocked out of her memory as a result of witnessing Japanese atrocities. Some Danes, similarly forced to learn German during the Nazi occupation of their country, report the same kind of memory block. Others who do remember the enforced language still hate to speak it.)

Dr. Ba Maw, however, did argue with the rulers of Burma about teaching their language, and the two Japanese who were then caught trying to assassinate him were not executed, only exiled.[4] To this day he believes

4 Thakin Nu: *Burma under the Japanese*, p. 54.

that he almost died for his refusal to order the teaching of Japanese.

In March, 1944, the Japanese mounted an offensive against the Allies in India that backfired and thus became the turning point of the war in Asia. The crucial battle was won at Imphal by the Allies, under Field Marshal Sir William Slim, who then pursued the Japanese into Burma. The defending Japanese applied scorched-earth tactics not only to the Burmese installations, but to the people. In a town near Pantanaw 200 Burmese were put to death for no reason. And U Khant, who fled the bombing of Rangoon with his family, taking refuge in Pantanaw, remembers that in nearby Myangmya, forty-nine persons, three of whom were friends of his, were massacred. As recalled in a letter twenty years later:

> I went and saw the old well on the outskirts of Myangmya, wherein the decapitated bodies of the forty-nine victims buried under tons of cement and bricks were exhumed, and on return to Pantanaw my unmanly nerves became unhinged, and I was down with typhoid fever for two and a half months . . . and I was on the verge of death that time.

U Thant too was in danger of death—not from illness but from the Japanese. Two one-time pupils who were police inspectors came to warn him, and even Lieutenant Oyama let fall a hint of imminent arrest. U Thant and his four friends, therefore, decided to destroy their short-wave radio. Thus, only a few weeks before the end of the war in Burma, they cut their contact with the outside world.

Even if they had kept the set, however, they would not have heard the dramatic story of the part played by the Burmese Resistance in the Allied race to reach Rangoon before the monsoon. U Thant later learned all the details of the story, for it was he who was chosen by the surviving chief actors in the drama to write its official history.

CHAPTER TEN

World War II
Engulfs a Country

The meeting at U Nu's house was held on the night of
August 1, 1944. Ostensibly called to celebrate the first
anniversary of Burmese "independence" under the Japanese, its purpose was to formalize the Resistance, the first
Burmese "united front" in history. Included were the
Burma National Army (under Aung San and Ne Win),
the Burma Revolutionary Party (under Thakin Mya, U
Kyaw Nyein, and U Ba Swe), the Communist Party
(founded the previous year by Thakins Soe and Thein Pe),
and members of no party, such as U Nu. The Burmese,
traditionally prolific in political parties, were finally able
to unite against the Japanese and subsequently against the
British.

The seeds of the Resistance movement, later named the

Anti-Fascist People's Freedom League (AFPFL), had been sown the previous year, 1943, at a meeting at Thakin Than Tun's house. Only the top members of the Ba Maw government knew of the movement, and not all of them took part. Dr. Ba Maw told U Nu, "Well, it looks as if Thakin Than Tun and his lot are playing with fire. So be careful. I don't want to stop anyone from doing what he thinks right. But you had better not tell me more about it. . . . The only thing I care about is independence."

As for Nu, his religiously motivated opposition to violence was often in conflict with his determination to force the Japanese out of Burma:

I was in with all the plans of our group, however secret they were and however dangerous. But I was not an active partner. . . . There was much that I approved and much that I disapproved. . . . But however much I disapproved, the others could be quite confident that I would never give them away or get them into trouble.[1]

Among the key activists, first in the Resistance and then in the AFPF League, were Aung San and Than Tun. Their wives became the Burmese equivalent of China's Soong sisters, married to leaders of their nation and remaining intimate despite the growing political differences between their respective husbands.[2] Aung San and Than Tun had been working in harness since the Thakin period. Now they wanted to broaden their political base. Together they traveled, in 1943, to the Delta to win the support of the Karens against the Japanese (their wives also had a brother married to a Karen). As U Nu wrote:

1 Thakin Nu: *Burma under the Japanese*, p. 104.
2 A third sister is married to U Tin Aung, Chief Accounts Officer of the State Agricultural Marketing Board. In China the Soong sisters were married to Sun Yat-sen, Chiang Kai-shek, and H. H. Kung.

For the great progress of the Karen-Burman reconciliation that was so important for the resistance movement we have to thank the magnetic personality of Aung San and the brains of Than Tun.[3]

Others who contributed to this reconciliation were General Ne Win, who established good relations with the Karen youth groups, and local leading Burmans such as U Thant who had been trusted during the communal strife in 1942 by the leaders of the local Karens.

One of the first acts of the Burmese underground was to make contact with the Allies in India and China. The officials in Simla were at first openly skeptical that the politically fragmented Burmese could work together. Their confidence, moreover, was not enhanced by the first Burmese emissary, Thakin Thein Pe, a Communist.

The British Intelligence Force 136, however, realized that the Burmese Communists, after Hitler's invasion of Russia in 1941, had genuinely become more anti-Axis than anti-British. But the official Allied decision to work with the Burmese Resistance was not made until Mountbatten took command in 1943. His reasoning was later made public in his Report to the Combined Chiefs of Staff:

Although the leader, Major General Aung San, was guilty of treason, since he had collaborated with the Japanese, he was one of those whose political convictions had led them to suppose that the true interests of their country lay in getting the Japanese to grant them political freedom. They had been mistaken, and their present course of action showed that they knew it. I submitted, therefore, that in supporting this uprising . . . we should be doing no more than . . . in Italy . . . where the satellites of a power that had let them down had been accepted as co-belligerents on our side.

[3] Thakin Nu: *Burma under the Japanese*, p. 99.

For the Burmese to support the Allies was not going to be easy. Japan, despite having declared Burma independent, had kept 150,000 of her troops in Burma. "The freedom we have today," Aung San told his ten-thousand-man Burma National Army, "is only on paper." The evils of colonialism, the Burmese were learning, could no longer be associated exclusively with the white man. On the other hand, the former white overlord, with Churchill at the helm, was against giving Burma independence after the war. ("I have not," Churchill announced, "become the King's First Minister in order to preside at the liquidation of the British Empire.") The British, furthermore, were allied with Burma's one-time enemy, the Chinese, and also with a relatively unknown quantity, the Americans, whose Christianizing activities among the Karens in the past had accentuated communal strife, yet whose medical and educational work had been a source of gratitude. Basically, the Burmese tended to lump the British and the Americans together. "The Americans are coming back," was the word that spread through Rangoon in 1945 when the Allied forces, led by the British, finally retook the capital from the Japanese. (Americans who took part in the China-Burma-India [CBI] Theater included members of [General Frank] Merrill's Marauders; General [Wild Bill] Donovan's 101 Detachment, "The Kachin Rangers"; General Claire Chennault's "Flying Tigers"; the intrepid birdmen who "flew the Hump," and various contingents under the command of General Joseph [Vinegar Joe] Stilwell.)

Lastly, there was the Burmese government in exile in Simla. Its officials had no love for the Thakins and the former student activists who were leading the Resistance. If the Simla government was the puppet of the British, and the Ba Maw government was, at least ostensibly, the puppet of the Japanese, and the Burmese Communists were, presumably, the puppets of Russia, how could Burma cease being a puppet nation and start pulling the strings of her own destiny?

Troubled as were Aung San and other Resistance leaders by these questions, there was no doubt that the first step was to get the Japanese out of Burma. And the Burmese were helped by the fact that the Japanese, like the British before them, had no inkling of the depth of Burmese resentment against them. It would seem that the imperialist-colonial relationship is one that cannot avoid breeding misunderstanding. In all events the Japanese, who were racially, religiously, and geographically closer to the Burmese than were the British, in the end were even more foreign in Burmese eyes than the British.

On March 17, 1945, eight months after the founding of the AFPF League, Aung San sent his wife and children into the countryside and marched the Burma National Army out of Rangoon to fight "the enemy." The Japanese assumed he would be fighting the British; the British, on the other hand, expected his forces to aid the Allied drive against the Japanese. For ten days Aung San and his troops marched northward. Dr. Ba Maw passes along a picture of the climactic day of March 27, 1945:

General Sakurai, the chief adviser to the BNA, was with Aung San at Prome the day he disappeared into the jungle to start his army's resistance against the Japanese. Sakurai told me that Aung San looked so taut and sullen . . . that he asked him the reason for it, and Aung San, clutching his head with both hands, replied that it was burning within and he was praying to Buddha to put the fire out. When Sakurai tried to calm him by speaking lightly of the dangers of . . . battle . . . Aung San shook his head vigorously and said, "No, no, you don't understand."

Even after Aung San had joined the Allies, Dr. Ba Maw says:

> The Japanese in Burma believed to the end in Aung San's "Japaneseness" . . . and that . . . it was politically imperative for him to join the [Allied] victors to prevent his political opponents, in particular the Communists, from gaining all the fruits of victory.

The Japanese fought the Allies, desperately and suicidally, for every inch. According to Sir William Slim, the hero of Imphal, "the individual Japanese soldier is the most formidable fighting insect in history." Nonetheless, on May 7, 1945, six weeks after Aung San had joined the Allies, Colonel Ne Win was back in Rangoon broadcasting a declaration of war by Burma against the "Japanese Fascists." This declaration was drafted by the leaders of the AFPF League, which had expanded to include Ba Maw's new Greater Burma Party, the All-Burma Trade Union Congress, the All-Burma Youth League, the All-Burma Peasant Organization, various monks' and women's groups, and representatives of the minorities such as the Karens, Shans, Kachins, Chins, and Arakanese.

Dr. Ba Maw and U Nu fled Rangoon with the Japanese (they would almost surely have been murdered if they had not). Ba Maw ultimately reached Japan, where the Americans took him into custody but released him after a year. U Nu rejoined his AFPF League comrades in Rangoon and shortly afterward withdrew from politics in order to pursue his long-postponed aim of writing plays and novels (one of his subsequent plays was an anti-Communist tract called *The People Win Through*). He also remained as vice president of the AFPF League.

The war of the battlefield was over, but the war for Government House was just beginning.

Fortunately for both sides, Aung San had developed a relationship of mutual respect, first with Sir William Slim, and then with Lord Mountbatten. Had these individuals not been, and recognized each other to be, men of courage whose word could be trusted, it is possible that Burma might promptly have gone to war against the British and, years later, like Indo-China, bloodied, exhausted, riven by internal chaos, would have been ripe for Communist intervention from the north.

Aung San retired from military service and in August, 1945, was elected president of the AFPF League. The League's aim was to be recognized as the provisional government of Burma. But when Governor Reginald Dorman Smith returned from Simla two months later he carried orders from Prime Minister Churchill to re-establish British control. This British White Paper of May 17, 1945, was actually retrogressive, since it abrogated the self-government provisions of the Government of Burma Act of 1935 and demanded British "direct rule" over the war-damaged country.

There was no question as to the extent of the damage. It has been estimated that Burma, together with the Philippines and Greece, suffered destruction worse than any other countries during World War II.[4]

There had, moreover, been an unintentional blow dealt to the Burmese peasants toward the end of Mountbatten's military administration. Instead of exchanging the inflated Japanese currency for British currency at a discount, he repudiated it. This step wiped out the peasants' savings and left them open to exploitation by the moneylenders (U Thant lost all his cash and such money as he had in the bank but not the family real estate holdings).

According to the British White Paper, "direct rule"

4 Frank Trager, *The New Leader,* July 4, 1955.

by the British would last up to three years in order to help
Burma back on her economic feet. After that, the 1935
Constitution would be restored and elections for the legislature could be held, with representatives chosen from
all parties to draft a constitution for Burmese self-government within the Commonwealth. Yet even after this
constitution had been approved by the British Government, the "hill areas" of Burma would be "excluded"
until their inhabitants voted to amalgamate with Burma
proper.

To the AFPF League this White Paper was a red flag.
Aung San, the day before it was officially issued, had confronted General Slim with the minimum Burmese re-
quirements:

1 Instead of abrogating the 1935 Constitution, its self-government provisions should be strengthened.
2 Instead of "direct rule" by the British, the AFPF League
should be recognized as the provisional government of
Burma competent to draw up a constitution.
3 Instead of being bound to the Commonwealth, the Burmese
people should be allowed to choose whether to join it or
form an independent republic.
4 Instead of the "hill areas" having the option not to join the
Union of Burma, they should be included.

Turning the clock back in Burma, the British soon
learned, was going to be more difficult than anticipated.
Not only had the Burmese leaders enjoyed at least the
trappings of independence under the Japanese, but the
United Nations, taking shape in San Francisco, was including a strong anti-colonialist plank, partly at the in-
stigation of the United States (which was in the process
of freeing her own colony, the Philippines). One of the
first steps the British took was to reduce the size of the
Burmese National Forces. But many of the demobilized

veterans joined in forming a People's Volunteer Army (PVO). These veterans, numbers of whom secretly kept their arms, were, for the most part, loyal to Aung San. Indeed, the British writer Foucar refers to them as "Aung San's private army [which] was at loggerheads with the Communist Party whose leader, Thakin Than Tun, was building up his own army." Yet some members of the People's Volunteer Army were sympathetic to communism. In fact, one reason for Aung San's distrust of the Burmese Communists was his fear that they might disclose the Burmese caches of arms to the British. On the other hand, he made certain in his conversations with the British that they knew such caches existed. And when speaking to the Burmese he reminded them of their own history of harassment against an alien occupier; on August 29, 1945, he said:

The Burmese are guerrillas by instinct and tradition. In the thirteenth century when Kublai Khan's hordes swept over Burma, the Burmese could not repel them by employment of elephants and heavy troops. So they broke up into guerrilla bands and harassed the invaders and forced them to withdraw. . . . We too have now consolidated our guerrilla forces under the banner of the AFPFL and stand ready to march to our freedom.[5]

Aung San was convinced that the British were not in a position to maintain more than four combat divisions in Burma. In the continuing war of nerves, he believed, time was on the Burmese side. On November 1, 1945, when Aung San was invited by Governor Dorman Smith to join a new Executive Council, he made the condition that the AFPF League constitute the Council's majority; when this condition was not met the League refused to join. Its boycott effectively reduced Governor Dorman Smith's power and prestige.

5 Quoted from Maung Maung: *Aung San of Burma*, p. 39.

Back in Great Britain, in August, 1945, the Conservative Party, led by Churchill, had been defeated at the polls by the Labour Party led by the mild Clement Attlee. Members of the new British Government had long favored "self-determination" for colonies in theory; now was their chance to put it into practice. On August 1, 1946, a year from their assumption of power, they did, in fact, sponsor an interim national government for India under Nehru —but still nothing was done for the younger sibling Burma.

Meanwhile the war-born unity of the AFPF League was beginning to show fissures. In February, 1946, at a meeting of the Central Committee, Thakin Soe broke with his fellow Communists and proceeded to form an independent "Red Flag" Communist Army. The Red Flag Communists were then officially outlawed by the AFPF League and are today still fighting the Union of Burma Government. Than Tun and his "White Flag" Communists remained with the AFPF League for a while longer, but the brothers-in-law Aung San and Than Tun were approaching a final parting of the ways.

Aung San's popularity, already great, was constantly increasing. To the Burmese he was "Bogyoke," the legendary commander with nigh magical powers.[6] He hoped to be able to spare his countrymen further bloodshed, but he had a premonition that he would not be spared. The predictions of the astrologers reinforced his premonition and he spoke, even in public, of his approaching death. This, if possible, made him even more precious to his countrymen.

A main obstacle to independence through peaceful means, in the eyes not only of the Burmese leaders, but

[6] Ho Chi Minh of North Vietnam today is said to hold a comparable position of respect among his own people for having been *their* George Washington.

eventually also of the British Labour Government, was Governor Dorman Smith. In the early part of 1946 he left Burma by sea for England. En route he was replaced by one of Mountbatten's chief wartime deputies, Sir Hubert Rance, who was well received by Aung San and other Burmese leaders. Yet the political controversies had become too complex to be readily resolved by the replacement of one man.

One point of controversy stemmed from the return of U Saw from British jail in Uganda in 1946. While the formation of a new Governing Council was being considered by Sir Hubert Rance in consultation with Aung San, U Saw openly challenged the AFPF League's claim to represent the majority of the Burmese people. Feverishly U Saw had been rebuilding his own Myochit Party to take its place. One night, on his way home from a party meeting, he was shot at, presumably by a political enemy. He lost the sight of one eye. Here, in human form, was the rogue elephant, wounded and bent on destruction.

Another point of controversy stemmed from the return of Dr. Ba Maw from jail in Japan, also in 1946. The AFPF League leaders offered him a post, but he did not wish to serve in a capacity subordinate to his former underlings whom he still refers to as "my boys," in a "boys will be boys" sort of way. So he too remained outside of, and somewhat antagonistic to, the AFPF League.

A few days after Sir Hubert Rance's arrival, a general strike, supported by the AFPF League, was put in motion. First the police, then the government workers, and finally the railway and oil workers left their jobs.

It was evident to Rance that the Governing Council "nominated" by his predecessor did not have the support of the Burmese people. He promptly abolished it and within five days, on September 26, 1946, he managed to form a new Council made up largely of AFPF League leaders, including Aung San. A week later the general strike ended. However, the White Flag Communists headed by Than Tun refused to accept the Governing Council's authority, nor would they, as the AFPF League leadership did, repudiate methods of extreme violence. This dual refusal caused them to be excluded from the AFPF League in October, 1946. According to Cady:

> This latter action occasioned . . . surprisingly little protest from Thakin Than Tun who made no secret of his intention to continue his revolutionary preparations in anticipation of the probable eventual failure of the AFPF League to reach an agreement with London.[7]

But such an agreement was precisely what Aung San was determined to achieve. If there were no blueprint for Burmese independence by early 1947, he informed Rance, he and the other AFPF League leaders would leave the Governing Council. At the last moment, just before the turn of the year, Prime Minister Attlee announced in the House of Commons a new policy for Burma. A Burmese delegation headed by Aung San was promptly invited to London and there agreed on a transfer of power.

Had King George III agreed to negotiate rather than go to war with the American Colonies, a comparable agreement might have been achieved. Such an agreement, presumably, would also have been supported by some colonials and not by others.

In any event, this is what happened in Burma. Among those who denounced the Aung San–Attlee agreement and demanded further concessions from Great Britain were U Saw, Dr. Ba Maw, the Communists, some members of the People's Volunteer Organization (PVO), and

7 Cady: *History of Modern Burma*, pp. 538–39.

separatists from the Arakan region whose feelings had been whipped up by the underground Red Flag Communists.

This problem of "separatism" was growing acute, especially among the Karens, who had expected to be rewarded for their loyal support of the British in early 1942 by being given their own separate region. But the British were making no moves in this direction.

Aung San, in order to forestall separatist violence, made a prolonged tour of the frontier areas to persuade not only Karens, but the Shan, Kachin, Chin, and Kayah leaders to from a united independent Burma. If they would join with the Burman majority, he solemnly promised, they would have political privileges within the Union of Burma and considerable local autonomy besides. So sincere was he that, in time, all the frontier peoples, though not the Karens, were persuaded, and on February 11, 1947, the Panglong Agreement was signed.

Two months later the elections for the Constituent Assembly were held. AFPF League candidates won more than 170 of the noncommunal seats, compared to only ten for the opposition. These ten, however, included seven Communists elected from the one district where they had run their own candidates. Elsewhere they had boycotted the election. Also boycotting it were the Ba Maw-U Saw group and the Karen National Union.

The Constituent Assembly drew up a constitution which has variously been termed "a scissors and paste job" (Richard Butwell) and "one of the most enlightened constitutions in the world" (Edgar Snow). It was a 78-page document which, according to Frank Trager and U Hla Maung, was "parliamentary in form, liberal democratic in political orientation, welfare-statist in economic outlook, and federal in structure."[8] Its first words, like those

[8] *Journal of International Affairs*, Columbia University, 1956.

of the United States Constitution, were "We, the people. . . ." Phrases and ideas were also borrowed from the constitutions of France, Yugoslavia, and Russia, and from precedents established in the days of the kings: no foreigner, for example, was allowed to own any sizable amount of land.[9]

As for Burma's membership in the Commonwealth, the British enthusiasm for this, as with the old issue of separation, had a chilling effect—and the Burmese opted against it.

This decision by the Burmese caused the Tory opposition in London to try to cancel Britain's promised contribution to Burma's governmental deficit (a similar attitude was shown by France a decade later when Guinea refused to join the French Community and De Gaulle cut off all aid). But the Labour Government remained steadfast and opened negotiations for aid with the new Burmese delegation arriving in London six days later. The delegation was headed by U Tin Tut, eldest brother of Dr. Htin Aung, and was joined by U Nu (Nu's delay having been caused by his election as President of the Assembly which voted Burma out of the Commonwealth). Many people have noted that nothing in Britain's history in Burma became her so much as her departure from that land. Said U Thant as a delegate to the UN Fourth Committee (on colonialism) in October, 1952:

I want to take this opportunity of expressing our heartfelt thanks to the United Kingdom for their foresight and magnanimity in granting independence—really genuine independence—without bloodshed, without resentment, without ill-feeling.

On July 9, 1947, Nu's friend Thant had moved to Rangoon with his wife and children. Thant's aim was to

9 The Constitution also provided for possible secession by the Hill areas after ten years.

found a national magazine along the lines of the *Atlantic Monthly*. In independent Burma, at last, he would have freedom to write and edit. He was investing his own savings and successfully raising funds from interested individuals. When Nu got back from London, Thant talked to him about the project. But Nu was not enthusiastic. He wanted Thant to work for the new Burmese government-in-the-making. But Thant had dreamed of his own magazine since boyhood and was not to be dissuaded.

It was a hopeful time in Burmese history: independence was soon to be achieved; the Governing Council was working overtime on reconstruction.

On Saturday morning, July 19, 1947, the Council had convened on the second floor of the main Secretariat Building. Though still in a monsoon month, the clouds parted and the sun was bright. People moved in and out of the building, watched by the uniformed but inexperienced young Burmese guards. At 10:40 A.M. four youths in uniform raced past the guards and up the stairs to the Council Chamber. With Sten and tommy guns they mowed down everyone in the room: Aung San, Thakin Mya, Aung San's older brother U Ba Win, and other irreplaceable Burmese leaders lay in their own and each other's blood. The assassins then dashed to U Nu's house, but he was not there.

This appalling act turned out to have been engineered by U Saw. The evidence against him was beyond doubt. He was tried and hanged.

As with the murder of Lincoln, after a previous long and bitter war, the divisive consequences for the nation were tragic. The impetus toward unity embodied in the national leader was lost and the country was riven for decades afterward.

The afternoon of the murder, Governor Hubert Rance called in U Nu and asked him to form a new Governing Council. U Nu accepted the post and within a week he summoned his friend Thant and asked him to take the job of Press Officer for the AFPF League. Thant had never joined a political party and never wanted to, and he was on the verge of fulfilling his journalistic dream. But if Burma was to avoid chaos, with independence only five months away, the hopes and plans of the new government needed to be communicated to the people. An experienced writer, fluent in English and Burmese, clearly was called for, and Burma had too few.

His hopes for the magazine were buried with Aung San.

CHAPTER ELEVEN

A Man
on the Wider Stage

Thant's magazine would have filled the gap left by the prewar demise of *The World of Books* and hopefully gone on to reach a wider audience. Clearly there was need in almost independent Burma for a journal to elucidate the social, political, and economic issues confronting the voters who for the first time would have real power over their own destiny.

Thant, by then, had become an ardent advocate of the democratic system. As he said in a broadcast on April 8, 1948:

It substitutes reason and persuasion for force . . . and it makes possible a change of government without a violent upheaval. . . . Democracy is the keystone of the arch of human freedom. . . . What are its other stones? The first is personal

freedom. . . . The second is the reign of law. . . . The third
. . . is freedom of thought, of worship, of speech, and of publication.[1]

But to publish a magazine had meant that U Thant
would have to move to Rangoon, and to extricate himself from Pantanaw had been difficult. His mother would
not be budged, and the members of the school board,
the teachers, and the students all begged him to stay.
Why could he not, they asked, remain High School Superintendent and write and edit on the side? Yet Daw Thein
Tin was pleased with the idea of the move. As a girl she
had been told by an astrologer that the man she married
would one day be world famous, a destiny unlikely to
be fulfilled if he stayed forever in Pantanaw.

Thant became ill. It was a mysterious illness. No one
could give it a name. For the first time, he, the energetic
and healthy one, was bedridden. Astrologers were summoned. U Khant recalls in a letter his mother's description of the occasion:

The abbot of Sein Monastery, Pantanaw . . . examined
U Thant's horoscope and predicted immense success in life
if he moved to Rangoon and sought pastures anew there.
He instructed [that] certain rites . . . be performed to ward
off evils. The rites . . . were, one night U Thant should
sleep with three bags of rice, one placed near his head, another about his middle, and the remaining near his feet. The
next morning the rice put near his head should be cooked
and offered to the Lord Buddha; the rice put near his middle
distributed to beggars, and the rice put near his feet should
be given away to the birds.

Thant today has no recollection of these rites but he
can well imagine that his wife or mother performed them

1 *Burma Speaks,* A Collection of Broadcast Talks, Government Printing
and Stationery Office, Rangoon, 1950.

while he was asleep. In all events, he soon improved. Once he regained his strength he made plans for his wife, himself, the three children, and some of their possessions to move to Rangoon. His library, for the time being, would remain in Pantanaw, together with his files and some of the furniture.

The date set, Thant went to pay his farewell visits. One of the most poignant was at the National High School where all the students assembled to hear him. Also in the audience was U Bo, then District Superintendent of Police, Maubin, who wrote in a letter sixteen years later:

The war had just ended . . . and near-chaotic conditions prevailed in the township of Pantanaw, the hotbed of the Karen insurgents. This was the time of my meeting with U Thant . . . and the fact that it left a deep impression on my mind is the measure of the man. . . .

I still remember a few words of counsel in his farewell speech. . . . He counseled his pupils thus:

"In this world, try to be both good and able men. If you do not become able men, at least try to be good men. The country has no use for able but bad men."

After this lapse of time, I could still recapture the mood of the students who heard his farewell speech, because I shared their mood of deep sorrow at losing him as their headmaster. I often asked myself what was there in those few words to make such a deep impression, and answering myself that it must be the depth of sincerity with which he spoke.

Rangoon, when the Thant family arrived, was still chaotic. Whole blocks of buildings had been bombed out, and into the empty spaces refugees had crowded, putting up bamboo and thatch huts and living, waterless, in stench and squalor. On the wide streets, little stalls had sprung up selling bits of food or sundries, cluttering the sidewalks so that people could hardly pass. Not only was water service inadequate but so were electricity and garbage removal. The Thant family finally found a habitable house with its own half-acre of land and outbuildings. In Burmese fashion, they were promptly joined by relatives—some close, some distant—who were welcomed to the outbuildings and who, in turn, helped with the housework, gardening, and care of the children.

The children were of school age and their father was determined that they should study hard. He had revised his 1942 blueprint for Burmese schools and it was published as a book in 1946. "Education must," he wrote, "be put in the forefront of the national reconstruction programme [since] democracy demands an enlightened electorate."[2] His daughter, shy like her mother, with her father's love of books, was happy to work toward becoming part of "an enlightened electorate," but the two high-spirited boys preferred the immediate joys of outdoor life to the long-term benefits their father insisted would accrue from indoor study. Joining them in their play was the family's first dog, partly pet and partly watchdog (his successor, the permissively brought up German shepherd in Riverdale, is optimistically named Balà, meaning Courage).

After U Thant became Press Officer for the AFPF League, he had little time to oversee his children's education. One of his most pleasant assignments was to escort Furnivall, summoned back from England as Adviser on National Planning, to the ceremony on January 4, 1948, marking Burma's independence. As the Union Jack was hauled down, the Union of Burma flag was raised; as some people wept, others exulted. Said U Ba U, soon to be the first Chief Justice:

[2] *The Burmese Review*, September 2, 1946, the first of a three-part series on education by U Thant.

So far as we were concerned we were sailing on an uncharted sea. Our captain was young and did not have much administrative experience, but he had some fine assets: he was honest, he was pious, he was sincere, and he had determination. He was also fortunate in having a band of young, enthusiastic, and loyal coadjutors. They were as honest, sincere, and dedicated as he.[3]

U Nu's coadjutors were under forty years of age. Shortly after U Nu had assumed the political mantle of Aung San, General Ne Win assumed the military one. Thant had met him in 1945 and found him "a sincere, handsome, and hard-working nationalist." For the second half of 1949 Ne Win, besides being in charge of the army, was a Deputy Prime Minister, the only soldier in U Nu's cabinet.

Other young "coadjutors" were the two Socialists, the brilliant, articulate U Kyaw Nyein and the popular, charming U Ba Swe; and M. A. Raschid (later called U Raschid) who, despite his Moslem Indian background, was a trusted member of the Government. On the civil service, as against the political side, was the man later described (by Hugh Tinker) as U Nu's *éminence grise*, U Thant.

For the five months preceding independence Thant had been gaining administrative experience at the Directorate of Information. He enjoyed picking up new skills, and he had long since learned how to encourage people of all ages and ranks to work together. "In every field of administration," he says today, "the public relations factor comes in: you have to size up each person you meet, what he wants: it boils down to the human factor."

Soon after independence, Thant was appointed Deputy

3 U Ba U: *My Burma* (New York: Taplinger Publishing Co.; 1958), p. 202.

to the Secretary of the Information Ministry, and subsequently also Director of Broadcasting. He was further asked to compile the history of the AFPF League. That he never skimped his office work is clear from the recollection in a letter from his chief, the late U Aung Than:

One day U Nu asked whether I would be willing to take on U Thant as my Deputy Secretary . . . and I readily gave my consent. From the moment he was taken on, I noticed that the work was disposed of with greater dispatch, with a distinct improvement in the standard of noting, as regards clarity, and the direct method of clinching cases. He began to take on more responsibilities day by day and I felt that I could place full trust in him. He was full of ideas and initiative. . . . He fears no man's frown and courts no man's favour. He has the courage to correct the obvious mistakes of his superiors, though in a courteous manner; and he is ready to acknowledge the debt of gratitude he owes to his superior for correcting his mistakes too. . . .

He knows how to get work done for him . . . and never fails to acknowledge it. . . . And although there may be hundreds of tasks which we well know that we must accomplish each day, he would take them one at a time in terms of what he taught his pupils in Pantanaw: "one thing at a time, and that done well, is a very good rule, as many can tell." We must think of our life as an hourglass. One grain of sand can pass through the narrow neck. . . . Anyone can carry his burden, however hard, until nightfall, anyone can do his work, however hard, for one day.

Aung Than was moved to another position in 1949 and shortly afterward Thant was promoted to Secretary. He had some 250 people working for him. One of his responsibilities was to supervise the publication of the *New Times of Burma*. Although deprived of his own magazine, Thant could work closely with the editor he had chosen for this journal. "I thought he showed good taste in choosing me," the irrepressible Dr. Maung Maung afterward wrote, "and I accepted. I'm glad I did. I had a wonderful time for a few months . . . working with U Thant."[4] Then the paper was sold.

But Thant did not lack for media. An official journal, the *Burma Weekly Bulletin,* was published regularly, and for several years he had a weekly radio program (he was sometimes referred to as the Ed Murrow of Burma; his pleasant voice grows even deeper over a microphone). He also became active in organizations outside the Government. In 1951 he founded the Society for the Extension of Democratic Ideals, and later he joined the Burmese Historical Commission and the Burmese Translation Society (which subsequently published an Encyclopedia Burmanica). He also became one of the charter members of the Burma Council of World Affairs. In 1952 he was appointed by U Nu as Chairman of the Burma Film Board, which involved viewing numerous movies (at 8:00 A.M.) and helping to select the local equivalents of Oscar winners for writing, acting, and directing.

Among his official responsibilities was to censor American and Russian propaganda when necessary. The Americans in the later forties had provided comic strips portraying the Russians as starving under communism, while the Russians presented the Americans as bloated capitalists and war-mongers. Both sides, Thant felt, were guilty of vast oversimplification, but in the interest of freedom of information he let the material go through. Then and later he gained insight into the intricacies—and difficulties—of psychological warfare. And today, despite his usual modesty, he calls himself "something of an expert" in that field.

As Secretary of Government for an important ministry, Thant had achieved the highest position open to a civil

4 *Guardian* magazine, August, 1956.

servant. At this time his mother-in-law, Daw Kyè, told his mother about a dream she had had when her daughter Daw Thein Tin was in her early teens. U Khant thus describes it in a letter:

In the dream Daw Kyè saw an amazing spectacle of the sun with the peacock emblem together with the portrait of her young daughter rising above the Eastern skies. In her dream Daw Kyè in amazement shouted at her husband to come and witness the heartening sight, but when he arrived the picture of his daughter had disappeared from the scene. Daw Kyè commented in her own way to mother that her late husband was not destined to see the greatness their daughter was married into.

Since almost all the civil servants in Burma had risen through the ranks of the ICS or BCS, some resentment was voiced at U Thant's having been transferred into their highest echelon. But he was so careful to stick to business and stay in the background that the resentment dwindled. As Alex Josey, a British journalist who served during the late 1940's and early 1950's in Burma, recalled:[5]

U Thant never intrigued. . . . First he was an administrator. He wanted to keep the wheels moving. For that reason, U Thant never became a leading political figure. He was content to be the man behind the scenes. He became something more than a political figure: he became a public figure.

Among Thant's duties as Secretary of Information was dealing with the foreign correspondents. Josey, himself one of their number, said:

He earned our gratitude by his strenuous efforts to help us. . . . Not only was he charming and friendly: he was also efficient and cared a great deal about presenting Burma to the world in the best possible light.

[5] *Guardian* newspaper, November 13, 1961.

Thant retained his "charming and friendly" manner even with his lowest-ranking subordinates. In the Secretariat Building in Rangoon, a great Victorian pile, the typical Secretary's office has an anteroom where the subordinates sit. Some Burmese officials, trained by the British, tap their bell in a peremptory manner. Thant seldom used his bell, preferring to walk to the door and politely request whatever he needed.

As for his subordinates, Thant encouraged them to make suggestions and to act on their own initiative. This too was unusual. Everett E. Hagen noted that one of the "barriers to efficient public administration in Burma [was] the ethic that a junior or subordinate should not express—much less act upon . . . his judgment in opposition to, or even independently of, an elder or superior," an attitude which had been "unwittingly reinforced by the colonial rulers."[6] Thant, a staunch believer not only in human freedom but in the value of learning by doing, considered such a system outdated and wasteful. From his point of view, it was better for a subordinate to err occasionally than to stagnate.

As for Thant's superiors, namely, the politicians, his patience and discretion enabled him to get along with them despite their increasingly factional activities. As he says today, after performing a similar function at the UN:

Reaching a compromise is an art, not a formula. You have to take the rights and wrongs of both sides into consideration and feel your way to a solution that is fair to them and all the other people affected by the decision. There are rarely only two sides to any problem.[7]

It is said that behind every successful man stands a woman; thus it might also be said that behind every

6 "The Economic Development of Burma," 1956, p. 62.
7 Interview with U Thant, New York, 1962.

successful politician stands at least one public servant with what President Roosevelt called "a passion for anonymity." It is he who searches for small clumps of common ground in the flood waters of political controversy— and often he who serves as a lightning rod for the anger of one or both antagonists. It takes courage to stand up to a political leader who has persuaded himself that he is selflessly fighting for a high principle. Some figures in public life have, as Disraeli termed it, "the instinct for the jugular"; others prefer the process of peacemaking. Certainly Thant, from headmastership through his decade as a civil servant in Rangoon, had ample opportunity to practice the "art" of reaching a compromise. Ironically, it was the self-effacing way he continued doing so as Burma's Ambassador to the UN that later caused his colleagues there to catapult him into the global limelight as Secretary-General.

Another way that his work in Rangoon helped prepare him for the later role was the repeated necessity of grasping quantities of new material. As the economist Robert R. Nathan recalled: "U Thant never let himself get bogged down in details. He was generally interested in a number of things and rarely probed too deeply into any one of them. He realized the difference between understanding an issue and mastering all its details."[8]

One issue that arose three months after independence nearly destroyed the Government. In March, 1948, the above-ground White Flag Communists under Than Tun staged several mass meetings that U Nu and the cabinet interpreted as a grab for political power. The Government issued orders for arrests, and the White Flag Communists, together with their labor arm, went underground. They and the Red Flag Communists were subsequently joined

[8] Interview With Robert R. Nathan, Washington, 1963.

by part of the People's Volunteer Organization (PVO) and some disaffected units of the Burmese army. Then, from the Government's point of view, came "the most unkindest cut of all," the defection of the Karen National Defense Organization (KNDO), which had never given up its hope for a separate Karen state. "Among all the insurgents," U Nu said on January 14, 1949, "the KNDOs were the most formidable and their rebellion put the Government into unprecedented straits."

Again the Delta was the area worst hit by the Karen rebellion. The Burmese army was no longer able to control the area. U Thant hurriedly moved his mother to Rangoon, and just in time, for in 1949 the Karens took over Pantanaw and burned it to the ground. "Oh, my home," Daw Thein Tin cried when she heard the news. "Oh, my books," U Thant groaned. His files, his early writings, the family photographs, all were ashes. Not only was the Thant home burned but so were all the other houses he and his wife had owned. There was no insurance. For the second time in his life his moderate wealth had vanished.

Anti-Karen feeling among many Burmans grew into ferocity and they accused the Burman, U Nu, of being "Karen Nu" because he tried to conciliate the Karens. The fact that the Karen outbreak had started in three Baptist missions further heightened Burman antagonism to Christians in general and to American missionaries in particular. Some Burmans called the Karen insurgency "The Baptist Rebellion," despite the oath previously sworn by American missionaries to take no part in Burmese political affairs. It was strange and bitter fruit that had grown upon the tree planted by the pious Adoniram Judson more than a century before.[9]

9 In nearby Vietnam, where French Jesuits rather than American Baptists had come in the nineteenth century, similar Buddhist-Christian controversies erupted—and still continue.

One of the emissaries sent by U Nu into the Karen area to try to arrange a cease-fire was U Thant. Thant's wife was stoical about the danger he faced, but the wife of Thant's driver went into hysterics and threatened divorce. The two men, nevertheless, drove to the Karen barricade, and, after explaining their mission, were permitted to pass. Thant was well received both by his old Pantanaw friend, Saw Hunter Tha Hmwe, and by the Karen chief, Saw Ba U Gyi, but the Karens refused to lay down their arms (it took thirteen more years, until 1964, for an agreement to be reached). Thant, on his return, wrote pamphlets to be dropped behind the Karen and other insurgents' lines.

The Karen rebellion (which still continues sporadically) was tragic from many points of view. The Karens felt betrayed by the Union of Burma Government, and the Government was forced, less than a year after the equivalent of the American Revolution, to fight the equivalent of the American Civil War. While George Washington had been a source of inspiration to Aung San, Nu spoke of his own role as paralleling Lincoln's:

> The reason that the United States is the strongest and most influential nation in the world is . . . that Abraham Lincoln . . . successfully prevented the southern states from secession . . . thus consolidating the whole country.[1]

By early 1949 the insurgents were within four miles of Rangoon. U Nu went on the radio to reassure the people. U Thant wrote a number of U Nu's speeches and delivered many of his own. Morale was maintained within the beleagured capital partly by a typically Burmese insouciance in the face of danger and partly by the Government's decision that life should go on as usual. But probably the chief factor in saving the Union was the

[1] Butwell: *U Nu,* p. 108.

inability of the various insurgents to act in concert. Either the two groups of Communists were in bitter disagreement with each other or with the KNDOs or the PVOs. On the other hand, there was also some dissention within Rangoon:

. . . The All-Burma Ministerial Services Union reacted to the January pay cut without consideration of the enemy at the gate, by calling a strike of government services. . . . There were mass demonstrations in the heart of Rangoon. . . . Amid the confusion, U Nu and his supporters kept at their jobs. Parliament continued to meet. . . . There were race meetings, cinemas, and for the more adventurous, special bus services to the Insein front where, for one rupee, you could take a pot-shot at the Karens; and all the while, in U Nu's words, "daylight dacoities were the order of the day, even in Rangoon."[2]

The Government leaders had all risked worse than death during the Japanese occupation; their nerve was not going to be shattered by their countrymen. Furthermore, they obtained arms from Great Britain, although these became insufficient for their needs. When Britain would give them no more, Burma's Foreign Minister, Dr. E. Maung, hurried to the United States to procure arms. But he returned empty-handed. The Burmese interpreted the American refusal as stemming from the same cause as the British refusal to provide further arms, namely, that the arms would be used against Karen Christians. Finally, the Burmese Government bought arms on the black market in Singapore and later received some military aid from India, Pakistan, and Yugoslavia, despite the precarious condition of these countries.

Through the summer of 1949 the Burmese Government continued to favor what Nu called "strong alliances."

2 Tinker: *The Union of Burma*, p. 41.

There is even mention of Burma's attempt, through Dr. E. Maung, to sound out Britain and the United States on a Pacific Alliance—a concept that later became embodied in the South East Asia Treaty Organization (SEATO). But when Burma's overtures were rebuffed she turned instead to neutralism. "She had," Frank Trager, says, "no alternative."

As for economic aid, as contrasted with military aid, there were many cooperative sources. Soon after independence, Burma, sponsored by Great Britain, the United States, and China (still under Chiang Kai-shek), had become the fifty-eighth member of the UN, and most agencies of the UN "family" have been helpful in Burma over the years.[3]

Multilateral aid came also from the Colombo Plan Organization. The Colombo Plan, not to be confused with the Colombo Powers (which were organized later, in 1954), was formed as Britain's Asian equivalent of the Marshall Plan for Europe. Its membership included the United Kingdom, Australia, New Zealand, the United States, Japan, and nations of South and Southeast Asia.

In September, 1950, after the worst of the insurgency was over, the United States signed an aid agreement for $8,000,000 with Burma. This was administered first by the American Economic Cooperation Administration (President Harry S. Truman's "Point Four"). Frank Trager became ECA-TCA Director in Burma (1951–1953) and found U Thant one of the few government officials able

[3] These include WHO (World Health Organization); UNICEF (UN International Children's Emergency Fund); ILO (International Labor Organization); FAO (Food and Agricultural Organization); UNESCO (UN Educational, Scientific and Cultural Organization); UNTAA (UN Technical Assistance Administration); the IBRD (International Bank for Reconstruction and Development—"the World Bank"); the IMF (International Monetary Fund); and ECAFE (Economic Commission for Asia and the Far East).

to cut red tape. The Ford and Asia Foundations, too, came to Burma to work in health and education. They started new projects and also took over some old ones run by the American missionaries before Burmese opinion hardened against them.

When U Nu signed the formal agreements with the American foundations he said he preferred to have aid come from private agencies than from governments. The essential, from his point of view, was that all aid be "without strings." Several years later, his successor, General Ne Win, also against "strings," reversed this position and asked that the private agencies depart and that aid be on a government-to-government basis.

By 1950 Burma was beginning to prosper. Trading in rice and teak became a state monopoly and the price of rice rose steeply after the Korean War began in June, 1950. Although India and Indonesia abstained, Burma had voted at the UN to condemn the aggression by the North Koreans. This action took courage in view of Communist China's support of the North Koreans. Burma's neutrality did not mean apathy in international affairs. The previous year, for example, when the Chinese Communists invaded Tibet, U Thant had gone on the air to voice the Burmese Government's strong disapproval.

With the increase in the world price of paddy, Burma sold her rice abroad for approximately twice the domestic price and thus gained needed foreign exchange for development. Helping to plan her development were three American enterprises with which U Thant worked closely: the Knappen, Tippett, Abbot Engineering Company, the Pierce Management, Inc. (mining), and the Robert R. Nathan Associates (economists). Together they prepared a Preliminary Report in 1952 which became the basis for Burma's Pyidawtha (or Eight-Year Welfare State) Plan. Although the original reports had been financed by

an American ECA grant, the Burmese Government was
so satisfied that on renewing the contract it assumed the
dollar costs involved. As Hugh Tinker says, "In 1951
and 1952 came the high-water mark between Burma and
the United States."[4] The year 1952 was also a period when
the Burmese were building a genuinely "mixed economy." They called it Democratic Socialism; Trager says
it was "a tropical variant of the Scandinavian pattern."
Farmers could own as much as fifty acres and private enterprise was permitted. But the basic means of production,
distribution, and transportation were in the public sector.
Had they remained in the private sector, Thant says,
"they would have been captured by foreigners," namely,
by the British, Indians, and Chinese whom Governor Dorman Smith had encouraged to return to Burma.[5] "Capitalism" in Burma had previously meant large-scale foreign
investment (and the accompanying hidden "strings").
Even the American form of capitalism, U Thant says, was
suspect because it was so thoroughly associated in the Burmese mind with British colonial practice. As U Nu said
of this kind of capitalism on September 24, 1947:

> We are out to crush that evil economic system whereby a
> handful of people hold the monopoly, while the masses of
> Burma remain in endless poverty. It is immaterial who caused
> the perpetration of this evil—British, Chinese or Burmese—
> the evil system must go.[6]

One of U Thant's jobs was to explain the Government's
plans to the Burmese people. On the radio, on April 8,
1948, he said that "Democratic Socialism . . . is not an

[4] Tinker: *The Union of Burma,* p. 367.
[5] In 1948 the Burmese had passed a law nationalizing large estates and
thus limiting the power of the Chettyars, Chinese, and British land-
holders and moneylenders. At the same time the Communist Party was
outlawed.
[6] U Nu's speech is quoted in Louis J. Walinsky: *Economic Development
in Burma, 1951–60* (New York: Twentieth Century Fund; 1963), p. 63

end in itself, but only the means of attaining conditions under which the fullest possible life will be available for all of us." Burma's ills, he later explained, could not be cured if laissez-faire capitalism were allowed full sway:

For one thing, so long as profit is the driving force . . . money . . . will be invested in those undertakings which will give the greatest profit, not in those our country needs most.

Secondly, Burma cannot accept the theory that wealth should still give access to the best education and to positions of influence and power. . . .

Thirdly, our leaders feel strongly that there is something wicked about a system . . . in which a successful trader can make a fortune but a successful teacher has to strike before he gets an adequate reward.

At the same time, the Pyidawtha Plan was explicitly based on the conviction that "if economic growth is to permeate the whole life of the nation, then planned government investment must be matched by all sorts of large and small investment by private individuals."[7]

U Thant, who in 1953 was made "Secretary for Projects in the Office of the Prime Minister," was learning first-hand about oil processing, mining, airport expansion, and a variety of other nation-building endeavors. He discussed these and other matters with the Prime Minister on their daily walks together at seven in the morning.

In 1951, the first general elections had been held for Parliament. The AFPF League won 90 per cent of the seats, the one from Pantanaw going to U Thant's brother, U Khant. The Executive Committee of the AFPF League became the Party leadership for the Government, and its Saturday meetings decided the agenda for the Cabinet meetings on Monday.

7 *Pyidawtha: the New Burma* (Rangoon: Economic and Social Board; 1914), p. 14.

One of the chief governmental organs through which the Executive Committee's decisions were implemented was the Economic and Social Board. Although U Thant was not a member of the Cabinet, he was appointed by U Nu to two positions which gave him considerable informal influence on it. The first, a position U Nu created in 1954, was that of "Secretary to the Prime Minister"; the second was as Secretary to the Economic and Social Board (1955). Administrative agencies were multiplying in Burma in the 1950s as they had during the American New Deal in the 1930s.

Since U Nu rarely freed Thant from a previous responsibility before piling another on him, Thant was overburdened. Nu had no conception of the complexities of administration. Said Louis Walinsky, who was working in Burma at the time U Thant was appointed Secretary of the Economic and Social Board:

On Thant's appointment I went around to congratulate him and see what priorities he wanted to establish. He told me, "I'm not for this. I haven't the least idea of this kind of thing. I'm not very happy about it. I told the Prime Minister I wasn't qualified for this kind of job. He said, 'What's so difficult about it? It's just an administrative job.' "[8]

The problems in "just an administrative job" in Burma were delineated by U Raschid (in a 1959 interview with Butwell):

Government in Burma is like nothing in the West. The degree of non-coordination and the casualness with which officials take their responsibilities is unimaginable to one who has not been outside the United States or Western Europe. There was a time, for example, when we sent five missions in a single month to China. The non-Communist

[8] Interview with Louis J. Walinsky, Washington, 1963.

embassies were much alarmed; they feared we were becoming pro-Communist. The truth is that nobody knew we had five missions visiting China at the same time.

Another example was given by Frank Trager; while, as he says, there may be twelve routine steps in the processing of a letter by the United States Government, in Burma there were thirty-eight.

In order to reward U Thant for his hard work U Nu gave him several titles comparable to the Queen's Honors List in Great Britain, one of which was *Thiri Pyanchi* (1949) which Aung Than said "might mean 'Flying Glory Bearer.' " The second was *Wunna Kyaw Htin* (1953), which Aung Than said "might mean 'Famed for Conspicuous Form or Beauty.' " The third was *Sithu* (1947), which Aung Than said "might mean 'Thriving Personality' or something of the sort." And the fourth was *Maha Thray Sithu,* which Aung Than said (U Thant agrees) is untranslatable.

The difficulty of rendering the Burmese language into English led to confusion, even for a bilingual word-smith like Thant. Hugh Tinker, for example, says:

> In many cases there is no term available so that cumbrous portmanteau words have to be invented . . . "free-empty-business" equals independence; . . ." Country-establishment-collection" equals Union.[9]

Whether because of the problems inherent in the Burmese language, or the Burmese administrative system, or both, Thant finally persuaded U Nu to let him drop

[9] Tinker: *The Union of Burma*, p. 178. Other Oriental languages have similar problems. William J. Coughlin in *Harper's*, March, 1953, suggests that if one Japanese word had been translated differently into English the atom bomb might never have been dropped on Hiroshima. The word was used to describe the Japanese cabinet's reaction to the Potsdam ultimatum. Its preferred meaning is "withholding comment" (pending a decision), but the Domei news agency sent it over the wires as "ignores."

the post as Secretary to the Economic and Social Board. An American then working in Burma says (in a letter):

Some persons interpreted this action as due simply to . . . U Thant's . . . aversion to a position requiring a good deal of pressures on agencies that were not performing adequately. My own judgment was that because of the erratic personality of U Nu and the fact that all machinery came to a complete stop until U Nu had made a decision, and also because of the tendency to inaction of some other Ministers, U Thant wanted to return from a formally more important position to one in which he could get some things done.

As Secretary to the Prime Minister, Thant's duties included writing speeches, having charge of appointments, corresponding with important international figures, accompanying the Prime Minister on his frequent trips abroad starting in 1951, and serving as a sounding board for his ideas. As Robert Nathan wrote in his diary:

I never went to see Nu but that I saw Thant. Sometimes if Nu was busy we'd talk to Thant instead. He was very frank and outspoken in his talk with us. He knew a lot about what was going on and was very useful for interpreting things and evaluating relationships and developments.

U Thant was always loyal to U Nu, but in private he argued with him in a way that many others dared not. Thant's chief leverage over the Prime Minister was his sincere desire to retire to private life. A week after he was first appointed he felt forced to threaten to resign. U Nu, always visionary and at times impractical, had wanted to establish a school in Rangoon to train 25,000 nurses in six months, one nurse for each of Burma's 25,000 villages. All village midwives would then be forbidden to practice and the nurses would take their place. Thant pointed out that in a free society a Rangoon girl could hardly be ordered to go live and work in a remote village. U Nu lost his temper. U Kyaw Nyein and U Ba Swe were in on the meeting but said nothing. Thant let Nu's temper run its course and then offered his resignation. Thant stayed—and so have many of the midwives in outlying areas.

Thant did not, however, always win his arguments with U Nu. An important disagreement took place over plans for the six-million-dollar monument and man-made "cave" that U Nu wanted built in Rangoon for the Sixth Great Buddhist Council planned for 1954. The convening of the Synod, the first since the days of King Mindon, would be a historic occasion, but Thant thought the building too expensive. The "cave" was nonetheless built and remains as a focus of pilgrimages from all Asia.

U Nu also used U Thant for help in personnel problems. Nu, for example, would say that he would like to promote X if only X's wife were not so crassly ambitious. Thant would then casually mention to X—not, of course, in connection with X himself—that the Prime Minister was allergic to scheming wives. . . .

The Prime Minister was also allergic to undue criticism from the press. After a less-than-discreet article by Edward Law Yone, the Sino-Burman Catholic editor of the Burmese *Nation,* Nu threatened to have him jailed for breaching the official secrets act. Thant stood up for Law Yone's loyalty while admitting that the article's criticism was out of line. Adopting Nu's own technique of using an old Burmese adage, Thant said of Law Yone, "It is his way," and then added: "Surely you don't want a good paper to suffer for the imprudence of its editor."

Thant's job as Secretary to the Prime Minister, like others high in the government, was known to be open to possibilities of bribery. But Thant was famous, as U Nyo Mya has said, for "having a record 'as clean as a hound's tooth.'"

Other officials were susceptible, however, and corruption grew. Nu was incensed and, in 1951, established a Bureau of Special Investigation, comparable to the FBI. Government officials at all levels were jailed; others lived in fear. In a brand-new country where the family, for millennia, has been the chief unit of society, one man's nepotism might be another man's responsible performance of filial duty. The accused, moreover, were often not brought to trial for years. Since "justice postponed is justice denied," grave injustices occurred in post-independence Burma, as they had in the United States under the Alien and Sedition Laws of 1798.[1]

Thant was not in danger of arrest, but he was in danger of breaking down under his work load. Edward Law Yone, in an article entitled *A Hard Look at Mr. Tender* (U Nu roughly translates as Mr. Tender), revealed the basic problem:

Who are U Nu's friends? We can parade in our mind's eye a succession of ministers, religious leaders, politicians, businessmen and clowns. Now and again we hear of someone who is extra-thick with him but never lasts. . . . Perhaps the only exception is U Thant, and U Thant never talks about him, not because he does not know or because it would take too long. To all questioners, U Thant answers with one word, "mercurial," and that is a very apt description. I am not sure that this lack of attachment on U Nu's part is not a virtue. When I recently told U Nu that U Thant was down with overwork, the reply I got was typical. "It's a miracle that he didn't go down last year or the year before that." It was not a callous remark, but coming from U Nu the best tribute

1 One of the people jailed for "treason" under Nu's administration was Dr. Gordon Seagrave, who had been convicted in 1950 of having given drugs and medical attention (as doctors are by oath required to do) to some Karen and Kachin rebels. Later his five-year term was commuted and he went back to work at his Namkham hospital until his death in 1965.

he could pay to a loyal friend. U Thant, too, knows how to speak his language.

"What keeps you so busy these days, Ko Thant?" U Nu . . . asked.

"You," was the unhesitating retort.[2]

Because U Thant was busy all day and late into the evening, he lost touch with the other crucial realm in his life, his home. The children missed him and one of them needed his firm hand. Saw Lwin, the foster son, had been departing in the morning, ostensibly for school. He would deposit his books in his "form" and then disappear. During his time of truancy he fell in love with a young girl. Not only was the boy going against his foster father's belief in the importance of education, but he was practicing deception, deliberately and over a long period. U Thant lost his temper and let his fist fly. Either the boy ducked or U Thant changed his mind at the last moment. U Thant's hand crashed through a glass door and was so badly cut that it needed repeated medical care.[3] Saw Lwin left home and eloped soon after. U Thant publicly disowned him. Daw Thein Tin, however, kept secretly in touch with the young couple and managed to help them with money without U Thant's knowledge.

In the public realm, Burma too was having trouble. The end of the Korean War in 1953 meant a sudden drop in the price of rice. Foreign exchange for development was reduced just at the time Burma needed it most —and instead of asking for more aid from the United States the Burmese Government felt forced to cancel such aid as she was receiving. Events had transpired to make her fear that without so drastic a step she might become a second Korea.

2 William C. Johnstone: *Burma's Foreign Policy, A Study in Neutralism* (Cambridge, Mass.: Harvard University Press; 1963), Appendix III.
3 Interview with U Khant, Rangoon, 1964.

CHAPTER TWELVE

A Country
on the Wider Scene

Burma's fear of becoming another Korea was based on the infiltration across her northeastern frontier of Kuomintang troops fleeing the new Peking regime in 1949. By 1952 some 12,000 Nationalist Chinese had illegally entered Burma and set up their own *de facto* government in the hills. While Burma's army, under General Ne Win, was fighting the Karen, the Red Flag, the White Flag, and other insurgents, it had little manpower to search out the Chinese troops who could, when necessary, hide in the dense forests.

These Kuomintang troops, simply by being on Burmese soil, provided ample provocation to the Communist Chinese to invade Burma. "We are a tender gourd surrounded by cactus," said U Nu; and U Kyaw Nyein com-

pared Burma's relations with China to Finland's with
Russia. The Burmese were trying to be as "correct" as
possible in regard to Mainland China; indeed they were
the first non-Communist country to recognize the Mao
Tse-tung regime; but they could not prevent the Kuomintang troops from recrossing the border in raids on their
erstwhile motherland. When some of these troops were
captured by the Burmese, they were armed with American
recoilless rifles and other equipment of recent manufac-
ture, supplied, presumably, by Chiang Kai-shek. The Cold
War thus had invaded Burma.

For two years, the Burmese Government urged the
United States to persuade Chaing Kai-shek to recall his
troops from Burma, but although it was the American
Seventh Fleet that was guarding Formosa, the General-
issimo was not to be persuaded.

Inside Burma the continued presence of the Kuomintang provided the Communist opposition to the U Nu
Government with a double-edged weapon. With one edge
they attacked Nu for being a lackey of British and American imperialists—else surely he would have succeeded in
ousting the Kuomintang—and with the other, they demanded that he join them in a united front to drive out
the invaders. Adding to the Government's embarrassment
was the widespread suspicion that the American Central
Intelligence Agency (CIA), the successor to the wartime
OSS, was directly involved in helping the Kuomintang
(three white corpses with American address books on them
were found after one of the battles).[1]

In March, 1953, Burma brought the Kuomintang
question before the UN. But the result of lengthy and
at times heated debate was a watered-down resolution.

[1] In 1965 this CIA involvement in Burma was casually admitted in a
New York Times report (May 18) about renewed Kuomintang attacks
from Burma on the Chinese province of Yunnan.

Still, some action resulted. A thousand Nationalist Chinese were airlifted out of Burma with the help of planes chartered by the United States, Thailand, and Nationalist China. But the people who departed were mostly elderly persons, women, and children, who turned in few arms. Eight months later, after negotiations had again stalled, Burma brought the issue back to the UN. More Kuomintang troops were moved out, but some 6,000 —about half the original number—remained. A third time, in August, 1954, Burma complained to the UN. The presence of the troops, her UN Ambassador, James Barrington, said, was posing "a threat not only to our country, but to the peace and tranquillity of . . . Southeast Asia."

Today, despite a joint Burmese and Mainland Chinese mopping-up operation in 1960, there are still some 700 Kuomintang troops in the northeast border region between Burma, Laos, and Thailand. This provides a smoldering cause for anti-American feeling, shared by General Ne Win.

When Burma was first preparing her UN case against the Kuomintang, U Nu feared that because Burma was getting American aid, her case against a fellow recipient, Chiang Kai-shek, might be weakened. He therefore announced in March, 1953, that United States aid to Burma would be canceled. In Rangoon, people were almost as surprised as in Washington.

Sudden as U Nu's action was, it was not capricious. For several other developments had caused American aid, welcome as it was in the beginning, to gall the Burmese. One was the change of name in 1951 of the United States Economic Cooperation Administration (ECA) to the Mutual Security Administration (MSA): "cooperation" was a word the Burmese approved; "security," with its military overtone, was not. Implications of this change of name were debated in the Burmese Parliament, with Cabinet Ministers and members of the opposition both alleging that the United States, by way of its aid, was trying to drag Burma into World War III.

A second development was the campaign statement on October 2, 1952, by Dwight D. Eisenhower in regard to Asia: "If there must be a war there, let it be Asians against Asians, with our support on the side of freedom." The phrase about Asians fighting Asians, when repeated out of context, coincided with the chip on many Asian shoulders put there by white colonialism.

A third development was the Japanese left-wing Socialist propaganda to the effect that the Americans had dropped the first atomic bombs on the Asian enemy, not the European one, for racial reasons. As U Thant later said, "Many Asians believed that these deadly bombs were dropped upon Japanese cities because the Japanese were nonwhites."[2] Realistic explanations for the act, that the A-bomb was not ready until Germany was collapsing, and that the invasion of the Japanese islands would have cost a million American lives, were accepted by thoughtful Burmese. But their suspicion was again aroused by United States support of its NATO allies, some of which, like Portugal, were still acting in the old-fashioned colonialist manner. The Burmese were further disturbed by statements of President Eisenhower's Secretary of State, John Foster Dulles: militarily he frightened them by threatening to "unleash Chiang Kai-shek"; morally he offended them by terming their neutralism "an immoral and short-sighted conception."

On the other hand, there were individual Americans who remained popular in Burma. The Knappen–Tippett–

2 Interview with U Thant, New York, 1963; also his press conference in Ottawa, May 26, 1964.

Robert Nathan technical advisers were retained on special contract after United States aid was officially canceled, and the American foundations were permitted to carry on their work. The general Burmese impression, U Thant says, was that the Americans were generous, sentimental people, less reserved than the British, and less dignified. American movies—like the British—were popular in Burma, although some highly placed Burmese deplored their hedonistic approach to sex. As Ambassador Thant said in Madison, Wisconsin, July 6, 1961:

It appears that there is a sort of high tide in sex which is not really connected with literary values. I notice that this epidemic is gradually catching on in Burma, too, both in the fields of literature and screen. This phenomenon is greatly resented . . . as alien invasion of Burmese culture.

Previously Dr. Maung Maung had criticized the Americans in a manner both more serious and more humorous. In 1953 he wrote a pamphlet, *Grim War Against KMT* (the Kuomintang), to which U Thant contributed a laudatory preface. Said Dr. Maung Maung:

Americans who have come out of the war as a world power are still rather confused as to what to do about it, and to cover that confusion they like to throw their weight about and indulge in big thoughts and big talk. . . . The average American is . . . too innocent and simple to think of harming people. Only he is a crusader. Once the crusade is over . . . he will, of course, slip quietly away and not talk about it at all except on nation-wide hookups of radio and television. . . .

That same year, 1953, three months after U Nu had canceled American aid, the Korean War ended and Burma was left with vast stores of rice for which she could no longer get a good price and which she could not store. The United States, in the meantime, had been selling her

[*215*]

rice surpluses to Japan and elsewhere on noncommercial terms. Since this reduced the market available to Burma, it injured her at a most vulnerable point.

Burma was forced to sell much of her rice at prices far lower than anticipated and to barter the rest. As Cady says, the resultant "anti-American attitude opened the door to more intimate Burmese relations with Communist China and the U.S.S.R." Among these relations were not only barter deals but gifts to Burma from the Soviet Union, namely, a technical institute, a hospital, a hotel, a theater, and a cultural and sports center.

But the proud Burmese never liked "gifts." U Nu said in April, 1954: "Burma is willing to accept . . . economic aid but we do not want it free. We prefer to pay for it as this forms a more solid basis of friendship."

Also, Burma had agreed to supply the local labor and materials for each Russian "gift" project, only to find that these were vitally needed for more basic development. She therefore canceled some of the gifts, thus balancing her rejection of aid from the West with rejection of aid from the Communist world. She was still trying to avoid too great a dependence on any outside power, particularly one involved in the Cold War.[3]

For Burma, as for many newly established countries, the achievement of political sovereignty had not brought about the anticipated degree of economic sovereignty. Not only was she dependent on the world price for her "primary product," rice, but foreigners still wielded power over her through investments, control of banking, shipping, and airlines (when this kind of control is by the

---

3 The Americans had not been alone in complicating their relations with Burma. The Russians, for example, sent cement during the monsoon rains in quantities sufficient to tie up the port of Rangoon for weeks. It appears to be impossible perfectly to arrange a cross-cultural aid program in a hurry, though countries can, and do, learn from their own and other countries' mistakes.

West, the term "neo-colonialism," originally coined by the Communists, is likely to be applied).

Although U Nu had canceled American aid in 1953, he had permitted the completion of projects already started. The cancellation, therefore, was phased out until 1955. That year he came to the United States, with U Thant, on a good will mission. Burmese antagonism to the United States having by then abated, U Nu proposed a system of exchange rather than aid. The United States agreed and signed a $2,000,000 three-way deal whereby she bought Burmese rice to be shipped to Pakistan, then in dire need of it, and paid through scholarships and other services desired by the Burmese. U Nu, in return, gave a "token" check for $5,000 to President Eisenhower for the families of American military men killed during the Burma campaign in World War II.

United States Government aid projects followed and are still, to a sharply reduced extent, continuing today. Burma, meanwhile, is also receiving aid from Russia and Mainland China. Unlike some countries in a similar position, however, Burma has steadfastly refused to play off one side against the other. Not only would this be immoral in her view but, as former Ambassador Barrington has pointed out, it would heighten the Cold War tensions that she, like many neutrals, is trying to reduce.

Burma's policy of neutralism had evolved after her time of troubles in 1948–49. The United States, as U Nu explained to a joint session of Congress in 1955, had similarly avoided "entangling alliances" for over a century after independence: "You are aware that this policy [Burma's] is not without its critics. Nor, for that matter, was yours."[4]

---

[4] Thomas Jefferson, who had first warned against "entangling alliances" (Washington having previously warned against "permanent alliances"), said in May, 1793, that a "sneaking neutrality" would probably be the

Burma described her version of neutralism first as "positive," then as "independent," and finally as "dynamic." By whatever name, it has been based on one fundamental postulate, the refusal to join a Cold War military alliance (as U Thant says, the neutrals are those countries that refuse to join NATO, SEATO, or the Warsaw Pact). Burma's neutralism has two further postulates—"no strings" to the economic aid she accepts, and "friendly relations" with all powers.

By refusing to join a military alliance, Burma feels she is guarding her independence. Twice, within the memory of her leaders, Burma had found herself a belligerent in a World War without having been consulted. The British Government, moreover, had retained control of Burma's foreign affairs and external defense to the very end. Said James Barrington:

> The ability of a nation to make its own foreign policy decisions, without outside domination or pressure, became in the eyes of the Burmese people the test of independence. It remains so today . . . Burma's neutrality is not neutrality as between right and wrong. It is neutrality in the sense that in an extended conflict in which neither side is absolutely right nor absolutely wrong, she refuses to line up absolutely with either side.[5]

At the UN she has voted both with the West and with the Communists but not consistently with either, nor, for that matter, with the other neutrals. Contrary to many of them, and together with the United States and the Soviet Union, for example, she voted to condemn the Anglo-French-Israeli action in Suez in 1956. She also voted, as many of them did not, to condemn Russian

American attitude toward the war between England and France. See Saul K. Padover: *Jefferson* (London: Jonathan Cape; 1942).
5 *Atlantic Supplement*, 1958.

action in Hungary in 1956: "There," said the Burmese Ambassador to the UN, "but for the grace of God go we." His successor a year later was even more explicit: "We remain convinced," said U Thant in September, 1957, "that what occurred in Hungary was essentially a nationalist uprising . . . that this . . . uprising was suppressed by the armed might of the Soviet Union, and that a Government not of their choice was imposed on the Hungarian people."

When SEATO was founded, after the French were forced to leave Indo-China in 1954, Burma, together with Ceylon, India, and Indonesia, refused to join. "We must not," U Nu said, "be caught in the clash of swords." Some Burmese feared that if SEATO became aggressive it might precipitate war with Peking. Others thought that SEATO might deter Peking's expansionism. If so, SEATO would be an insurance policy on which the local neutrals were paying no premium, or as a Cold Warrior has said, a form of representation without taxation.

Burma, like a number of nonaligned countries, occasionally makes moral pronouncements on international affairs that strike people in the Cold War nations as self-righteous. Having eschewed military responsibility for other countries, she feels free to condemn both sides of the Cold War for their enormous military expenditures, even though each side considers these essential to guard itself and its allies—and, in some instances, the neutrals too—against depredations from the other. That there is an element of self-interest in Burmese anti-militarism was admitted with typical honesty by U Nu when he said that nuclear war must be avoided at all costs because, even if the neutrals survived, the donor countries would not, and there would thus be no source of funds for the underdeveloped countries.

Another potential shield for Burma is the UN and its willingness, at least at times, to help the small country victimized by outside aggression. U Thant, when serving as Burma's UN Ambassador, said, "It is in the UN that most of us have pinned our only hope for the future."

Walter Lippmann, a writer admired by U Thant, has pointed out that the United States was the beneficiary of similar shieldlike protection for more than a century after independence, in that her neutrality was tacitly dependent on British control of the seas. Only when the Germans sank British shipping in World War I, thus piercing the unadmitted shield, did the United States find it in her self-interest to enter the fighting.

Because the United States was neutral for so long, many a Burmese is puzzled by Americans' lack of sympathy for today's form of neutralism. One cause for their lack of sympathy is the suspicion that the neutrals are indifferent to the dangers of communism; yet Burma, among others, has been fighting local Communists since 1948. Another cause is the suspicion that the neutrals are inhibited in their international judgments for fear of offending one side or the other in the Cold War; yet Burma, among others, has voted in the UN against the Soviet Union on Congo issues and against the United States on seating Mainland China. (U Thant, as Burma's Permanent Representative, 1957–61, often commented forcefully on seating Mainland China, pointing out that the UN could hardly be strengthened by keeping out fully one-fourth of the world's people.) A third cause is the suspicion that the neutrals refuse to recognize that the Cold War, in Adlai Stevenson's phrase, "is not a private struggle between two great super-powers [but] a world civil war, a contest between the pluralistic world and the monolithic world," and hence these neutrals contribute nothing militarily to the pluralistic side; yet Burma, among others, is so underdeveloped that her contribution would at best be meager and yet would be enough to starve desperately needed projects at home. As Ambassador Barrington said at Colby College, March 18, 1954:

The most urgent need is for Burma to strengthen her economic and social foundations; and in order that she may do this, the Union needs peace above all else. . . . Those who accuse us of timidity little know how much moral courage it requires . . . to remain uncommitted.

Burma's policy of nonalignment has elicited a policy of "correctness" on the part of Mainland China. Not only has the Peking regime refrained from giving military aid to the Red Flag or to the White Flag Communists, but the Chinese-Burmese border negotiations, started in 1954 and concluded in 1960, gave Burma the best of a good bargain. She kept more land than she gave up and was able to receive into Burma the people who wished to come—and all of them did—from the three areas ceded to Mainland China. Peking also provided Burma with a $30 million interest-free loan to be repaid in ten years.[6]

Conjectures abound as to why Mainland China has behaved in so exemplary a fashion. The former United States Ambassador to Burma, John Scott Everton, thinks that the Chinese view Burma as they do Hong Kong, a place they could overrun any time but that they prefer to leave alone because it provides them with a listening post and a trade outlet. A Burmese former diplomat stresses the "cousin" relationship which predisposes the Chinese more favorably toward the Burmese than toward

[6] General Ne Win, late in 1965, closed down all privately owned foreign-language newspapers in Rangoon, including four Chinese papers with a pro-Peking slant and a combined circulation of 20,000.

other of their neighbors, and also the friendship between
Chou En-lai and, first, U Nu, and then General Ne Win,
and the long-time residence in Peking of Burma's then
Ambassador, "one of the architects of that friendship,"
U Myint Thein.

The competition between Peking and Moscow for
friends among the nonaligned countries is undoubtedly
also a factor. At a banquet in Peking given in honor of
U Nu on December 2, 1954, Chou En-lai said:

> The equal and mutually beneficial—not unequal and mu-
> tually harmful—relations between our two countries give the
> whole world cogent proof that countries with different social
> systems and different ideologies not only should but perfectly
> well can coexist peacefully and that no country is any excep-
> tion.[7]

Lastly, the Chinese not only saved face in the border
negotiations by solving an age-old problem in a way
satisfactory to both sides but they added to their prestige
in Africa as well as Asia. As Amaury de Riencourt says
in *The Soul of China,* the rulers of Peking have a profound desire to make their country a respected and influential member of the nonwhite community.

William C. Johnstone, an American political scientist,
takes Burma to task for her "cult of neutralism" and her
posture toward Mainland China. Burma, he says, holds to
a "double standard": being less fearful of antagonizing
the West than the Communists, she gives in more frequently to the Communists. Furthermore, he says:

> There is the risk that continued adherence to neutralism
> . . . induces a psychology of compromise. Fear of offending
> a "friendly" nation often leads a government to place undue

[7] This speech at which Thant was present was printed in the Peking
supplement to *People's China,* January 1, 1955.

value on settlement of any differences to the point where peaceful settlement . . . becomes an end in itself.[8]

Neutralism may also lead the Burmese unconsciously to play down Mainland China's aggressive intentions toward other of her neighbors. Whereas Burma had officially denounced China's invasion of Tibet in 1949, she was silent on the bloody repression of the Tibetans by the Chinese ten years later. Privately, the reason was given that since Tibet, by then, was part of China, what happened there was an "internal" matter.[9] Similarly, during the China-India border battles of 1962, Burma did not criticize the Chinese. Privately, the reason given was that the Indians, too, had been at fault, first, for insisting that the old British McMahon Line was sacrosanct although it had never been ratified by Peking; and secondly, for ignoring two years of Chinese incursions on the Indian side of the line, thus allowing the Chinese to build roads and otherwise establish a form of squatters' rights.

Other critics claim that many neutrals, instead of fearing the Communists too much, fear them not enough. Oscar Handlin points to the naïveté of those countries that place faith in Communist professions of concern with peace.[1] Having suffered under Western colonial exploitation in the past, these countries, he feels, are too often blinded to the greater dangers of exploitation by Mainland China as well as Russia in the future.

Yet U Kyaw Nyein, then a Cabinet Minister, had said at an Asian Socialist meeting in 1954 that Russia's "new imperialism" was more dangerous than the old-type colonialism because it was "more ruthless, more systematic

[8] Johnstone: *Burma's Foreign Policy,* p. 295.
[9] A group of Buddhists meeting in Rangoon did send a sharp protest to Peking.
[1] Oscar Handlin: "The Gullibility of Neutrals," *The Atlantic,* March, 1963.

and more blatantly justified in the name of world Communist Revolution." And U Nu in 1957 expressed his anticommunism in, for him, the most meaningful terms, those of religion: Buddhism and Communist Marxism, he said, were irreconcilable.

As for the Western view of neutralism, there have been many long steps taken from the Dulles position that those who are not for the Americans must be against virtue. In the United States there is a new appreciation of genuine, not bogus, neutrality as the best that can be expected in small countries bordering on Mainland China, such as Burma, Laos, and hopefully the Vietnams. The argument has also been made that genuine neutrals have helped to maintain peace in the Cold War period. Like the godparents of a young child whose father and mother are embattled, they are less interested in which side has the greater grievance than in staving off nuclear divorce. And their presence at international meetings, according to the Canadian political scientist, Thomas Franck, "has undoubtedly inspired both . . . Russia and the United States . . . to present more reasoned, consistent, and moderate arguments . . . and to behave toward the neutral participants almost as to a jury—no matter how often they might have felt like slamming the book, uttering an oath and walking out."[2] Even General De Gaulle, on February 8, 1965, made a speech in which he praised the neutral countries for their useful role in the UN.

Although the neutral countries are often lumped together, they do not constitute a "bloc." Their membership covers a complete spectrum of viewpoint on non-Cold War issues, such as the subject of Israel. And at the Cairo Conference of Nonaligned Nations in October, 1964, countries like Cuba, which follow one of the Com-

[2] Professor Franck's as yet uncompleted manuscript is titled "The Structure of Impartiality."

munist lines, were included, as well as countries like Venezuela, which remain ideologically close to the West.

Resolutions passed by such conferences upholding the UN do not make headlines; reporters are more likely to stress the anticolonialist planks that seem deliberately to tweak the British Lion's tail or Uncle Sam's beard. There is sometimes a "look, Ma, I'm dancing" quality to these statements, almost as if the new countries, for home consumption or to impress one another, were flaunting their newly won independence.

The first of these conferences was held in cool, breezy Bandung in April, 1955. U Thant had helped U Nu plan for it during the previous year when the Prime Ministers of Burma, Ceylon, India, Indonesia, and Pakistan (the Colombo Powers) met. There were many disagreements. One was when Burma joined with Ceylon and Pakistan in favoring a resolution, opposed by India and Indonesia, that was critical of the Soviet Union as well as of the West. Another was when Burma introduced a resolution inviting Israel to Bandung despite the hostility of the Arab nations (this resolution failed, as did the one inviting another friend of Burma's, Yugoslavia). The Conference ended up being wholly Asian and African, and many people have said that the geographic and racial togetherness of its 29 participants was more of a cementing force than the bruited neutralism.

Very much in evidence was Chou En-lai; indeed Bandung was his "coming-out party." Also prominent was U Nu, who, according to Robert Alden in *The New York Times,* "seemed to grow in stature." With him was U Thant, characterized by a top Burmese official as "probably the only man who can be said to have been a personal adviser in the foreign field."[3]

3 Butwell: *U Nu,* pp. 185 and 191.

1955 was the high water mark of Burmese influence in international affairs. U Nu even succeeded to a limited extent in bridging the seemingly unbridgeable gap between Mainland China and the United States by persuading them to open official negotiations in Geneva for the return of prisoners taken in the Korean War. Also that year came the signing of the joint Burmese-Chinese "Five Principles of Peaceful Co-Existence:

1 mutual respect for territorial integrity,
2 nonaggression,
3 noninterference in each other's internal affairs,
4 equality and mutual benefits,
5 peaceful co-existence.[4]

Furthermore a reparations agreement with Japan had recently been signed whereby from 1954 to 1964 Japan would pay Burma $250 million. Burma did not, however, press her claims on Thailand for damage suffered during World War II; in fact U Nu, during a good will visit to Bangkok (with U Thant) apologized for the "misdeeds" perpetrated against Thailand by the Burmese kings of old, and offered 100,000 Burmese Kyats ($20,000) for the rebuilding of the ancient capital, Ayuthia, sacked by the Burmese in 1767.

As U Nu explained it to his own people, he was trying to build a "friendship curtain" around Burma. An important panel in this curtain was the Sixth Great Buddhist Council, comparable to the Vatican Council for the Roman Catholics and the Ecumenical Councils for the Protestants. As a Briton observed in 1961:

Burma is . . . in many ways becoming the acknowledged center of the Buddhist world. . . . Such intercourse across

4 India signed a similar agreement with Peking which did not, however, protect her from invasion in 1962. It is said that Nehru's sense of betrayal by his friend Chou En-lai contributed to his death soon afterward (Jacques Marcuse, *The New York Times Magazine*, July 11, 1965).

Asia among Buddhist pilgrims has not been seen since ancient times.[5]

Other panels in the friendship curtain were new technical assistance agreements signed in 1956 with the United States, Yugoslavia, and Israel.

But behind the friendship curtain Burma's internal unity was falling apart. In 1956 elections were held, and although the AFPF League won (U Khant, for political reasons, did not seek re-election), its margin was noticeably reduced. This reduction led to soul-searching among the leaders and to recriminations between them. Yet bitter as the personal feelings grew between U Nu on the one side and U Ba Swe and U Kyaw Nyein on the other, U Thant managed to remain friends with them all.

So disillusioned was U Nu over political developments that he revised his views that government ownership was the answer to the production of essential goods and services. These, he said in 1957, "should not be entrusted solely to those who are only interested in getting salaries. They should be entrusted also to those who have profit motives."[6] Yet when asked whether the Government was abandoning socialism he said, "The answer is No." The leadership, as he explained it, "were modifying their ideas as to what socialism was and how it could be best put into practice." One of these modifications was to spur the development of cooperatives.

Disillusioned as U Nu was with some of the politicians and civil servants, he was still satisfied with his own role as diplomat. And like a salesman depressed by the intramural friction in the home office, he was often glad to summon his loyal assistant and take to the road.

[5] Tinker: *The Union of Burma*, p. 175.
[6] Quoted from Frank N. Trager: *Building a Welfare State in Burma, 1948–56*, p. 118.

CHAPTER THIRTEEN

A Man
of the World

Everywhere that Nu went, Thant was sure to go.

Never having left his native shores until 1951, Thant was then rarely in Burma for more than a few months at a time. Not having worn Western dress until 1952 when he went to New York as a member of the Burmese delegation to the UN, he had to get used to it later. (His taste runs to dark business suits with white shirts and conservative ties during the week, and a light-gray flannel suit for weekends. In 1952 he wore bow ties; now he wears four-in-hands. Also in 1952 he began wearing glasses.) He had built a comfortable yellow stucco house on Windermere Road in Rangoon in 1955, but hardly had a chance to live in it. "The last few years," Dr. Maung Maung wrote in 1956, "U Thant has lived in a suitcase."

A Man of the World

U Thant has omnivorous curiosity about people and he enjoyed many of the trips. He had, moreover, read so widely that he found the countries he visited not far different from what he had expected. This was true not only of England in 1951 where he was particularly pleased to meet Maurice Collis, but also of the United States in 1952 where he was particularly impressed by Adlai Stevenson's campaign speeches (on that trip and later, U Thant traveled to more than twenty states).

Thant also met many of the world's leaders. In 1954, shortly before Khrushchev became Premier, Thant visited him and found him "a down-to-earth kind of person" with a sense of humor and without the deceptive smoothness of the professional diplomat or politician. Thant also met Leonid Brezhnev, whom he described later as "a friendly, warm, and unaffected gentleman with a deep knowledge of affairs," and Alexei Kosygin, about whom Thant said later, "He is one of the most unostentatious men I have ever met," adding that both Kosygin and Brezhnev "have a realistic appraisal of the world situation."[1]

In Peking, Thant met Mao Tse-tung and Chou En-lai and noted the same lack of freedom of the press as in Russia. But in private he found the Chinese people more willing than the Russians to joke about their leaders. These leaders, he learned, were genuinely worried about American encirclement of China from the west (Iran), from the east (the Ryukyus and Taiwan), and from the south (Thailand). "China," as a non-Communist Indian points out today, "was the Asian country most humiliated in the past by Western powers; its current fear of Western encirclement may not be rational but it is understandable."

[1] Earl W. Foell: *Christian Science Monitor*, October 24, 1964.

[229]

At the banquet in honor of U Nu in Peking on December 2, 1954, Chou En-lai vigorously attacked SEATO as the divisive force preventing peace. U Nu, known to be no friend of SEATO, concentrated on thanking Peking for its self-restraint in regard to the Kuomintang problem in Burma and gently reminding his Chinese audience that those Chinese rulers who had gone against the wishes of the Chinese people by invading Burma in the thirteenth and eighteenth centuries had been thrown out by the Burmese.

On their way to Peking U Nu and U Thant had visited Hanoi, where they found Ho Chi Minh frank, friendly, and contagiously enthusiastic about the excellent French food that he served.

Two countries that overwhelmed Nu and Thant with their friendliness were Israel and Yugoslavia. As Thant wrote on his return home in the Burmese *Guardian*, September, 1955:

In Haifa I saw old women shedding tears of joy at the sight of U Nu, and in Tel Aviv men and women struggled and broke the police cordon just to touch U Nu. . . . Perhaps, both the government and the people of Israel consider Burma . . . as Israel's greatest friend. . . . Israel and Burma are the only two countries in Asia with Socialism in power. . . . In the sphere of international affairs too the two countries have an almost identical approach.

Following U Nu's visit, a mutual-aid agreement was signed and a number of Israeli technicians came to Burma to help in her development. Most of these, including those who set up kibbutzim in the north, have since returned home, but the Burmese have not forgotten the sharing by Israel of her then meager resources; and Israel, on the basis of her experience in Burma, has gone on to provide valued technical assistance to 53 other countries, mostly African.

As for Yugoslavia, Thant said in that same *Guardian* article:

Equally tumultuous receptions awaited us. . . . Marshal Tito took a deep personal interest in the comfort of U Nu, and Madame Broz Tito was a most charming hostess. . . . The joint Tito-Nu communiqué . . . revealed the agreement to sign a five-year economic pact by which Yugoslavia will buy Burmese rice to enable Burma to purchase consumer and capital goods in Yugoslavia. The communiqué also states that the policy of active co-existence is gaining support as the only sure way of attaining peace.

After visits of state, return visits are in order. International personages began arriving in Rangoon: Bulganin and Khrushchev, Chou En-lai, Ho Chi Minh, Nehru, Tito, John Foster Dulles, Richard Nixon, Lord Louis Mountbatten, and Adlai Stevenson. U Thant took charge of correspondence with them beforehand and attending all the functions in their honor. (In his eulogy of Stevenson at the UN on July 19, 1965, U Thant mentioned how impressed he had been during Stevenson's visit to Burma in 1953 by "his depth of intellect and his breadth of vision.")

When the elections of 1956 showed the AFPF League to have lost ground, U Nu decided to resign. He had several purposes in mind, one being to purify himself through a prolonged visit to a monastery; another being to purify the AFPF League through visits around the country to inspire the honest members and weed out the corrupt ones. He therefore turned over the premiership to U Ba Swe.

For U Thant the change in Prime Ministers meant staying on the job. He accompanied U Ba Swe to the Socialist

Conference in Bombay and the third Colombo Conference in New Delhi, and at home continued his administrative duties.

In 1957 Nu returned as Prime Minister—but his relationship with U Ba Swe and U Kyaw Nyein was rapidly deteriorating. These men had been working in close quarters under almost intolerable tension for two decades. They were tired—and tired of each other (their wives, according to a Westerner, "had figuratively reached the hair-pulling stage"). U Ba Swe and U Kyaw Nyein accused U Nu of dictatorial tendencies; he accused them of disrespect and disloyalty.

Among the issues that divided them was whether Buddhism should be made the state religion. U Nu stated at the end of the two-year Sixth Great Buddhist Synod in 1956 that he had a "burning desire" to see Buddhism declared the state religion. U Kyaw Nyein and U Ba Swe, as well as General Ne Win and U Thant, though good Buddhists, wanted no state religion. The political pongyis began to line up on one side and the secularists on the other.

In 1957, U Nu offered U Thant the post of Burma's Permanent Representative to the UN. Thant was enthusiastic about the offer; his wife was not, but, like Naomi, her attitude was, "Wheresoever thou goest, I shall go." Her health had weakened and she needed specialized medical attention. Besides, Thant hoped that, once out of Rangoon, he would have more time with his children than he could ever get by being at U Nu's constant call.

In Rangoon, Dr. Maung Maung says, there was "general belief that if Thant had been around . . . to heal and harmonize, the split [in the AFPFL] would not have happened," and many Western observers agree. Others dispute this view. Butwell, for one, says:

Unquestionably the placid Thant was a stabilizing influence on Nu and an intellectually stimulating one whose ideas and good sense helped his friend clarify his own thoughts in . . . important areas. . . . It is very easy, however, to overrate Thant's role in view of his subsequent skillful execution of the duties of Secretary General. . . . U Thant was not interested in politics, and he did not involve himself in AFPFL in-fighting, let alone electioneering.[2]

Certainly the job of Secretary to the Prime Minister, the post U Nu had created for Thant, was hard to fill. After Thant's departure three people were asked to take it; two refused and the third fled after only a few months.

Thant and his four professional colleagues in the Burmese Mission to the UN were sorely missed in Rangoon. An official complained wistfully to William Johnstone, "If I could have just half the persons who are busy representing Burma at the UN sessions . . . on full-time duty in the Foreign Office, we would have much more efficient conduct of our foreign relations."[3]

When U Thant, his wife, daughter, and son boarded the transoceanic plane at Mingadalon Airport outside Rangoon, his mother and three brothers were there to wave good-by. U Khant by then was a free-lance journalist, while both U Thaung and U Tin Maung had reached the peak of civil service, U Thaung being Secretary in the Division of Public Administration, and U Tin Maung, Secretary in the Ministry of Trade Development. Since all now lived in Rangoon, their mother could move easily from the house of one to that of another. U Thant's own house was rented to a European family. U Thant's wife, who hates flying, was miserable during the trip. U Thant, who does not mind flying, cannot, however, sleep on

2 Butwell: *U Nu*, p. 142.
3 Johnstone: *Burma's Foreign Policy*, p. 209.

planes, and the two children were in a state of excitement.

New York was vast, crowded, and noisy, but at least there was no language problem for U Thant and the children. The family eventually found an apartment on East 72nd Street.[4] Aye Aye took time in making friends at school, but Tin Maung soon filled the apartment with boys and girls of several nationalities. Keeping a dog in a Manhattan apartment would have been difficult; the family, however, acquired several cats. Later there was a problem with the Manhattan landlord, who, like some, did not welcome diplomatic tenants, especially those from Asia or Africa.

The Burmese Mission to the UN was small and its staff was overworked. The UN General Assembly has seven committees, in which each nation is represented, as well as its plenary sessions. There are also caucuses of important groups such as the Asian-African group, which got its impetus from Bandung. U Thant, by nature and training a delegator, gave his subordinates a free hand. Actually there was not time enough in the day for him to summon the kind of staff meetings the larger missions hold. As one of his then assistants, U Paw Htin, recalls, "We were on our own."[5] Since cable contact with the opposite side of the world takes time, and since Rangoon officials are not famous for the speedy dispatch of their paper work, Thant, like the Permanent Representatives from many new and distant countries, was also often on his own.

Part of Thant's job was to portray Burma's viewpoint both to his UN colleagues and to the many American groups that invited him to speak. In Philadelphia (April 11, 1958), he said:

[4] See the page from U Thant's diary on page 235.
[5] Interview with U Paw Htin, Bangkok, 1964.

AUGUST

Su	Mo	Tu	We	Th	Fr	Sa
				1	2	3
4	5	6	7	8	9	10
11	12	13	14	15	16	17
18	19	20	21	22	23	24
25	26	27	28	29	30	31

WEDNESDAY

14

AUGUST

SEPTEMBER

Su	Mo	Tu	We	Th	Fr	Sa
1	2	3	4	5	6	7
8	9	10	11	12	13	14
15	16	17	18	19	20	21
22	23	24	25	26	27	28
29	30					

8ºº a.m. Office at 9.30 and went over the documents on the S.A.

9ºº Discussed Residential accomodation with Jimmy. So difficult to find a

10ºº suitable apartment of about ten rooms (furnished) within the sanctioned rent of

11ºº $1000/ a month. Dictated a few correspondence and went to U.N. at 10.45 to present my

12ºº credentials. Mr. Hammarskjöld received me very warmly and recounted our meeting

1ºº p.m. in July 1955 when he entertained U Nu, James and me to a small lunch. He has

2ºº a high esteem for U Nu for his moral and

3ºº spiritual qualities. His knowledge of Buddhist philosophy, though not profound, is far

4ºº from superficial. I am impressed by his interest in the moral and spiritual aspects

5ºº of life. He makes some references to the

6ºº affinity of approach between a German philosopher (?) and Lord Buddha. I

7ºº attempted to straighten him out on the theory of Karma. A very pleasant and

8ºº rewarding 30 minutes.

Weather reminded me of Burma in April — hot and humid.

14 AUG. Read Max Lerner's "America as a Civilization" — P— 123 – 266.

This page from U Thant's 1957 diary was photographed by Saw Lwin, his foster son.

"Jimmy" is U Paw Htin, a Burmese diplomat then with the Burmese Mission to the UN, now Chargé d'Affaires in Thailand.

"James" is Ambassador James Barrington, U Thant's predecessor and successor as Burma's Permanent Representative at the UN.

The "German philosopher" is probably Martin Buber, according to Joseph P. Lash, biographer of Hammarskjöld, who says that in 1957 Hammarskjöld was translating some of Buber's writings from German into Swedish. Buber's universalism might well have lent itself to a comparison with some aspects of Buddhism.

The Burmese . . . attitude toward political systems . . . in other countries is governed solely by considerations of peace. We are convinced that it is not the path of wisdom to form military blocs, to enter into a hectic armaments race, and to rant hysterically at each other. . . . If the world's great religions like Islam and Christianity, after a prolonged and bloody war for centuries, can flourish side by side in peace and amity, why should not Communist and non-Communist systems be permitted to co-exist peacefully?[6]

He added the hope that just as religious tolerance was once considered not merely deplorable but actually sinful—and is so no longer—so in the political sphere a similar relaxation may develop:

I do not wish to be misunderstood. I look upon free institutions as not only the most desirable of political systems but also as those most congenial to the flowering of human genius. . . . But these beliefs and convictions do not shut me off from the knowledge that there are others who believe differently. To put it plainly, the plane of ideas between the culture of democracy and the culture of communism cannot be reconciled [but] in the plane of diplomacy and international relations . . . co-existence is possible and desirable.

Co-existence is possible on the negative side, he says, because neither the United States nor the Soviet Union can afford a nuclear war in which "the only winner is death." Co-existence is possible on the positive side, he says, because the tension between the West and the Communists is not, in the long run, the most crucial one: "The more essential issue is the division of the world into the weak and the strong, the prosperous and the abject poor, the ruler and the ruled, the master race and the subhuman." In short, the purpose of nuclear peace is not merely survival but the rapid improvement in the

6 *The Annals of the American Academy of Political and Social Science,* July, 1958.

subhuman economic and social conditions prevailing in the underprivileged two-thirds of the world. And in this tension between " 'North' and 'South,' " he admits, "I cannot be neutral."

One ground for Thant's optimism—the University of California, in granting him an honorary Doctor of Laws in 1964, termed him a "cautious optimist"—was having seen for himself the peoples of the world. As he had written after traveling on both sides of the Iron Curtain:[7]

> One of the impressions I have gained . . . is the essential similarity of national characters on which a world-wide understanding can be built and global solidarity can rest. Everywhere, men and women, young and old, love peace, enjoy a good joke and lead affectionate family lives. No doubt mass media . . . have bred in the minds of people certain prejudices and bias. I met people who are violently critical or adulatory of something or other, but I believe that the same mass media . . . can turn such people into their real selves.
>
> I do not mean to insinuate that we should not have likes and dislikes, but I do mean that in matters like politics and political systems we . . . should be prepared to hear what the other side has to say.

At the UN he was hearing what a hundred other governments had to say—and some of what he heard he did not like. He placed the blame not on the peoples of the world, but on those politicians or diplomats whom he named "so-called statesmen," a phrase reminiscent of his student blast at Burma's "so-called leaders." In a speech before "Israel Horizons" in New York, October, 1958, it was plain that Thant's optimism had been tempered by a year's service at the UN:

> Our destiny is being determined by so-called statesmen, trained more in manipulation than insight and imagination. They pay lip service to justice and democracy, while ma-

7 *Guardian* magazine, September, 1955.

neuvering for positions of advantage and superiority for themselves and those whom they seemingly represent. Behind their smooth facade of words, there goes on all the time bitter haggling, accentuated by bland international blackmail and power-threats, euphemistically called diplomacy.[8]

On the other hand, U Thant himself had been forced to become a "diplomat." His favorite definition, he says, comes from Talleyrand. A guest at a crowded inn opened the door to the public bathroom and found a lady in the tub. Had he been an ordinary citizen, he would have said, "I'm sorry, madam," but being a diplomat, he said, "I'm sorry, sir."

As a school principal U Thant had been relatively free to speak and write as he pleased. But as a diplomat, he complained to a group of American elementary school principals on July 6, 1961, he was forced to "confine my remarks within the four corners of my government's set policy and statements."

His government's policy had not changed when U Ba Swe followed U Nu as Premier, nor when U Nu resumed the premiership, nor when U Nu stepped down in favor of General Ne Win and his "caretaker government" in 1958. Nor did General Ne Win change the personnel of the Burmese Mission to the UN. Thant remained in New York, half a world away from the events occurring in his homeland. But since he knew all the protagonists he was able to picture their encounters, and in January, 1961, during his only trip home during four years as Burma's Permanent Representative, he agreed with Dr. Maung Maung's estimate, that in "young Burma . . . democracy is going through its teething times."

[8] U Thant would never reveal whom he had in mind, but this was the period of Krishna Menon's heyday, and some reporters were presenting that flamboyant Indian headline hunter as what he was not—a typical "neutralist."

Even before General Ne Win's self-imposed time limit
of two years, he resigned and U Nu again became Premier
in 1960. Ne Win for reasons of health then paid his first
visit to the United States. Unfortunately his wife had
an unhappy experience in Walter Reed Hospital in Washington, because Mrs. Mamie Eisenhower, the President's
wife, was expected, and Mrs. Ne Win was unceremoni-
ously ushered out of the waiting room on her husband's
floor. (U Nu and U Thant had had a similar experience
in Washington in 1955. When they appeared on time for
their appointment with Ezra Taft Benson, then Secretary
of Agriculture, his receptionist, insufficiently briefed and
overly protective toward her chief, wanted to know who
they were and why they wanted to see the Secretary, and
let them wait. U Nu and U Thant left. The State Department was acutely embarrassed and Secretary Benson tried
to make amends by hurrying around to Blair House to
call on U Nu. U Thant had to take at least twenty calls
from the press. "It was all rather unusual," he says un-
smilingly in retrospect.)[9]

U Thant entertained General and Mrs. Ne Win when
they came to New York and invited American scholars
as well as diplomats to meet him. The dinner is reported
by one of the guests to have been a great success, but
apparently General Ne Win still felt that the Americans
had not given him as warm a welcome as they might have
and he never forgot it.

In April, 1958, the AFPF League had finally split into
the Nu and Kyaw Nyein–Ba Swe factions. In June Parliament was called and Nu was able to secure a majority
only by forming a coalition with the National United
Front. This NUF had its inception in 1950 when some

[9] This was another example of U Thant's giving information only in
response to a direct question. If U Khant had not written in a letter
about this episode, I would never have known enough to ask about it.

AFPF League leaders, opposed to Burma's support of the UN in Korea, had split off and founded the Burma Workers and Peasants Party. In the 1956 elections the NUF showed growing strength, and by 1958 it included twenty organizations ranging from the above-ground un-admitted Communists to the largely right-wing Justice Party led by U Nu's former Foreign Minister, E Maung. After the AFPF League split, some NUF leaders realized that if they joined the Nu faction and helped it survive the vote in Parliament, they would cease being the opposition and might hold the balance of power within the Government.

Their hopes were realized, as Nu won the vote by a margin of only eight. But then the NUF began to break up. The Burmese, without a tradition of democratic give and take within the parties as well as between them, not only went their own way, but in many cases also, as in the days before independence, developed their own "pocket armies."[1]

In 1960, U Nu continued Burma's foreign policy un-changed. He also kept U Thant at the UN. By that time U Thant was very much at home there and was speaking out on a number of issues. He deplored the "wanton costliness" of the race to the moon, and he took an active part in trying to find a solution for the militarily riven Congo. He was a prominent member of the Afro-Asian group which itself had assumed a role of UN leadership during the Suez crisis of 1956. He was also Chairman of the UN Development Fund, and of the then-powerful Working Committee on Algerian Freedom. "That was the job I enjoyed the most," he says in retrospect, "al-

[1] The PVO had been described as Aung San's pocket army; actually armed bands for protective purposes dated back to the time of the kings; by 1958, the AFPF League had its own armed bands as did the All Burma Peasants' Organization and other groups.

though I was not so popular with France for a long time."[2]

One reason for Thant's popularity at the UN was his willingness to work long and hard behind the scenes; another was his friendliness. "Being Permanent Representative was more relaxed and more fun than Secretary-General," he says today; "I definitely enjoyed the receptions and taking friends to a Chinese restaurant afterward [there is no Burmese restaurant in New York]; as Secretary-General I haven't been to a restaurant in over three years." Still another reason was Thant's humor. Dr. Hla Bu, in a letter, reports Thant's *bon mot* at the time Cold War tensions had mounted to almost unbearable proportions over the U-2 incident in 1960:

In the UN lobby delegates were taking sides and raising heat over it. As U Thant walked in, he sensed the highly charged atmosphere. With a smile he remarked, "Gentlemen, it's a case of U 2 and I too, isn't it?" The group immediately exploded in laughter.

When the question arose of who should preside over the Congo Conciliation Commission, a formidable and ticklish job, Hammarskjöld and others opted for Thant, who was duly elected. Ralph Bunche remembers Hammarskjöld's comment as they passed Thant in the corridor: "There's a man who would make a good Secretary-General."[3]

One of the problems Thant confronted as chairman of these various UN groups was when to extend debate in hopes of dissolving differences and when to take a vote. He, like many delegates from Asia and Africa, tries

[2] Interview with U Thant, New York, 1965. General de Gaulle, however, appears to have forgiven Thant, and welcomed him warmly when, as Secretary-General, Thant visited France in 1964. U Thant receives Christmas cards signed by the General and his wife.
[3] Interview with Under-Secretary Bunche, New York, 1964.

to avoid premature crystallization of an issue by voting. As Dr. Maung Maung said in his January 1962, *Guardian* article on U Thant:

There can be no victory in resolutions passed by mere majority votes, there can be no victory in numbers which . . . possess no substance unless all the members, big and small, consent and move along together.[4]

In the summer of 1961 U Thant accompanied U Nu to the Second Conference of Unaligned Nations in Belgrade. This time Yugoslavia was included while Mainland China was not. Just before the meeting convened, the Soviet Union unilaterally broke the bomb-testing moratorium. The chiefs of state meeting in Belgrade refused to single out the Soviet Union for criticism. Instead, they called upon both the Soviet Union and the NATO countries to refrain from further tests.

The defense by the neutrals—including Burma—for this action took several forms. One argument was that the United States had got so far ahead of Russia before the original nuclear test moratorium that Russia, in her fear of NATO, with its Turkish bases adjacent to the Soviet Union, felt bound to shorten the gap. Another argument was that although the United States had honored her word and refrained from testing, her ally, France, had not (and moreover had exploded a "dirty" bomb in a nonwhite continent). A third argument was that although every country at Belgrade individually deplored Russia's break of the test ban, many did not wish collectively to accentuate East-West tensions by an official declaration at a conference called to reduce those tensions.

4 The United States delegate to the UN Trusteeship Council, who was elected as its President in 1962, reports that the Trusteeship Council was often able to achieve this kind of consensus in many of its reports. Jonathan Bingham says: "The consensus gave the reports much greater influence than they would have had otherwise."

A Man of the World

U Thant had received from U Nu some good news about Burma. Thant's two volumes of history of the Burmese independence movement had been published by the Government and were being distributed to high schools and colleges throughout the country. But other news was seriously disquieting. U Nu's Union Party, like the AFPF League before it, was about to split: one-tenth of the country was still under Communist or Karen insurgent rule; separatist demands were being pressed by Shan leaders, Arakanese, Kachins, and Mons. As Johnstone later epitomized the situation, Burma was a "state," but she was not yet a "nation."[5] Thant was increasingly concerned about Burma and the several other new countries that had established national independence only to find themselves incapable of making democracy work. As he said on July 6, 1962, in London:

In many newly independent countries, it is most unlikely that there will be a two-party system for many years to come. The nationalist movements are very powerful indeed. They will control governments without there being any effective challenge to them from within. And any challenge from the outside would only strengthen them. As was the case in many European countries, it might take some time before it would be possible for political opposition to be expressed in constitutional forms. Moreover, it is worth bearing in mind that the democratic system . . . is perhaps the most difficult form of government to operate.

U Nu had returned from Belgrade bone-weary—and traits such as his superstitiousness, which had been kept under control, were now rampant. He publicly worshiped the Nat spirits; he forbade the butchering (and eating) of beef; and he issued orders that on a certain Saturday (he himself being Saturday-born), sixty thou-

5 Johnstone: *Burma's Foreign Policy,* p. 10.

sand pagodas should be built of sand. As the Rangoon *Guardian* later commented, "To build that many pagodas would have taken 12 million tons of sand—we don't have that much sand in Burma."

The pagodas were never built. On March 2, 1962, Ne Win came again to power, this time not as Prime Minister of a caretaker government but as the military leader of a seventeen-man Revolutionary Council Government. "Parliamentary democracy," said Ne Win and the Revolutionary Council, "came into existence in history with the British, American and French revolutions against feudalism. It happens to be the best in comparison with all its preceding systems;" but when this system was "tried and tested" in Burma it did not work: there were too many "weaknesses and loopholes, abuses and the absence of a mature public opinion."[6]

Three months later, in June, 1962, the *Guardian* newspaper echoed his feeling, particularly about Burma's lack of "a matured public opinion." As for parliamentary democracy, the editorial said, "it was a bit premature."

In its place General Ne Win saw a temporary dictatorship as the only solution. He suspended the Constitution, replaced the courts by military tribunals, and dissolved Parliament. More businesses were taken over by the Government. He placed the leading politicians, most of the Shan hereditary chiefs, and some journalists under detention: U Nu, U Ba Swe, U Kyaw Nyein, U Raschid, Dr. E Maung, U Myint Thein, Bo Let Ya, U Edward Law Yone, U Nyo Mya, Mi Mi Khaing's husband, and others are today well fed and housed, but can see their families but rarely. They can read, but not write, what they wish. Ne Win also took steps against foreigners in Burma. The American Ford and Asia Foundations were asked

6 Quoted by Jerry A. Rose: *The Reporter*, January 3, 1963.

to close up shop.[7] Many wealthy Indians were encouraged to depart and required to leave most of their possessions behind; large numbers of Indian "coolies" also departed. In January, 1964, just after a Baptist convention in Rangoon, General Ne Win reduced the ten-day transit visa to twenty-four hours. "Burma is in the process of spring cleaning," is the unofficial explanation; "we would like our visitors later." Yet when the General, or someone he trusts, knows the visitors, their visas may well be extended. In Burmese law, since the days a monk could throw his robe over the accused, or one member of the Hlutdaw could talk back to the king, room has always been made for the judicious exception.

In other ways Burma under Ne Win is like Burma under the kings. The villages have again been given a certain amount of autonomy, combined, however, with central economic control, foreigners are viewed with suspicion, and emigration is allowed only with the ruler's permission. If an individual under stress can return to a previous manner of behavior, perhaps a country may too. Yet at the same time there are evidences of national maturity in Burma. She is today, as she was not under many of her kings, at peace with her neighbors, and she firmly supports the UN despite Mainland China's and Indonesia's pressures to the contrary. "The Burmese Way to Socialism" has been proclaimed as the national goal, and General Ne Win is explicit in his criticism of "communism" on the one hand and "feudal landlordism and

[7] General Ne Win had feared the American CIA since Kuomintang days. His suspicion that the CIA was using American foundations as a "cover" appeared to many people as xenophobic until the revelations in *The New York Times*, August 31, 1964, by Congressman Wright Patman of Texas, who named a small foundation as having been used for this purpose. Like Premier Sukarno of Indonesia and various African leaders, General Ne Win is said to have carefully read *The Invisible Government* by David Wise and Thomas B. Ross about the CIA.

capitalism" on the other. Through a combination of austerity and hard work, he is hoping to raise the living standard of the people and make Burma "Viet-Cong-proof."

Under the Revolutionary Council Government Burma is sending some students abroad, though far fewer than previously. Those with Government scholarships go, not to the West, but to the less affluent, less civil-libertarian countries of Eastern Europe: "There is not so much of an adjustment when they return," is one explanation.

At Rangoon University the Student Union Building, used as a meeting place by a group of neo-Communists, was burned by the Army in July, 1962, under orders of General Ne Win. For over a year the University was closed. Reopened in November, 1964, it now stresses technical subjects, such as agronomy and engineering, and a disciplined understanding of Marxist principles.

Burma, in short, is no longer an Asian parliamentary democracy, such as India or Japan, but a unitary state, such as Pakistan or Thailand.

Burma has continued her policy of neutralism between the West and the Soviet Union, and between the Soviet Union and Mainland China, and her UN Ambassadors have spoken out articulately on its behalf. The Ambassador who both preceded and succeeded U Thant was James Barrington.

For on November 3, 1961, U Thant had changed jobs.

CHAPTER FOURTEEN

The World
Chooses a Man

The crash of the plane was heard around the world.

Near Ndola in Central Africa on September 17, 1961, a mission of peace for the Congo had ended in flames. Hammarskjöld the golden, the poet-statesman, the irreplaceable one, was gone. The capitals were stunned and the multitudes grieved. Would the UN survive as a force for peace? Who could possibly be found to take his place?

Rumblings of an earthquake that might well cause fissures in the UN's effectiveness had been heard for a year. The Russians, who had turned against Hammarskjöld because of his actions in the Congo, proposed dividing the job of Secretary-General, like Gaul, into three parts. According to this "troika" plan, there would be three Secretaries-General, one representing the Communist world, one the West, and one the nonaligned countries, with all having to agree before action could be taken. Five months before Hammarskjöld's death Premier Nikita Khrushchev had revealed his reasoning to Walter Lippmann:

While there are neutral countries, there are no neutral men. You would not accept a Communist administrator, and I cannot accept a non-Communist administrator. I will never entrust the security of the Soviet Union to any foreigner. We cannot have another Hammarskjöld, no matter where he comes from among the neutral countries.[1]

Among the neutral countries' representatives were some who could see a certain logic to the Russian proposal. If it was true, as the Russians believed and the United States did not, that the world in truth was a troika world, with three well-defined and inwardly consistent blocs, then perhaps it made sense for each to be represented at the peak of Secretariat power.

In time, however, these neutral representatives became convinced that, even if the world were so neat in its divisions, the introduction of the veto power at the top level of the Secretariat would paralyze the UN. Yet for a single Secretary-General to be elected in the usual manner, the Russian veto in the Security Council would have to be avoided; the candidate would have to be acceptable to the Soviet Union as well as to the other four Permanent Members: the United States, Great Britain, France, and (Nationalist) China. For under the Charter it is the Security Council which nominates the Secretary-General whereas the General Assembly votes him into office.

1 New York *Herald Tribune,* April 17, 1961.

Within the UN, turmoil arose from two other factors. One had preceded Hammarskjöld's death but was intensified by it: the formidable drain of UN life and funds in the Congo. The other was a direct result of Hammarskjöld's death: a sharp drop in the morale of the 3,500 Secretariat members in New York and the 14,500 in the field. Humanly difficult as it is to make sacrifices for a unified and permanent-seeming world organization, it is even harder when the organization is riven and appears impermanent. With no new Secretary-General in sight, UN officials were uncertain about who was responsible for specific decisions and whether, if a decision was reached, it might not be reversed.

Something had to be done, and fast. Discussions began on several fronts even before Hammarskjöld's state funeral in Uppsala, Sweden. One front was an informal trio of small-power Permanent Representatives who happened also to be friends—the gracious, blue-eyed Ambassador from Norway, Sievert Nielsen; the jovial, blue-eyed Ambassador from Ireland, Frederick Boland; and the imperturbable, brown-eyed Ambassador from Burma, U Thant.[2]

Another front was the larger Steering Committee of which these three were members, together with the Permanent Representatives of India, Mexico, the United Arab Republic, Venezuela, and Yugoslavia. Two further fronts were the sunny modern office of Ambassador Adlai Stevenson in the United States Mission to the UN, and the cavernous old Park Avenue residence where Foreign Minister Andrei Gromyko and Ambassador Valerian Zorin of the Soviet Union were at work.

[2] Interviews with Boland, New York, 1962, and Dublin, 1964; interview with Nielson by telephone, 1962; interviews with Stevenson, New York, 1962 and 1963. Thant declined to comment when questioned about this period.

In these offices, bilateral consultations were held as well as consultations with members of the trio. Within the UN's insulated meeting rooms and carpeted corridors, no idea was left unexplored, no Permanent Representative was left unconsulted. The world has shrunk but it is still a vast place from which to choose a lone Secretary-General whose decisions may make or break the organization.

The late Ambassador Stevenson, whose UN experience had dated from San Francisco in 1945, became convinced that the best procedure would be, first, to find a man on whom most nations could agree, and only then to let the troika battle run its course. His position was firmly expressed on October 2, 1961. Although, as he said, "due regard" should be given to the "geographical" factor, "it would be contrary to the . . . Charter . . . to introduce . . . political representation . . . into the upper levels of the Secretariat."

But who was the man on whom there would be general, if not unanimous, agreement? Among the possibilities was Ambassador Boland of Ireland, who had just completed a term as President of the General Assembly. Another was the intelligent and subtle Ambassador Mongi Slim of Tunisia, who had been elected President of the General Assembly thirty-two hours after the death of Hammarskjöld. But Boland, convinced that the new Secretary-General should not be another European, withdrew his name, and Slim was perplexed as to which of the two jobs he should take or whether, against his wish, but at the insistence of a few, he should try to do both. Were he to become the subject of a draft for Secretary-General, he felt, he would have no choice but to accept.

If he were the choice, moreover, a new element might

enter the picture. The Security Council, with its need for unanimity among the great powers, might then be by-passed: the General Assembly could, if it chose to, vote to add the powers of the Secretary-General to those of its already elected President. The Russian veto, in effect, might thus be vetoed.

While all these points and persons were under con-sideration two of the trio, Boland of Ireland and Thant of Burma, called on Soviet Foreign Minister Andrei Gromyko. They told him what he undoubtedly already knew, that there was absolutely no support for the troika outside the Communist group, and that even Yugoslavia, which often votes with the group, was opposed to it.

"Oh well," Boland remembers Gromyko saying, "we can have one Secretary-General, but why not three *Under-Secretaries?*"

"That's not troika," Boland answered, "that's quad-riga." Gromyko, according to Boland, "smiled a wintry smile."

The two emissaries, however, went on to assure Gro-myko that they were against the idea of bypassing the Security Council. "We told him," says Boland, "we felt the Charter should be followed."

Soon after this meeting the Soviet Ambassador gave an interview to the press. At the end of it, almost off the cuff, Zorin accused one of the two American Under-Secretaries, Andrew Cordier, then *chef de cabinet,* of usurping the powers of the Secretary-General. Gratuitous as the attack was, it put the Soviet Union in the position of having to make some further move, one that, unlike the troika proposal, would have a chance of finding sup-port among the UN membership.

Meanwhile Ambassador Stevenson was having the feel-ing of *déjà vu.* When he had served as chief of the

United States delegation to the UN Preparatory Commission in London in 1945–46 he had seen a deadlock develop between the West, whose candidate for Secretary-General was Lester B. Pearson, now Prime Minister of Canada, and the Communist world, whose candidate was Stanoje Simic of Yugoslavia. Eventually both sides had compromised on a man whose nation lay far afield from either candidate's—Norway's Trygve Lie. Now too it might be possible to compromise on someone from far afield. With most of the UN's new members being African and Asian it began to look, as Boland said, as if "the best card to lead with would be an Afro-Asian card."

Stevenson had become increasingly impressed with U Thant through the long nights and days of negotiation. During World War II, before the UN was founded, President Roosevelt had suggested that the new organization's chief executive be named the "Moderator," since such would be his primary role. Thant seemed eminently suited for it. He listened far more than he spoke, and when he spoke, it was with empathy toward all reasonable points of view. Nor had he the slightest reluctance to stand up either to the United States or the Soviet Union or, if necessary, to both. Thant also clearly believed in the need for a truly international Secretariat whose members would be responsible solely to the organization. Yet he knew from experience that such an attitude takes training and self-discipline; that whereas patriotism flourishes like a wild flower on almost any soil, international objectivity is a hothouse bloom that must be consciously nurtured until it attains full growth. (After it is full grown, however, it can be as hard to uproot as patriotism.)

As Thant said on television five days before his election

as Secretary-General: "It will be very difficult for a [UN official] to be neutral on the burning issues of the day. . . ."

"You mean," Stevenson asked him, that "there can be no moral neutrality?"

"That is true," Thant said. "Whoever occupies the office of the Secretary-General must be impartial, but not necessarily neutral. . . . I think the judges of the . . . Supreme Court must be impartial. . . . But they are not neutral as regards who is the criminal and who is the person on whom the crime has been committed. . . . There are many men not only in the UN but outside the UN who are impartial, who are imbued with the spirit of service, who can override their national and ideological considerations."[3]

Just when Thant began to appear to his fellow negotiators as the logical candidate, no one is quite certain. But Thant was one of the last to hear of it. As he said on television, "Of course I had no idea. To be frank, I had no idea, not the faintest idea, that I would be . . . directly involved in this." In a way, he was like the marital go-between who finds himself chosen by the lady in place of the suitor whose cause he was pleading. Stevenson said it was Boland who first had the idea; Boland says the idea stemmed from Hammarskjöld's having recommended Thant as the best man to act as chairman of the Congo Conciliation Commission. Others say it was the kind of idea that was in the wind; several persons thought of it independently and others, after hearing of it, wondered why they had not thought of it themselves.

When Thant understood that he was the likely candidate he withdrew from the negotiations. He was, more-

[3] WABC-TV, "Adlai Stevenson Reports," October 29, 1961.

over, not certain about taking the job, although his government endorsed his doing so. Hammarskjöld, a bachelor, had established a killing pace of work—sixteen hours a day—and Thant, although a hard worker, had his family to consider. He also craves a certain amount of solitude for meditation. The job that would demand every bit of wisdom and inner calm might paradoxically deny him the time to tap their sources. On the other hand, to be chosen Secretary-General was an honor to his country as well, and if his colleagues agreed that he was the man, there would be, on his part, neither false modesty nor demand for a draft.

Some did, at first, object to Thant. Hammarskjöld had been a linguist; Thant knows only Burmese and English. His lack of French particularly was felt to be a serious hindrance. (The brilliant Foreign Minister of Belgium, Paul-Henri Spaak, had once been ruled out for Secretary-General because he lacked fluency in English.) Members of the Arab world were worried lest Burma's friendship with Israel prevent a Burmese from being impartial concerning problems of the Middle East. Some nations, such as France, were opposed to a strong UN; Thant was in favor of it. Still other nations felt concerned, as Thomas Hamilton of *The New York Times* recalled on March 25, 1963, that Thant might be "neutralist to the point of naïveté," or that because Thant believed neither side of the Cold War to be 100 per cent correct, he might hover near a middle position because it was middle rather than because it was right. Yet Burma's neutrality had not prevented her from making independent judgments in regard to the Cold War, and her Ambassador to the UN was known for his forceful expression of these judgments.

The Communist group, moreover, knew that Thant

and Burma, from the beginning, had been urging admission of Mainland China to the UN. Also, it is said, Premier Khrushchev was influenced by his personal good impression of Thant and by the enthusiastic support for Thant promptly voiced by Burma's neighbors, Premier Nehru of India, President Sukarno of Indonesia, and Prince Norodom Sihanouk of Cambodia.

Not only did Thant have no enemies in the UN, but his relaxed manner with prestigious officials of the great powers was reassuring to representatives of the small powers. One delegate says that, while still in doubt as to whether to support Thant, he attended an October Sunday boatride around Manhattan Island, given in honor of Secretary of State Dean Rusk. Rusk had served in the China-Burma-India theatre during World War II under General Joseph Stilwell, and the ease of conversation between him and Thant persuaded the delegate that Thant could, after all, handle not only the issues but the personalities that the job would confront him with.

As more and more delegates swung over to Thant, the hold-outs began to climb aboard the bandwagon, including those who had the feeling that always seems to arise when a basically superhuman job is about to be filled: that somewhere, somehow, there must be someone better.

Meanwhile, the question of how many Under-Secretaries there should be, and from which countries, was being hotly debated. There were several issues at stake. One was the political nature of the Under-Secretaries: would they "represent" the various political forces in the world or serve as international civil servants? The second was how much control the Under-Secretaries would be given over the Secretary-General: would he have to obtain their "agreement" before acting, or "consult" with them and then make up his own mind? A third issue was whether the Secretary-General should or should not be "committed" on these or other issues as a condition of his election.

There followed what all concerned still wearily refer to as the "numbers game." The Soviet Union had fallen back from the original troika to a position of "double troika" or six Under-Secretaries, two from each of the three so-called political divisions of the world. The United States insisted that geographical, not political, considerations should prevail in the distribution of Under-Secretaries. Every whole number from one to fifteen was proposed in regard to the quantity of these, and if human beings could actually, as they can statistically, be divided, there would have been fractions as well.

Meanwhile the Congo situation was deteriorating and the UN was rapidly going broke. After weeks of negotiations the "numbers game" was no nearer solution.

Early one morning, in his Waldorf Towers apartment, Adlai Stevenson, like Archimedes, leaped from his bathtub, having found the solution to his problem. The Russians, he had suddenly realized, despite their apparent seriousness, had no intention of agreeing on the "numbers game." Its continuance and the resultant delay in finding an executive head for the UN were serving their purpose in the Congo and elsewhere only too well. Later in the day, Stevenson informed the Soviet Mission that the United States was prepared to propose unconditionally that U Thant, on whom there was by now general agreement, should be elected Secretary-General. Since the Africans and Asians were sure to go along with such a plan, the Soviet Union could block it only at the cost of appearing unfriendly to Africans and Asians. The Russians countered by saying that they were unwilling for Thant to be elected for a full five-year term or to have the full title of Secretary-General, that at most he should serve out the remaining year and a half of Hammarskjöld's term with the title "Acting." They would thus be "buying" him only "on approval."

Ambassador Stevenson's official statement to the General Assembly was made on November 1, 1961:

> There will be no Troika and no veto in the Secretariat. The new incumbent . . . will appoint his own staff, and consult them in a manner consistent with the Charter. . . . Whether he chooses to have several advisers or none is for him to determine, in our opinion. . . . Moreover there is general agreement on the individual to fill the office. Ambassador U Thant of Burma is a man of the highest character and ability. . . . In spite of our preference that he should have not only the full powers but also the full title of Secretary-General we have indicated that we would acquiesce, in a spirit of conciliation, if the U.S.S.R. continues to hold the view that he should serve in an "acting" capacity.

In April, 1963, when time came for Thant's re-election, he had no competition, Russian-backed or otherwise. Yet he himself requested that his previous year and a half be credited to his new five-year term. He is consequently serving only until November, 1966.

Thant's election as Acting Secretary-General was unanimous (as was his re-election one and a half years later). In diplomatic but unmistakable terms his acceptance speech revealed his intentions toward his Under-Secretaries:

> It is my intention to invite a limited number of persons . . . to act as my principal advisers on important questions. . . . I intend to include among these advisers Dr. Ralph J. Bunche and Mr. Georgy Petrovitch Arkadiev. It is also my intention to work together with these colleagues in close

collaboration and consultation in a spirit of mutual understanding. I am sure that they will seek to work with me in the same manner.[4]

After "consulting" with the great powers and the small ones he announced that there would be eight key Under-Secretaries, one each from the United States, the U.S.S.R., Western Europe, Eastern Europe, Latin America, the Middle East, Africa, and Asia. India's C. V. Narasimhan, a former ICS officer, had already been scheduled by Hammarskjöld to be *chef de cabinet* after the retirement of Andrew Cordier because of age, and U Thant went along with this plan.

In Burma the news that their Permanent Representative had been elected chief executive of the UN—and the rebroadcast of his acceptance speech—caused no great excitement. The front pages of the Rangoon newspapers that day were full of a campaign U Thant would have liked to support, namely, for greater freedom of the press. As William Johnstone notes:

There is very little knowledge about the history of operations of the United Nations among the literate public in Burma. . . . Material produced about the United Nations is not easily available and what little is available does not get distribution. . . . The United Nations . . . is still something of a far-away abstraction.[5]

This was still the period before General Ne Win's second take-over. As it happened, Premier U Nu had

4 U Thant's speech to the General Assembly, November 3, 1961.
5 Johnstone: *Burma's Foreign Policy*, p. 236. To the Burmese, moreover, the Secretary-General's annual salary (tax-free) of $27,000, plus $22,500 for "representation," plus the use of a house, seems astronomical. They find it hard to believe that, because of daily luncheons for as many as twenty persons and an occasional reception for as many as five hundred, added to the high cost of living in New York, the Secretary-General is sometimes temporarily out of pocket. Yet he refused a raise in pay when this was privately suggested at the time the Justices of the International Court were given increases in salary.

scheduled U Thant for the nation's second highest award, *Thedo Thiri Thudhama.* But once U Thant had moved from being the servant of Burma to being the servant of the UN he thought it inappropriate to accept an award. He has, in fact, deliberately dropped all contact with his native land except for Burmese newspapers and occasional letters from family and friends. He has been back only once, for a three-day state visit in July, 1964. That was the occasion when he was asked by reporters in Rangoon for a statement about Mainland China's admission to the UN. Said Thant: "In regard to such questions, please try to remember that there are two U Thants—the U Thant who represented Burma before 1961 and the U Thant of post-1961 as the Secretary-General of the UN. The 1964 U Thant is not supposed to have views in that capacity on such matters."[6]

On that same visit, he contrasted the UN favorably with the League of Nations, which he termed "primarily a European Club." The UN, representing people from every continent, he said, is not just a debating society: although "it is not a Big Power with its own army, navy and airforce . . . it is the cumulative result of massive public opinion."[7]

In trying to be the servant of this "massive public opinion," Thant makes a continuous effort to expunge from himself such nationalistic feelings as would blind him to views that differ from those of the Burmese:

If a Burmese boxer, maybe a middleweight, fights a U.S. boxer, I will not feel any emotions. I've reached this stage. It has taken much training and meditation. The parochial concept of "our town," "our country," is disappearing. I've been trained to be as objective as possible. This should be

6 *The Working People's Daily*, Rangoon, July 26, 1964.
7 *Guardian* newspaper, July 28, 1964.

our aspiration. I feel very strongly about it. If we can think of one human species, it is only wisdom [to do so].[8]

Thant remains on guard against bias not only in himself, but in the Secretariat. As he says, one cannot *automatically* expect a person from the United States or the U.S.S.R. to be unbiased on the Cold War; or a person from a new nation to be unbiased on colonialism; or a person from Asia, where the horrors of nuclear fall-out are particularly vivid because of Japan's experiences, to be impartial on nuclear testing.

As Burma's Ambassador, U Thant was bound by the "four corners of [his] nation's policy"; as Secretary-General he is bound by the Charter, the resolutions passed by the UN bodies, and a growing bulk of UN precedent. But personally and as a Buddhist U Thant also feels bound in fellowship to the mute hundreds of millions of people, who, except for him, have no other single voice. In his identical cables to President Kennedy and Premier Khrushchev at the height of the Cuban crisis, he appealed to them, both in his UN capacity and "as a human being."

He is a human being, moreover, who has never craved power or its perquisites (he tries to avoid, when traveling, the red-carpet treatment). On the other hand, the former schoolteacher could scarcely object to his lessons being blazoned across the front pages of the world. Hammarskjöld was a man of few words but of occasional impulsive action; he would be on a plane headed for a personal confrontation in a trouble spot virtually before the cable about it had been decoded. Thant, the writer, is cautious in action but ready with words. He likes to draft his own speeches, savoring a neat turn of phrase

[8] U Thant was quoted by Robert Moskin in *Look,* September 24, 1963.

such as "using the force of argument instead of the argument of force," and his habitual expression is, "If I may say so."

In the Foreign Offices and the news media there are people whose reaction is, "No, you may not say so." Thant is therefore torn between the courage of his convictions and the concern lest by saying the wrong thing, or the right thing at the wrong time, he jeopardize the office of Secretary-General. For, as he has found through his successes and his ability to learn from his mistakes, it is through judicious handling of that office that the UN can sometimes take its most far-reaching steps toward peace.

The View
from the 38th Floor

U Thant inhabits a glass tower but not an ivory one.

On the stark modern desk he inherited from Ham-marskjöld lie documents concerning the major inter-national problems. Sometimes the problems are not officially before the UN, and even when they are, the appropriate UN organ may not have been able to agree on more than the vaguest of instructions for the Secre-tary-General. By *not* speaking out or taking action, he is taking a form of action. To intervene or not to inter-vene, that is often the question.

His office is rectangular, with one long side overlooking the East River. The only changes he has made are to keep the office, like his home, at a temperature of eighty degrees; to have an embossed silver cheroot box on the round wooden table and, on the walls, some undramatic Impressionists chosen for him by José Rolz-Bennett and Brian Urquhart from those on loan from the Metropolitan Museum of Art (Hammarskjöld always chose his own paintings and tended to favor Braque).

Most of the Secretary-General's work is never mentioned in the press. The political part is often secret, and the nonpolitical and largest part is often not deemed newsworthy. Eighty-five per cent of the daily operation of the Secretariat concerns economic, social, and educational endeavors in the underdeveloped countries. Perhaps because U Thant comes from one of these countries he feels free to abandon the customary euphemism, "developing." As he said on March 23, 1964, "These areas are in fact not developing, or are not developing enough; they are suffering from . . . acute and persistent underdevelopment."

Despite all multilateral and bilateral aid, the gap between their standard of living and that of the developed countries has been widening rather than narrowing; and although their rate of growth is often faster than that of the developed countries, their increasing population keeps living standards low. (In general, U Thant believes in population control but says that it is up to each country to determine the method best suited to itself.) The Development Decade, proposed by President Kennedy in 1961 and enthusiastically implemented by U Thant, has thus far had disappointing results.[1]

But these results could readily be improved. U Thant, like the historian Arnold Toynbee, thinks that the most historic advance in the twentieth century is that for

[1] "The overall level of performance . . . of the underdeveloped countries," Under-Secretary Philippe de Seynes informed the General Assembly on October 5, 1965, "is lower than that of the 1950s."

the first time enough food can be produced to feed mankind. Thant says: "It is no longer resources that limit
decisions. It is the decision that makes resources." Consequently, hungry people have been given rising expec-
tations, and affluent people have been given "a revolutionary freedom . . . the freedom to help or not help
their . . . neighbors who do not yet command the means
to help themselves."[2]

This freedom no longer involves the simple moral
imperative of the "haves" cutting the "have-nots" in on
the pie: it involves the most complex expansion of the
pie through modern means of technology, organization,
capital investment, and fiscal policy. As U Thant says:

> I do not think it is true any longer that one nation can
> become rich only by beggaring its neighbor. I believe that it
> is possible for the advanced countries . . . to contribute to
> the economic development of the less advanced and in so
> doing to gain greater prosperity for themselves.[3]

There can be, Thant says, still another creative by-
product: "The economic development of underdeveloped
countries lends itself, in all its major aspects, to cooperation between the United States and the Soviet Union."
This cooperation, by reducing Cold War tensions, might
well "bring them closer to the goal of an agreement for
securing lasting peace."[4]

One step in this direction was the partial nuclear test
ban treaty of 1963. U Thant reported being "thrilled"
to be invited to Moscow for the signing. Any reasonable
step toward disarmament not only reduces the danger of
war but frees the resources of the rich nations to help
the poor ones (the world, on both sides of the iron

2 Speech in Copenhagen, May 8, 1962.
3 Convocation address, Carleton University, May 25, 1962.
4 U Thant's interview with David Sureck.

curtain, he points out, is spending some $120 billion a year for military items, the equivalent roughly to the entire national income of the underdeveloped countries).

The underdeveloped countries, on their side, Thant says, must make comparable exertions. They must draw up plans for expanding their production, agricultural as well as industrial, and then use much of the money earned for further planned development. Yet here too they are largely dependent on the rich nations which have it in their power to accept or reject the primary products of the new nations. A fair price—and not a too fluctuating one—must be paid for these products, or the benefits of foreign aid will be more than offset by the resulting economic stagnation and human distress. Although the UN Trade and Development Conference of 1964 did not produce the hoped-for solution to the problem of marketing primary products, it did establish machinery for working out such a solution: "It was a positive advance," U Thant said: "trade and aid will never be quite the same again."[5]

Subsequently, on February 8, 1965, sixty nations agreed at Geneva that the reduction of trade barriers between the rich nations would be extended to the poor nations without demanding reciprocal concessions from them.

U Thant's patience in regard to such long-term developments is based partly on his firsthand experience in Burma with the complications of putting foreign aid to constructive use:

The transfer of scientific knowledge and technical know-how to societies whose habits and thinking and way of life are largely unprepared for them can give rise to serious disruptions and it is not a process that can be accomplished very

[5] Interview with U Thant, New York, 1965.

quickly in the best of circumstances. A great deal will depend on a general rise in standards of education.[6]

As the former teacher, Thant stresses education; as the former Secretary for Projects in the Burmese Government, he stresses development; as the former Ambassador from a neutral country, he stresses tolerance (he particularly liked President Kennedy's phrase, "a world safe for diversity"); as Secretary-General, he stresses the UN's role: "The greatest event in the twentieth century," he says, "was the signing of the UN Charter."

As a former Press Secretary he has developed many friends among the reporters. He supplies them with his daily appointment schedule, chats with them in the corridors, and on occasion holds a major press conference. Yet here too he has his problems. "He is a trusting person," says one of Thant's aides, "too trusting at times, and some members of the press have manufactured headlines rather than solid news."

In *The New York Times*, September 8, 1965, the unsigned "profile" of U Thant says that "his principal aides try to divert him from accidental meetings with reporters because the aides fear he is too kind about answering unexpected questions." (Hammarskjöld never answered such questions.) The reporters, however, the article says, suspect that "in most cases the questions are not really unexpected and that Mr. Thant has his answer ready."

Within a person's own culture it is extraordinarily difficult to predict which aspect of a lengthly press conference will be chosen for the headline and the lead. To U Thant from Asia, with a press officer from the Middle East, some American news stories have come as a jolt. Nor does

6 U Thant's interview with David Sureck.

Thant make his job any easier for himself by indulging in the kind of moral pronouncement that is common in Burma but not in the West.[7] "Thant's elliptical Buddhist phrases," says one American, "are useful in the search for compromise between antagonists because each can interpret them somewhat differently and thus reach an agreement that might otherwise not be possible; but using such phrases at a press conference is asking for trouble."

An example was U Thant's annual press conference following the General Assembly which he held on February 24, 1965 (this was the occasion when he pointed to Burma's handling of local Communists as a model for Vietnam). In answer to a question about the recently begun American reprisals against North Vietnam, U Thant stated generally that "in times of war and of hostilities the first casualty is truth," and specifically that "the great American people, if only they knew the true facts and the background to the developments in South Vietnam, would agree with me that further bloodshed is unnecessary."

If one test of a press conference is the lack of demand for subsequent explanations, this conference was Thant's least successful one. For days he had to issue clarifications, one of which was that American public opinion is "among the best informed in the world." Some high officials, including President Lyndon B. Johnson, were reported as enraged by Thant's phrase about Americans not being given "the true facts," having, it was said, interpreted it in a more military context than Thant intended. There was, furthermore, a White House denial of having received the "concrete ideas and proposals"

7 Lucian W. Pye does not mention U Thant in *Politics, Personality and Nation Building*, but on page 142 of his book he makes the generalization that "the Burmese are oddly insensitive to the possibility that moralistic injunctions could appear provocative to others."

Thant said he had sent to both sides of the Vietnam conflict as well as to other powers (including, presumably, the Soviet Union, Great Britain, and France). Not long afterward Dean Rusk confirmed that the United States had been consulting with the Secretary-General on these matters over a two-year period but that Thant's recent proposals had been procedural rather than substantive: questions of where and how to call a conference rather than what subjects were to be negotiated.

On April 7, 1965, President Johnson, speaking about Vietnam at Johns Hopkins University in Baltimore, said that the United States was willing to hold "unconditional discussions." On April 8 the Secretary-General publicly praised the President's speech. On April 9 a Peking broadcast attacked the Secretary-General, saying that although he considers himself an Asian, a European such as Bertrand Russell understands Asia better than does U Thant.

Three months later, on July 29, 1965, Ambassador Arthur J. Goldberg, who succeeded Stevenson, brought to U Thant a letter from President Johnson asking the Secretary-General to renew his good offices in the Vietnam conflict and saying that U Thant's past efforts "are very much appreciated and highly valued by my Government." U Thant's answer was interpreted by the press as courteously recording his awareness that events had caused a modification of the President's attitude. Said Thant:

Please allow me to thank you for your kind words about my efforts in the past to find some way to remove the dispute over Vietnam from the battlefield to the negotiating table. I am heartened by your wish that my efforts should be continued.

In November, 1965, four months thereafter, Eric Sevareid published his interpretation of a post-midnight conversation with Adlai Stevenson two nights before Stevenson's death on July 12. Stevenson, according to Sevareid, had described U Thant's long months of effort, starting in the early autumn of 1964, to win United States agreement to discussions with a Hanoi representative in Rangoon.[8] Washington's eventual refusal, presumably, had been one of the "facts" U Thant had in mind when he said that the American people were not being given them all. Following the Sevareid article the State Department admitted the Secretary-General's past diplomatic initiative but explained its own rejection of it and subsequent secrecy as having been based on fear that the then-shaky Saigon government might be further weakened, thus harming the war effort.

U Thant has lectured not only governments but also the news media. There is, he said on April 22, 1965, to the American Publishers' Association, "a section of the press in most countries which lives on sensationalism" and thus exacerbates tensions; this is the group to which "good news is no news." In turn, Thant cheerfully, if wryly, accepted criticism of himself and his colleagues as part of his job: "At the UN we are the regular recipients of an immense flow of criticism and admonition . . . , a form of stimulus which we should welcome, although, of course, it can, like all good things, be overdone."

Thant also credits the news media, together with the Non-Governmental Organizations (NGOs), with helping to build an informed world opinion. For him world opinion is an important reality although its existence cannot be proved to those who, like former Secretary of State Dean Acheson, deny it. While Buddhist meditation gives

[8] *Look,* November 30, 1965.

Thant strength from within, world opinion gives him strength from without. It is, he says, "an invisible presence which . . . is very real and comforting: the yearning for peace and brotherhood of untold millions."[9]

World opinion, particularly in the era of instant communication, is both malleable and potent. As U Thant said at the UN's twentieth anniversary on June 26, 1965, in San Francisco, "Patriotism, national pride, or ideological conviction can and must take new and more creative forms." He himself had succeeded in overcoming the Burman prejudice against the Karens, the Asian prejudice against the white colonialists, the Burmese war-born prejudice against the Japanese, and the neutralist prejudice against the Cold Warriors. Anything he could do, others could do—if not better, at least equally well. His modesty, thus, is a foundation stone of his optimism.

On the other hand, he admitted privately to American friends after his return from San Francisco that he had been shocked at the placards there denouncing President Johnson in four-letter words. He also was dismayed at some of the treatment of the President, not to mention the UN, in sections of the American news media. "Liberty in the United States," he said, "has become license. If the American brand of liberty were transported to the new countries where there is no comparable degree of education, the result would be chaos."

Also in private the Secretary-General has deplored the practice of making public those American Congressional hearings in which leaders of other countries are criticized for their personal behavior: "News of these attacks is not made much of in the American press but it is blown up in the country itself and doesn't make for good international relations."

[9] U Thant's interview with David Sureck.

Privately as well as publicly the Secretary-General is courteous to the representatives of all countries, whether or not he agrees with their international or internal policies. And in return, the representatives exhibit courtesy toward him. In 1962, for example, the French Ambassador to the United States, reflecting General de Gaulle's disdain for what he termed "The Disunited Nations," had planned to seat the Secretary-General at an unsuitably low table at the dinner honoring the arrival in New York of the *Mona Lisa*. When news of this slap at the organization leaked out, almost all the Permanent Representatives—as well as U Thant and the other high Secretariat officials—sent their regrets. Later, alone, U Thant paid a call on the *Mona Lisa*. He liked her.

One of U Thant's perennial problems is the staffing of the Secretariat. (To add to the short supply of civil servants from the new nations, U Thant has helped to establish a UN Institute with training and research facilities in New York and Geneva.) For years the Soviet Union has demanded that the Secretary-General take more of her own and her satellites' nationals. At the same time, she refuses to permit recruitment by the Secretary-General's representatives within these countries. Instead, she confronts him with a list—a practice wholly at variance with that of the rest of the world. If, furthermore, he accepts the list, he may keep the people on it for only two or three years.

U Thant, despite these limiting conditions, has added to the number of Communists in the Secretariat, but this has not satisfied the Russians. They keep asking for more to be hired and for more sensitive positions to be given those who are hired. In November, 1965, the Russians publicly demanded that the Secretary-General virtually treble the number of short-term Secretariat appointments from all nations and correspondingly decrease the long-term ones. U Thant, who believes in a career international civil service, has quietly maintained the ratio at 29 per cent short-term, as against the 75 per cent demanded by the Soviet Union.

The Secretary-General has kept, among the eight Under-Secretaries who serve as his special aides, a Russian and an Eastern European, but his closest working associates are the same as Hammarskjöld's, Under-Secretaries Narasimhan and Ralph Bunche, with the addition of José Rolz-Bennett. They, like Thant, have had years of practice in the discreet handling of conflicts. They know how important is secrecy for the guarding of fluidity, so that rigid postures may, in private, without loss of face, be made elastic. As U Thant said on November 3, 1962, his first anniversary as "SG:"

When the future of mankind is at stake, no country or interest-group can afford to . . . claim that its position is the only right one and that others must take it or leave it. No difficult problem can be solved to the satisfaction of all sides. We live in an imperfect world and have to accept imperfect solutions, which become more acceptable as we learn to live with them and as time passes by.

This view has been criticized by, among others, Professor Hans Morgenthau.[1] Thant, according to Morgenthau, has overstressed the value of compromise, elevating it to "a universal principle of foreign policy" rather than keeping it as one of many possibilities, suitable in some instances but not in others. U Thant denies that he considers compromise an absolute. It must always, he says, "be coupled with negotiation"; in effect, it does not stand

[1] *Commentary*, January, 1963. When asked by letter in the spring of 1965 whether, in view of Vietnam, he had changed his mind about U Thant, Morgenthau replied that he had not.

alone. The door to talk must never be locked, but repeatedly pried ajar in hope that discussion will provoke new ideas or that fresh developments will occur. Not only a Buddhist believing in impermanence, but anyone who has lived through the last quarter century when Russia, the ally of the West, became its enemy at the very time that the West's enemies, Japan and Germany, were becoming its allies, realizes that the appearance of the unpredictable is, in time, almost predictable.

A small news item in the New York *Herald Tribune* (February 25, 1964) provides evidence that Thant practices what he preaches; the guarantors of the 1960 Cyprus treaty, Greece, Turkey, and Great Britain, were at loggerheads with the Cypriot Government:

> After ten days of intensive negotiations neither the Cypriots nor the guarantors are willing to modify their positions. Nevertheless Mr. Thant plans to continue the negotiations.

Thant's patience is reinforced by his conviction that all conflicts have more than two sides, those of the two antagonists and that of "the rest of the world [as] an interested party" both in the present and in the future.[2] He likes to describe this world community in the words of Pierre Teilhard de Chardin, "a common soul in this vast body." Thant also points to the fact that all conflicts have a history that must be understood in depth before new solutions will find acceptance. As he said in a controversial speech at Johns Hopkins in December, 1962:

> Russia's obsessive fear of encirclement probably has its roots in her memories of 1919, and leads her to think in terms which are no longer valid in this thermonuclear age. The United States . . . too, seems to me a prisoner of her past. She

[2] U Thant's speech to the Security Council on the Cuban crisis, October 23, 1962.

was rudely dragged into the center of the world stage, much against her will, by the unprovoked attack on Pearl Harbor. It seems to me that the fear that such a catastrophic surprise attack will be repeated dominates the thinking in Washington, and a surprise attack is seen in the United States as the supreme risk. This fear stems from the same assumption that history will repeat itself.

But history, Thant often says, "does *not* repeat itself." Despite recurring patterns, there is always likely to be a novel element. And one of the oldest assumptions, that because wars have always occurred in the past, they must occur in the future, in Thant's view, is both a mistaken and uncreative hypothesis. He has had several experiences at the UN, such as in the Cuban crisis of October, 1962, when what might have been a *casus belli* in the pre-nuclear age was negotiated to a mutually bearable stalemate. In this negotiation the UN had played a signal role. By simultaneously asking the Soviet Union for a moratorium on the shipment of arms to Cuba, and the United States for a moratorium on the blockade of such shipments, its Secretary-General provided an interval during which both sides could come to an agreement.

At one stage U Thant had members of the United States Mission in his conference room, and of the Soviet Mission in his adjoining office. He commuted between them bearing his own analysis of each proposal as it emerged and thus "helped to narrow the gap in their thinking."[3]

Besides easing tension in the Cuban crisis, another source of satisfaction to U Thant was "when the military phase of the United Nations operation in the Congo was brought to an . . . almost bloodless conclusion with the end of the secession in Katanga."[4] At the height of that

[3] Gertrude Samuel: "The Meditation of U Thant," *The New York Times Magazine*, December 13, 1964.
[4] U Thant's interview with David Sureck.

operation, U Thant, no pacifist, had been, like Hammarskjöld before him, in charge of 20,000 officers and men.

A third development that gave him satisfaction, he said,
was the "compromise solution of the New Guinea crisis
with the UN acting as a temporary executive authority
for the transfer of administration of that territory." This
was the first time that the UN had directly administered
a large area and, thanks to the 1,500 Pakistanis whose
salaries were paid jointly by the Netherlands and Indonesia, the job was effectively handled for six months.
The area, also called West Irian, was then turned over
to Indonesia with Dutch consent.

Another "first" for the UN during U Thant's term of
office was the prelude to the founding of Malaysia. Here
the Secretary-General laid down as a condition of his
sending a requested fact-finding mission to North Borneo
that he would later act on the basis of its decision. On
one side was the claim by Indonesia, backed by the Communist "East," and on the other was the claim of Malaya,
backed by the non-Communist "West." The UN fact-
finders reported a clear preference by the natives to be
united with Malaya, and Thant acted on the report despite warlike behavior by Indonesia.

The cease-fire between India and Pakistan over Kashmir
in September, 1965, was widely heralded as a success for
the UN. In the Security Council the permanent members
had acted in the kind of unison envisaged by the Charter,
and the Secretary-General had promptly flown to New
Delhi and Rawalpindi to carry on the delicate process of
negotiation. After their acceptance of the cease-fire he
sent additional UN observers to the field, and in New
York he pressed the Security Council to follow up its
peace-keeping efforts with peace-making decisions.

An extraordinary further impetus toward basic and

peaceful solution of world conflicts was provided by Pope Paul VI when he accepted U Thant's invitation to address the UN on October 4, 1965. "He gave us a tremendous shot in the arm," U Thant says.

In addition to the eighteen-year-old stalemate in Kashmir there have been other long-term UN peace-keeping operations, such as in the Gaza Strip, and also sudden conflagrations such as in Cyprus, where the UN dispatched improvised forces within two weeks. In the battle over Yemen a sizable team of UN observers was sent and kept there for the agreed time, their expenses shared by the two warring sides, Saudi Arabia and the United Arab Republic. When the allotted period ended, Thant withdrew the observers, saying in his report of September 2, 1964, that the two countries should settle "their needless and now senseless dispute." (The settlement, however, did not come about until a year later.)

Blunt language like the above is not unusual from the Secretary-General. He may, for years, avoid speaking out on an issue, but when he does, some old-school diplomats jump. As early as April 29, 1964, for example, he stated that a political rather than a military solution must be found for South Vietnam; military efforts had failed there in 1954: "I don't see any reason why they would succeed ten years later." Some Western diplomats termed Thant's comments "extraordinarily bold," and the South Vietnamese Government complained that Thant was "going beyond his duties."[5] Since the Vietnam problem was not officially before the UN, it is certainly arguable that Thant was going beyond his duties. Yet any "threat to the peace" is, according to Article 99 of the UN Charter, within the province of the Secretary-General. Moreover,

5 *Mainichi Daily News,* Osaka, Japan, July 26, 1964 (the only newspaper available to me on that day when I was en route to Rangoon).

Thant had been told by some delegates that silence by him might be misconstrued as agreement with the United States military intervention.

In flatly stating controversial views, Thant leaves himself open not only to disagreement but to misinterpretation. In the March, 1964, *Reader's Digest,* for example, Noel Busch wrote of Thant that "in the world-wide struggle between the free world and communism he finds little to choose between adversaries." Yet Thant has long been on record as saying, "I am averse to totalitarian systems in any shape or form," and his view of history not repeating is antithetical to Marxist determinism.

When Thant re-entered the Vietnam dispute with his controversial press conference of February 24, 1965, he was greeted with even more strenuous objections in the American press. The following day the Washington *Evening Star* editorialized that Thant was "exceeding his authority with shocking impropriety," and the Washington *Post* columnist William S. White, a close friend of President Johnson, said:

> With a rarely matched twisting of the truth, but at least with a certain insolent candor, Secretary-General U Thant . . . has now openly become an apologist and propagandist for Communist aggression in South East Asia.

What White called a "twisting of the truth" was an honest disagreement about the facts. U Thant's information from world-wide press and radio, as well as from various diplomats, was such as to persuade him that the North Vietnamese had not militarily intervened in the south until after the American military assistance there had become sizable. The American White Paper, on the other hand, insisted that American military assistance had not become sizable until after the North Vietnamese

[277]

had militarily intervened in the south. With American secret intelligence not available to anyone outside the highest echelons of the United States Government, this cart-and-horse argument about facts may continue for a long time.

Aside from disagreement about facts, there is also question as to whether the Secretary-General should inject himself into an issue when three of the four countries involved, South and North Vietnam and Mainland China, are not members of the UN.

Similarly there was question whether the Secretary-General should have injected himself into a further issue that, on the surface, was an internal matter within the country. On October 23, 1964, U Thant issued a public appeal to Khrushchev's successors to permit Khrushchev to reveal to the world the circumstances leading to his exit from power. The Russians never answered the appeal—yet Thant remained persuaded that silence on his part might have led to potentially hazardous international misunderstanding of Russia's intentions in the field of foreign policy.

Other times when Thant speaks out, it is less the substance than the manner that flutters the dovecotes. Some Westerners are taken aback at his repeated praise for Hegel's theory of "thesis, antithesis, and synthesis," since these terms have collected clouds of Marxian implication. Indeed the John Birch Society book *None Dare Call It Treason* quotes Thant's use of this terminology to prove, as it claims, that "by 1963, the UN was headed by avowed Marxists."

On the other hand, those truly avowed Marxists, the leaders in Peking, responded with scorn to Thant's offer in April, 1965 to travel there in the interest of peace in Vietnam. And in September they said that in his peace mission to India and Pakistan he was "merely acting as Washington's political broker."[6]

The Secretary-General is philosophic when attacked. He agrees with Hammarskjöld's extemporaneous statement in Mexico City:

> In following a . . . line of independence . . . a Secretary-General . . . may antagonize one group today and another group tomorrow, or a third group the day after tomorrow, but that is nothing to worry about as member governments come to realize that they have much to gain and little to lose through such independence of the Secretary-General in international conflicts.[7]

The question of who should be Secretary-General when Thant's term expires on November 3, 1966, will surely be discussed during the 21st General Assembly in September, 1966. Some would-be candidates are beginning unconvincingly to deny that they are candidates; some enthusiasts for U Thant are beginning to insist that there is no substitute for experience.

The United States has by no means agreed with everything Thant has said and done; as a *New York Times* writer has said, "He is not our man." At the same time, the Russians have also not agreed with everything Thant has said and done; yet as a Secretariat official who is a Westerner says, "The Russians have had to admit that Thant is honest and objective." During the lengthy UN financial crisis that paralyzed the 19th General Assembly, a news report on December 20, 1964, noted that "the Soviet Government recently agreed to make a commitment to Mr. Thant personally, but to no one else, on

6 Seymour Topping, *The New York Times*, September 15, 1965, quoting *Jenmin Jih Pao*.
7 Joseph P. Lash: *Dag Hammarskjöld* (New York: Doubleday and Co., Inc.; 1961), p. 210.

the amount it would pay." But then a month later another news report said that "the Soviet Union accused . . . U Thant today of siding with the United States in the financial crisis. . . . The tone of the assault was similar to previous breaks [with] Lie and Hammarskjöld." (Before Trygve Lie resigned in 1953, the Russians, enraged by UN actions in Korea, had refused to speak to him. Before Hammarskjöld's death in 1961, the same thing happened because of the Congo. Thus, to date, Secretaries-General have resembled the previous husbands of the queen whom Theseus briefly married, being regularly treated as objects of sacrifice.)

Whether U Thant will be able to keep his balance on the high wire strung between the two poles of the Cold War to the end of his term, no one knows. Whether he would then wish to serve for another five years, or perhaps for one and a half years (to round out the balance of his elected five-year term), is problematic: "there is no indispensable man," he says. Personally he would be happy to start again, after a period of rest and meditation, with teaching and writing and speech-making. But his sense of duty has always been stronger than his personal desires, and his caution more calculated than felt. If, for example, a major power appeared to be manipulating some crisis in order to damage the UN, he might remain to defend the organization with the same passion he formerly exhibited on behalf of individual freedom.

U Thant sometimes refers to his role in the UN as he did his role as Secretary to the Prime Minister of Burma: as a "catalyst." But for a catalytic agent to be successful, the various necessary elements must be present. One such element may be more agreement than currently exists among the neutral powers; another may be a greater willingness to give and take than currently exists between the United States and the Soviet Union.

Another possibility is that the majority of UN members, including at least some of the great powers, might insist on Thant's staying on so that the organization would not be paralyzed by the attempt to agree on a successor (the memory of the old "numbers game" dies hard at the UN). As Adlai Stevenson said when Thant was first elected, he was "the only human being out of a hundred nations represented at the UN who was acceptable to everybody." And although U Thant does not believe in history repeating, this is one instance when it may.

Meanwhile, as the Sunshine Biscuit sign lights up across the East River and the beacons of the Long Island airports probe the darkening sky, the Secretary-General stands at his 38th-floor window. The view, he says, is conducive to meditation. Surely the lights and people he can see—a minuscule fraction of those the world over—cannot, must not, be reduced to radioactive ash by the conflicts of the nations. Thant frequently quotes the words of the UNESCO Charter: "Since wars begin in the minds of men, it is in the minds of men that the defenses of peace must be constructed." Indeed, with the nuclear stalemate and resultant diminished influence of purely military factors, he believes that the political and social and economic forces that make history may in the future play a larger role than in the past.

The winter sun has set—and is on its way to Burma. The Burmese do not customarily take vacations—their festivals provide sufficient holidays—and U Thant's only respite from work is, when possible, to add a few hours of late Saturday afternoon to Sunday's rest. This being a relatively quiet Saturday, he summons his car at five-thirty.

He puts on his black overcoat and his Homburg—he

still hates hats, but New York is cold for more than half the year as measured by the Burmese blood stream. The drive home takes twenty-five minutes. He does not meditate but looks with curiosity from the window. He has a phone in the car for emergencies but it does not ring. He walks in the door, greets his wife and daughter who go back upstairs, leaving his son-in-law in the study. The phone rings. U Thant takes the call. More trouble: a cable from overseas. As he listens to his assistant, he sees an American couple at the front door. The wife is bringing him the typescript of a book she has insisted on writing about him and Burma. A biography must not be allowed to turn into an autobiography. He smiles and waves at them to wait. In a moment he will tell them he will not read the draft. They may not like this, but a Secretary-General cannot please all of the people all of the time. He puts down the phone and, smiling, goes to greet his visitors.

Seeing their faces light up, he thinks, as he has so often, that Kipling, in presuming to predict the future of East and West, was only writing the epitaph of their past. Today both versions of East and West—the geographic and the ideological—have the choice of whether to be bound by this past—by some of its accomplishments as well as its mistakes—or whether to move forward, often with frustration, sometimes with injured pride, but with determination, open-mindedness, and awareness of the possibilities of change, toward the unique promises of the future. These promises, the obverse of the nuclear threat, include the peaceful, free, and abundant life for all people that it is his job at the UN to implement. Whether he or anyone else can succeed will depend primarily upon the governments of the world. Yet they, ultimately, depend on their own people. And for U Thant, where there are people, there is hope.

APPENDIX I

Marco Polo's description of the invasion of Burma by the Mongols (or Tartars) led by Kublai Khan is as circumstantial as if he had been there:

In the year 1277 . . . when the king of Mien [Burma] heard that an army of Tartars had arrived . . . he took the resolution of advancing immediately to attack it. . . . For this purpose he assembled a very large army, including a multitude of elephants . . . upon whose backs were placed battlements or castles of wood, capable of containing to the number of . . . fourteen [men] in each. With these and a numerous army of horse and foot, he took the road.

But the Tartars had two advantages, armor and better bows and arrows:

All their weapons being directed against the elephants, these were soon covered with arrows, and suddenly giving way, fell back upon their own people in the rear, who were thereby thrown into confusion. It soon became impossible for their drivers to manage them. . . . Smarting under the pain of their wounds, and terrified by the shouting of the assailants . . . they rushed into a part of the wood not occupied by the Tartars. The consequence . . . was that from the closeness of the branches of large trees, they broke, with loud crashes, the battlements or castles that were upon their backs. . . . On the part of the king's troops there was no want of valor. And he himself went among the ranks entreating them to stand firm. . . . But the Tartars were finally victorious.

APPENDIX II

"We, who are the Ministers and Generals of the King of
Burma, the Overlord of all the Kings of the Orient, the most
Powerful Sun-rising King . . . the Lord of Many White Elephants, and the Great Righteous Ruler . . . write this letter
to the President and Ministers who are the rulers of both
Washington and the countries of the West. The Powerful
and Righteous Ruler who occupies the throne and rules all
the countries of the ancestors . . . wishes to negotiate a royal
treaty between Burma and America. When the American
Teacher, Mr. Kincaid, came under the Golden Feet he was
allowed to come in and go out of the Palace and to behold
the Golden Face of the King and to send in the petition without any obstructions. If the treaty is made between Burma
and America and if it be lasting from sons to grandsons and
from grandsons to great grandsons, there will be advantages
both for traders and common people. Seeing this advantage
I send this letter to you through Teacher Kincaid."

Eugenio Kincaid, an American missionary, brought the
letter to President Pierce, but it was not answered until the
following year, 1857, and then by Pierce's successor, President James Buchanan. The answer ignored the request for
a treaty but it included a prescient sentence about Burmese-
American relations:

Appendices

"As we have no interest the promotion of which so far as can be foreseen, would render it necessary to desire that your majesty's sovereignty should be diminished or in any way put in jeopardy, we trust that peace and good will may be perpetual between us."

APPENDIX III

THE BUDDHIST NOBLE EIGHTFOLD PATH

On the wheel of Buddha's law, "the spokes are the rules of pure conduct; justice is the uniformity of their length; wisdom is the tire; modesty and thoughtfulness are the hub in which the immovable axle of truth is fixed."

The rules of pure conduct, the Middle Way, include the Noble Eightfold Path. Their interrelationship is as follows:

The first two edicts of the Noble Eightfold Path, right views and right aspiration, fit under the first aspect of the Middle Way, mental discipline. Only through right understanding of the nature of life can one avoid thinking the wrong thoughts or proceed to thinking the right ones. In so doing, one can become aware of the very process of thinking and thereby learn to control it.

The third, fourth, and fifth edicts of the Noble Eightfold Path, right speech, right conduct, and the right means of livelihood, fit under the second aspect of the Middle Way, ethical conduct. Right speech means to avoid saying hurtful things and to try to say compassionate ones. "Noble silence" is enjoined when right speech is impossible; in the West there is a comparable adage, "If you can't say something nice, don't say anything at all." Similarly, right action means to be motivated by concern more for others than for self. Right means of livelihood permits honest competition with other humans for

[286]

business (except in arms, lethal weapons, and intoxicants) but forbids the killing of animals or fish for any reason. Laziness, moreover, is abjured: "A life of indolence is an abomination. . . ."

The last three edicts of the Noble Eightfold Path, right effort, right mindfulness, and right concentration, fit under the third aspect of the Middle Way, wisdom. Right effort leads to right mindfulness or awareness; when the clamorings of the self are stilled the true needs of others become plain. In right concentration there is first a withdrawal from outer stimuli; second, a stilling of the intellect; third, a reviewing of the virtues of the Buddha, in such a way that these become not merely intellectually but existentially real; and lastly, pure equanimity.[1]

[1] The author is indebted to Dr. Htin Aung and U Khant for translation from the Pali and for elucidation of the text.

APPENDIX IV

This, U Thant's best-known pre-war article, was printed in *The World of Books,* September, 1939.

OH! WE BURMANS

We Burmans as a people have one most conspicuous shortcoming which is a condition of maldevelopment. Americans might have called this deficiency "Adult infantilism." There is much to indicate that we are a nation of adult infants, and not a little to prove it. This defect is responsible for more intellectual vagrancy than any disease of mind and body. And the number of Burmese thus afflicted seems to be increasing. What is it and where is it leading us?

We often hear a child say to his playmate: "My house is bigger than yours"—"I can run faster than you"—"My father can lick yours any day," etc., etc. Parents tend to correct this childish boasting, but in reality it often amuses them. Carried into adult life, it is manifest when U Ngwe makes a big diamond comb for his wife after his neighbour U Shwe has made one. It often prompts such statements as "Our Burmese kings had conquered Siam, Assam and Manipur," "Bandula was unrivalled as a military tactician and at last he purposely sought death," etc., etc. It accounts for that self-satisfaction with which we hold aloof from the affairs of other nations, and for that self-esteem which leads us to believe in the superiority of our people and the righteousness of our conduct. Our personal achievements and accomplishments evoke a similar childish emotional response. We pride ourselves grossly on what we have done; we experience a glow of satisfaction when we have succeeded in defeating an adversary; and we are loud in our self-praise and laudation. So are children. "I got the best mark and I am the cleverest of all" is the keynote that echoes our masterful lives.

Proportionately, we have more places of worship than any other country of the world and yet we are the least religious-minded and the least cultured. We have a religion which forbids its priests to meddle in worldly affairs, yet some of our priests are more worldly and more debauched than any other religious brotherhood. Our country is one of the most productive and most resourceful countries in the world, yet we do not attempt to take full advantage of it. Why? Because so many of us are emotionally infantile.

We praise a young man for his delicate limbs, soft complexion and feminine meekness. And we abhor a muscular youth with an aptitude for sports and a flair for adventure. We are one of the most artistic people on earth, yet we look down on actors and artists as social low-brows. Among the Burmese, it is universally regarded as degrading to sit on the same floor with actors and actresses. We often condemn alien ways and modes of thinking. We are adult infants and we enjoy it. We do not experience pleasure or fulfilment in the thought that we are grown up individuals prepared to meet struggle and hardship. We think that the longer we remain impervious to life's warning the luckier we are; that if life could only spare us its blows we should be happy.

Children do not like to carry a thing to its logical conclusion; they do not like to think connectedly; they do not like to think at all. They like to have others do it for them. Grown-up Burmans experience similar likes and dislikes. They leave it to their priests, students and newspapers to think for them.

Foreign visitors to this country are amused at us and often describe us as very gay people, never worrying our heads about the morrow. We take pride in being remarked such, as a child delights in being flattered by a good-humoured gentleman. Our childishness is most conspicuous when we are together; our wit banal, our conversation trivial, our conduct herdish, our thought superficial. Our aim is to be seen, heard and envied as children wish to be in the limelight and to have the attention of others directed towards their activities. Englishmen and educated Indians tell us we are clever and resourceful, but they tell one another behind our backs that we are childish.

Our thought is standardized because we refuse to grow up and think for ourselves; we are unable to purge ourselves of the fear of ridicule. This is particularly true of our literature. One can hardly picture H. G. Wells, D. H. Lawrence and Gogol developing in this country. When one of their types originates here we treat him as a pariah; we call him bad names, we impute his personal morality, and we warn the public to shun him. The same is true of Burmese politics. We estimate the worth of a politician in terms of our personal likes and dislikes and if any statesman of the calibre of Neville Chamberlain appears in Burma he is not likely to be kept in office for more than six months. At present Burmese politics have no meaning save to keep the Burmese newspapers busy and to provide fat jobs for half a dozen men who could not otherwise make a living. We have two political parties: the members of one oppose the other, but neither can tell wherein they differ. It seems that all our politicians are out "to wreck the constitution"; but at the first available opportunity the loudest-lunged politician will not hesitate to swallow his own spit—as the Burmese saying goes. The politician who is *"agin the guvment"* is always popular with the masses, because the Burmese regard Government as one of the five major enemies of the people. Our political views are for the most part emotional attitudes. Judgement does not enter into our conclusions, it leaves the road free to prejudice and to what we call tradition—that is to our newspapers' ideas and beliefs.

Children never remain long at one thing; they tire of it as soon as it has yielded its first glamour of novelty, their attention and interest are directed towards the next thing until that too loses its savour. We are as bad as children in this respect. A newspaper report of a romantic elopement would claim a nation-wide interest for a couple of weeks until it gave way to a newly-cropped-up non-confidence motion in the ministry.

Burma is said to be ideal soil for Democracy and the lack of so-called class distinctions among the Burmans is often stressed by foreign observers. Yet we say to our son or daughter, "Don't play with so-and-so, dear, he is not nice." Or we say to each other, "You know U Than Tha and Daw Pike San can't like Myogale; their children have no one to associate with. Their neighbours are all clerks and school teachers."

This is a picture of the Burmans as one of them sees them, but we need not despair. Recognition and detection of the causes of a malady are half the cure.

Maung Thant

APPENDIX V

BIBLIOGRAPHY

Sources listed are those quoted in the text and those that laymen might want to explore. Sometimes the two coincide; sometimes not.

BOOKS

Ba U, U: *My Burma:* New York: Taplinger Publishing Co.; 1958.

Butwell, Richard: *U Nu.* Stanford, Calif.: Stanford University Press; 1963.

Byles, Marie B.: *Journey into Burmese Silence.* London: George Allen and Unwin, Ltd.; 1962.

Cady, John F.: *A History of Modern Burma.* Ithaca, N.Y.: Cornell University Press; 1958.

Carus, Paul: *The Gospel of Buddha.* London: The Open Court Publishing Co.; 1907.

Christian, John Leroy: *Modern Burma.* Berkeley, Calif.: University of California Press; 1942.

————: *Burma.* London: Collins; 1945.

Churchill, Winston S.: *The Hinge of Fate.* Boston: Houghton Mifflin Company; 1950.

Collis, Maurice: *Into Hidden Burma.* London: Faber & Faber, Ltd.; 1953.

————: *Last and First in Burma.* London: Faber & Faber, Ltd.; 1956.

Bibliography

Conze, Edward: *Buddhism: Its Essence and Development.* New York: Torchbook, Harper & Brothers; 1959.

Cordier, Andrew W., and Wilder Foot (eds.): *The Quest for Peace* ("The Dag Hammarskjöld Memorial Lecture Series"). New York: Columbia University Press; 1965.

De Riencourt, Amaury: *The Soul of China.* London: Jonathan Cape, Ltd.; 1959.

Duff Cooper, Lord Alfred: *Old Men Forget.* London: Rupert Hart-Davis; 1953.

Estorick, Eric: *Stafford Cripps: Prophetic Rebel.* New York: The John Day Company; 1941.

Foot, Sir Hugh: *A Start in Freedom.* New York: Harper & Row; 1964.

Foucar, E. C. V.: *I Lived in Burma.* London: Dennis Dobson; 1953.

Furnivall, John S.: *Colonial Policy and Practice.* Cambridge: Cambridge University Press; 1948.

———: *The Governance of Burma.* Second edition. New York: Institute of Pacific Relations; 1960.

———: *The Story of Burma.* Rangoon: Ramakrishna Mission Society; 1954.

Gunther, John: *Inside Asia.* New York: Harper and Brothers; 1939.

Hagen, Everett E.: *On the Theory of Social Change.* Homewood, Ill.: Dorsey Press; 1962.

Hall, H. Fielding: *The Soul of a People.* London: Macmillan & Co., Ltd.; 1899.

———: *A People at School.* London: Macmillan & Co., Ltd.; 1906.

Hammarskjöld, Dag: *Markings.* New York: Alfred A. Knopf, Inc.; 1964.

Harvey, G. E.: *History of Burma from Earliest Times to 10 March 1824—The Beginning of the English Conquest.* New York: Longmans, Green & Co.; 1925.

———: *British Rule in Burma (1824–1942).* London: Faber & Faber, Ltd.; 1946.

Hla Pe, U: *Narrative of the Japanese Occupation of Burma;*

Bibliography

Recorded by U Khin; Data Paper 41; Southeast Asia Program. Ithaca, N.Y.: Cornell University; 1961.

Htin Aung, Dr.: *Burmese Drama*. London: Oxford University Press; 1937.

——: *Burmese Folk Tales*. London: Oxford University Press; 1948.

——: *Folk Elements in Burmese Buddhism*. London: Oxford University Press; 1962.

Johnstone, William C.: *Burma's Foreign Policy: A Study in Neutralism*. Cambridge, Mass.: Harvard University Press; 1963.

Judson, Edward: *Adoniram Judson, by His Son Edward Judson*. New York: Anson D. F. Randolph; 1883.

Kipling, Rudyard: *Definitive Edition of His Verse*. New York: Doubleday & Company, Inc.; 1939.

Lash, Joseph P.: *Dag Hammarskjöld: Custodian of the Brushfire Peace*. New York: Doubleday & Company, Inc.; 1961.

Lewis, C. S.: *Letters to Malcolm*. New York: Harcourt, Brace, and World, Inc.; 1964.

Maraini, Fosco: *Secret Tibet*. London: Hutchinson & Co., Ltd.; 1952.

Masters, John: *The Road Past Mandalay*. London: Four Square Books; 1964.

Maung Maung, Dr.: *Burma's Constitution*. The Hague: N. V. Martinus Nijhoff; 1959.

——: (compiler) *Aung San of Burma*. The Hague: N. V. Martinus Nijhoff; 1962.

Maxwell-Lefroy, C.: *The Land and People of Burma*. London: A. & C. Black Ltd.; 1963.

Mi Mi Khaing: *Burmese Family*. Bloomington, Ind.: Indiana University Press; 1962.

Nu, Thakin: *Burma under the Japanese*. New York: The Macmillan Company; 1954.

Nyanaponika Thera: *The Heart of Buddhist Meditation*. Colombo, Ceylon: The World of the Buddha Publishing Company; 1956.

Orwell, George: *Burmese Days*. New York: Harper and Brothers; 1934.

Parkinson, C. Northcote: *East and West*. Boston: Houghton Mifflin Company; 1963.

Pye, Lucian W.: *Politics, Personality and Nation Building*. New Haven, Conn.: Yale University Press; 1963.

Pyidawtha: *The New Burma*. Rangoon: Economic and Social Board; 1954.

Quaison-Sackey, Alex: *Africa Unbound*. New York: Frederick A. Praeger, Inc.; 1963.

Radcliffe, Lord: *The Problem of Power*. London: Martin Secker & Warburg, Ltd.; 1952.

Rahula Walpola: *What the Buddha Taught*. New York: Evergreen Books; 1962.

Rossi, Mario: *The Third World*. New York: Funk & Wagnalls; 1963.

Seagrave, Gordon: *The Life of a Burma Surgeon*. New York: W. W. Norton & Company; 1943.

Shattuck, Rear Admiral E. H.: *An Experiment in Mindfulness*. London: Rider & Co.; 1958.

Shway Yoe (Sir James Scott): *The Burman: His Life and Notions*. New York: W. W. Norton & Company; 1963.

Sinai, I. R.: *The Challenge of Modernisation: The West's Impact on The Non-Western World*. London: Chatto and Windus; 1964.

Slim, Field Marshal Sir William: *Defeat into Victory*. London: Cassell & Co., Ltd.; 1956.

Stevenson, Adlai E.: *Looking Outward*. Edited, with commentary, by Robert L. and Selma Schiffer. New York: Harper & Row; 1963.

Stilwell, General Joseph W.: *The Stilwell Papers*. Edited by Theodore H. White. New York: William Sloane Associates; 1948.

Thant, U: *Toward World Peace*. Speeches and Public Statements, 1957–1963. Edited by Jacob Baal Teshuva. New York: Thomas Yoseloff; 1964.

———: *The Secretary-General Speaks*. New York: UN Office of Public Information 1965.

Bibliography

Tinker, Hugh: *The Union of Burma*. London: Oxford University Press; 1961.

Trager, Frank N.: *Building a Welfare State in Burma, 1948–1956*. New York: Institute of Pacific Relations; 1958.

—— (editor): *Marxism in Southeast Asia*. Stanford, Calif.: Stanford University Press; 1951.

—— and Associates: *Burma*. Subcontractor's Monograph. New Haven, Conn.: Human Relations Area Files, Inc.; 1956.

Trumbull, Robert: *The Scrutable East*. New York: David McKay Co.; 1964.

Walinsky, Louis J.: *Economic Development in Burma, 1951–60*. New York: Twentieth Century Fund; 1963.

White, Sir Herbert Thirkell: *A Civil Servant in Burma*. London: Edward Arnold; 1913.

BROCHURES AND ENTIRE ISSUES OF MAGAZINES

Asia. A Selection of Papers Delivered before the Asia Society. Spring, 1964.

Burma Speaks. A Collection of Broadcast Talks. Rangoon: Government Printing and Stationery Office; 1950.

The Chinthe. Rangoon: Burma Council on World Affairs; April, 1951.

Hagen, Everett E.: *The Economic Development of Burma*. National Planning Association; 1956.

Maung Maung, Dr: *Burma's Teething Time*. With a Foreword by U Thant. Rangoon: Bama "AR" Publishing Co.; 1949.

——: *Grim War against KMT*. With a Foreword by U Thant. Rangoon: Nu Yin Press; 1953.

Nu, U: *An Asian Speaks*. Washington, D.C.: Embassy of the Union of Burma; 1955.

On Kin, Rev. U: *Burma under the Japanese*. Lucknow, India: Lucknow Publishing House; 1947.

Orient Review and Literary Digest. Burma Issue. July, 1956.

People's China. Peking Supplement. January 1, 1955.

Bibliography

"Perspectives of Burma." *Atlantic Monthly Supplement,* 1958.

Southeast Asia in Transition. Journal of International Affairs. New York: Columbia University; 1956.

The Specific Characteristics of the Burma Socialist Programme Party. Rangoon: Union of Burma Government; 1964.

(Than Tun), A Journalist: *Under Duress.* Rangoon: Khitaya Public Enlightenment Co.; October, 1945.

Trager, Frank N.: *Burma and China.* Reprinted from the *Journal of Southeast Asian History,* March, 1964.

————: *Reflections on Buddhism and the Social Order in Southeast Asia.* 1959.

————, Patricia Wolgemuth, and Lu-Yu Kiang: *Burma's Role in the United Nations 1948–55.* New York: Institute of Pacific Relations; 1956.

UN Monthly Chronicle. August–September, 1964.

MAGAZINE AND NEWSPAPER ARTICLES

Ball, Ian M.: "U Thant's First Two Years." *Daily Telegraph* (London), November 4, 1963.

"Burma's Foreign Policy, 1948–1956." *Journal of Asian Studies,* November, 1956.

Busch, Noel: "U Thant." *Reader's Digest,* March, 1964.

"A Half Hour with the Secretary-General." *Secretariat News,* January 16, 1964.

Hamilton, Thomas: "An Estimate of U Thant." *The New York Times* (San Francisco and Paris editions), March 25, 1963.

Htin Aung, Dr.: "The Spirit of the Burmese Folk Tale." *Asia,* Spring, 1965.

Jhabvala, Darius S.: "UN's Success and Failure." The New York *Herald Tribune,* October 10, 1965.

Khant, U: "Burma in August 1946." *Guardian* magazine (Rangoon), November, 1955.

Kiester, Ed: "U Thant of UN." *Parade,* December 30, 1962.

Kraft, Joseph: "Letdown at the UN." *Harper's,* January, 1965.

Lewis, Reba: "Burmese Marriage Through Western Eyes." *The Burman,* September 10, 1958.

Maung Maung, Dr.: "U Thant." *Guardian* magazine (Rangoon), August, 1956, and January, 1962.

Middleton, Drew: "On Peace, Thant Takes Long View." *The New York Times,* November 4, 1965.

Morgenthau, Hans J.: "The New Secretary-General." *Commentary,* January, 1963.

Moskin, J. Robert: "Morality USA." *Look,* September 24, 1963.

Mya Sein, U: "Buddhism." *Guardian* magazine (Rangoon), August, 1961.

Pick, Hella: "U Thant's Achievement at the UN." *The Guardian* (Manchester), December 6, 1962.

Rosen, Jane Krieger: "U Thant of the U.N." *This Month,* June, 1962.

Rovere, Richard H.: "The World Is in His Debt." *Saturday Evening Post,* September 21, 1963.

Samuel, Gertrude: "An Estimate of U Thant." *The New York Times Magazine,* December 13, 1964.

Snow, Edgar: "The Rover Boys Rule Burma." *Saturday Evening Post,* May 29, 1948.

Sureck, David: "U Thant Speaks His Mind." *Saturday Evening Post,* September 21, 1963; *UN Review,* January, 1964.

Teatsworth, Ralph: "U Thant, the Peacemaker." *Guardian* magazine (Rangoon), March, 1963.

Thant, U: "Education" (a series). *The Burmese Review,* September 2; September 30; and October 21, 1946.

———: "Round the World." *Guardian magazine* (Rangoon), September, 1955.

———: "Burma and Her Neighbors." *Guardian* magazine (Rangoon), January, 1958.

———: columns and articles in *The World of Books* in the issues of January, 1935; February, 1935; April, 1935; May, 1935, January–February, 1939; September, 1939.

Bibliography

Tinker, Hugh: "Short History of Pre-Colonial Burma." *Guardian* magazine (Rangoon), December, 1961.

Trager, Frank N.: "Political Divorce in Burma." *Foreign Affairs,* January, 1955.

————: "Burma, Ten Year of Independence." *Guardian* magazine (Rangoon), January, 1958.

————: "The Propaganda Battle in India and Burma." *Political and Social Science,* July, 1959.

————: "Burma, the Rooted Culture." *The New Leader,* June 13, 1960.

United Nations Review, December, 1961, pp. 16–21; November, 1962, pp. 7–8; December, 1962, pp. 13–15.

"U Nu and Burma." *Time,* August 30, 1955.

Urquhart, Brian: "The Point of Rest." *The New Yorker,* October 31, 1964.

TELEVISION INTERVIEWS

"Adlai Stevenson Reports" (W. R. Arnold Michaelis): December 23, 1962.

U Thant with Adlai Stevenson: WABC, October 29, 1961.

U Thant with Alistair Cooke: WNBC, April 22, 1962; WNBC, November 6, 1963.

UNPUBLISHED MATERIAL

Ba Maw: *Memoirs.* Vol. I.

Bekker, Sarah McInteer: *The Burmese Concept of Anadé: Its Function and Meaning in Interpersonal Relations.* Ph.D. dissertation, George Washington University, December 2, 1963.

Clubb, Oliver Edmund, Jr.: *The Dynamics of Burmese Independence. Ph.D. dissertation, Johns Hopkins University,* 1960.

Franck, Thomas: *The Structure of Impartiality* (an early draft).

Nathan, Robert: Diary excerpts.

Seplow, Ellen N.: *The Assimilation of Chinese Minorities into Southeast Asian Societies.*

INDEX

[*i*]

Index

Index

Index

Index

Index

A NOTE ABOUT THE AUTHOR

JUNE ROSSBACH BINGHAM

grew up in New York, attended Vassar, married Jonathan B. Bingham, and was graduated from Barnard. Her first book, written with Dr. Fritz Redlich, was The Inside Story: Psychiatry and Everyday Life (1953, 1960). Her second was Courage to Change: An Introduction to the Life and Thought of Reinhold Niebuhr (1961). Her articles have appeared in The New York Times Magazine, The American Journal of Psychiatry, and Mademoiselle, among others. Mrs. Bingham has traveled extensively in the less-developed countries (including Burma) both while her husband was Deputy Director of the Point Four Program and later. When he was an American Ambassador to the UN she became acquainted with delegates from all over the world (including, in January, 1961, Ambassador Thant of Burma). When Jonathan Bingham ran for Congress in 1964 she became engulfed by politics. Congressman and Mrs. Bingham now commute between the Bronx and Washington. They have four children.

January 1966

A NOTE ON THE TYPE

The text of this book was set on the Linotype in Basker-
ville. The punches for this face were cut under the super-
vision of George W. Jones, an eminent English printer.
Linotype Baskerville is a facsimile cutting from type cast
from the original matrices of a face designed by John
Baskerville. The original face was the forerunner of the
"modern" group of type faces.

   John Baskerville (1706–75), of Birmingham, England, a
writing-master, with a special renown for cutting inscrip-
tions in stone, began experimenting about 1750 with
punch-cutting and making typographical material. It was
not until 1757 that he published his first work, a Virgil in
royal quarto, with great-primer letters. This was followed
by his famous editions of Milton, the Bible, the Book of
Common Prayer, and several Latin classic authors. His
types, at first criticized as unnecessarily slender, delicate,
and feminine, in time were recognized as both distinct and
elegant, and both his types and his printing were greatly
admired. Printers, however, preferred the stronger types of
Caslon, and Baskerville before his death repented of having
attempted the business of printing. For four years after his
death his widow continued to conduct his business. She
then sold all his punches and matrices to the Société Lit-
téraire-typographique, which used some of the types for
the sumptuous Kehl edition of Voltaire's works in seventy
volumes.

   The book was designed by Betty Anderson and was
composed, printed, and bound by The Haddon Craftsmen,
Inc., Scranton, Pennsylvania. Illustrations by Halliday
Lithograph Corporation, West Hannover, Massachusetts.